D0064678

HARVARD ECONOMIC STUDIES

VOLUME CXXVI

# *Consumer Demand in the United States, 1929–1970*

## Analyses and Projections

*by*

H. S. HOUTHAKKER

*and*

LESTER D. TAYLOR

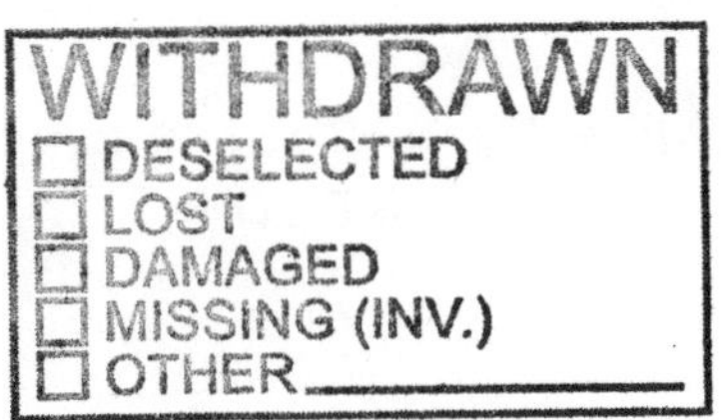


HARVARD UNIVERSITY PRESS
CAMBRIDGE, MASSACHUSETTS
1966

Distributed in Great Britain by Oxford University Press, London



Library of Congress Catalog Card Number: 65–22070

Printed in the United States of America

# *Preface*

In the modern economy the decisive voice in the level and composition of output belongs to consumers. Of the goods and services produced in the United States, some 65 percent are ultimately sold to consumers, as compared with 21 percent to the government and 14 percent to business for investment. To understand the past and future development of the economy as a whole, it is therefore essential to study the pattern of consumption. This is the primary purpose of the present book.

We approach the analysis of consumer demand through the historical record, which is available from 1929 on. For each of 83 items of consumption we estimate demand equations are used in turn to project consumption in 1970 under certain assumptions. Underlying our procedure is a belief in the basic relationships that determine actual patterns of demand. This belief is supported by the satisfactory agreement of our equations with the observations, but it may come as a surprise to those who think of the consumer either as inherently capricious or as the passive victim of advertising and the arbitrary dictates of fashion. The length of women's skirts or of automobile fenders, or the distribution of the toothpaste market between Brand X and Brand Y, would indeed be hard to analyze by our methods, but our concern is not with such details. We work with a breakdown of consumption in which fashion and product differentiation do not show up to any great extent.

This book is addressed to readers of three types. The general economist, we hope, will be interested in the dynamic theory of demand set out in Chapter 1, in at least a few of the results for particular commodities set out in Chapter 4 and discussed in Chapter 5, and perhaps most of all in the analysis of total consumption and savings in Chapter 6. Those interested in particular industries or groups of products, or in forecasting generally, may find Chapters 4 and 5 rewarding. The specialist in econometric methods, finally, is encouraged to turn to Chapters 1, 3, and 7.

It goes without saying that an undertaking as large as ours has benefited from the assistance and advice of numerous others. Most of the work was carried out at the Harvard Economic Research Project, of which Wassily Leontief is Director. Elizabeth W. Gilboy, Associate Director, shared in the supervision and was in charge of administrative aspects. Charlotte Taskier, a staff member of the Project, devoted much time to problems of data interpretation and classification. Karen R. Polenske, Yoel Haitovsky, Madabushanam V. Chari, Armando Lago, Barclay M. Hudson, and Judith L. Rice provided conscientious and imaginative research assistance. Apart from the above, useful advice and other help was also received from Jack Alterman, W. Duane Evans, and Hyman B. Kaitz of the Bureau of Labor Statistics and from Thomas A. Wilson, Clopper Almon, Jr., Richard Oveson, and Ronald Bodkin. Patricia M. Anderson provided invaluable programming assistance. Alvene P. Williams, Elizabeth Barnes, Marie-Claire Sempé, Beverlee Bell, Susan I. Tomkin, Lyndia Harvey, Mary Louise Fisher, Laura P. Hoffman, and Carolyn Mullins gave able and cheerful secretarial assistance.

Most of the research on this book was done under contract with the United States Department of Labor, which gave us access to unpublished data mostly originating in the Department of Commerce and provided certain assumptions for use in the 1970 projections. Earlier versions of Chapters 1, 2, 3, and 4 were supplied to the Department as reports under the contract. We are grateful to the Bureau of Labor Statistics for permitting their publication. It is to be understood that the Bureau does not endorse any of the opinions, methods, and conclusions contained in this book; we bear sole responsibility.

Cambridge, Mass.
June 1965

H.S.H.
L.D.T.

# Contents

# *List of Expenditure Categories in Chapter 4*

# *Introduction*

This monograph is first of all an econometric demand study designed for projecting all items of United States private consumption expenditure (PCE) in future years, particularly in 1970. It presents the results of research done under a contract between the U.S. Bureau of Labor Statistics and the Harvard Economic Research Project; this work was started in the spring of 1962 and completed in the summer of 1964. The projection of the PCE items is one of several components of the Interagency Growth Study, a comprehensive investigation of the quantitative structure of the American economy in conditions of full employment and steady growth. Since these components are interrelated, the projections had to be flexible enough to fit in with a variety of assumptions concerning the determinants of demand. This means, in fact, that a system of demand functions had to be estimated. The classification of consumption in this system is virtually the same as in the annual PCE table published by the U.S. Department of Commerce, which is the principal source of data. Pending the completion of the other components of the Interagency Growth Study, the Bureau of Labor Statistics provided us with four sets of tentative assumptions for which preliminary projections of the pattern of consumer demand in 1970 are reported in this monograph. We have also investigated the relation between total PCE or savings and personal income.

Practical considerations have necessarily had a large influence on the design and development of this study. Since one of its main results had to be a set of plausible projections for 1970, the sobering test of common sense was applied at nearly every step of the empirical research, so that the demand equations finally reported in Chapter 4 are the result of a long process of experimentation and elimination. For several items, ten or more equations were estimated and projected before a final equation was selected. In this selection process the plausibility of the projection (often a matter of opinion) was only one of the criteria; the economic and statistical characteristics of each equation were usually given greater weight.

Apart from this primary objective, the present study also pursues more strictly scientific goals. The analysis of consumer demand is one of the most developed branches of econometrics, actively practiced in North America and no less so in Europe and Asia. To see what progress its students have made, we venture to suggest a comparison of our results with the pioneering work of

Schultz (1938)[1] and perhaps with the more recent but already classic investigations of Wold and Jureen (1953) and Stone (1954). If we have been able to advance beyond these illustrious predecessors, it may be mostly because of a greater attention to the dynamic aspects of demand, though improvements in basic data and computing techniques have certainly contributed as well. There is of course nothing new in emphasizing the role of time in demand analysis, but the means of translating this emphasis into an adequate and workable method have only become available in the last few years, thanks to the work of Koyck (1954), Nerlove (1958), Stone and Rowe (1958), and others. It is also only recently that the quantitative importance of dynamic effects has been fully recognized; some evidence on this may be found in Houthakker (1965).

The dynamic model on which most of our work is based generalizes an idea long adopted in demand studies for durables: that current purchases depend not only on current income and prices, but also on the pre-existing inventory of the item in question. Current purchases then are regarded as an attempt to bring inventories in line with some desired or equilibrium level. It follows also that the effect of, say, a change in income can be analyzed into a short-term effect (the change in current purchases for given stocks) and a long-term effect (the change in purchases after stocks have reached the desired level). In the case of durables, the short-term effect will be greater than the long-term effect.

This idea can easily be extended to nondurable commodities, where habit formation is the exact counterpart of stock adjustment. Although the "inventories" can no longer be given a concrete interpretation, the formal difference between habit formation and stock adjustment is only in the sign of the parameter relating stocks to current purchases. For habit-forming commodities, the long-term effect is larger than the short-term effect, and their consumption is less dependent on income change than are purchases of durables. In our model the concept of habit formation, studied earlier by Duesenberry (1948), Farrell (1952), Brown (1952), Tsujimura and Sato (1964), and others, becomes amenable to more conclusive analysis than had hitherto been possible, and our empirical results show it to be of very wide applicability.

The implementation of our dynamic model raises various problems of statistical technique, some of which are discussed in this book. In particular we have made much use of a new estimation method, developed by Taylor and Wilson (1964), for equations containing lagged values of the dependent variable and serially correlated errors. Projection from dynamic equations also raises difficult problems which, in the absence of sufficiently pertinent theory, we have often had to resolve by Monte Carlo experiments. Students of econometric methods may also be interested in our principal-components analysis of the explanatory variables used in the final demand equations, which confirms the predominant role of total PCE or personal income.

We shall now summarize the seven chapters of the book. Chapter 1 deals

[1] All citations in this form are to the list of references at the back of the volume.

mostly with the economic background. It explains why time-series analysis has been preferred over cross-section analysis, sets out the basic dynamic model of demand mentioned above (both formally and by numerical examples) with its various special cases, and presents an alternative and simpler dynamic model that has been used for a few commodities.

The second chapter discusses the underlying data and the explanatory variables used in the equations; it also goes into the consequence of using per capita rather than aggregate data. Chapter 3 is devoted to statistical problems, particularly those arising in projection. It also contains a brief description of the Taylor–Wilson method of "three-pass least squares," compares the merits of different estimation and projection techniques by Monte Carlo experiments, and discusses the "adding-up problem," which arises from the failure of our system of demand functions to equate the sum of the individual demand projections to the given total PCE.

Chapter 4 contains the main results of our work: the demand equations for 83 commodities as finally selected, together with one or more alternative equations for each commodity and four projections for 1970. Most of the final equations are dynamic (with habit formation predominant) and rely on total PCE for most or all of their explanatory power. In nearly all instances the goodness of fit, the plausibility of the estimated parameters, and the serial correlation of the disturbances range from satisfactory to excellent, but a number of problem items remain. Each commodity is discussed in some detail. In Chapter 5 some broader conclusions are drawn from the results of Chapter 4 and the projections are regrouped in various ways to bring out their implications. As a test of the equations, projections are then made for 1962 and 1963, for which actual data became available after the equations were estimated. Although there are some large discrepancies between projected and actual data, for the most part the test provides encouragement concerning the usefulness of our approach. Further encouragement is derived from a comparison with actual and projected consumption data for six European countries. This comparison suggests that international differences in demand functions are fairly small.

Chapter 6 deals with total PCE as a function of personal disposable income (the "consumption function"). The basic data are annual for 1929–1961 and quarterly for 1947–1962, and refer not only to the United States but also to Canada. Our basic dynamic model is again found to give good results, especially with quarterly data. A version of Friedman's permanent-income hypothesis was incorporated into this model, but the results are disappointing. The assumption that saving is the accumulation of nondepreciating assets turns out to be more useful.

Chapter 7 is an evaluation of the results as a whole. It contains, among other things, a principal-component analysis of the 55 variables (45 of them prices) that appear in the final equations. It appears that no less than 92 percent of the total variance can be attributed to total PCE, which explains the relative unimportance of the other variables in the equations, most of which would only introduce multicollinearity if used more widely.

In several respects this book is a counterpart to an earlier one in which one of the present authors participated (Prais and Houthakker, 1955). There consumption patterns were analyzed from cross-section data, mostly British, here from time series, mostly American. The first point of similarity between the two works is that, although the general approach in each is suggested by economic theory, it is kept flexible enough so as not to become a straitjacket. Second, while novel statistical techniques are developed and applied in both, neither is exclusively or even primarily methodological: the substantive results are an end in themselves and not merely an illustration of the methods. In fact, both originated in requests from government departments interested in concrete economic problems.[2] Third, in both studies the whole range of consumers' expenditure is covered, not just the foodstuffs and durables that have received most attention in the literature. Fourth, in each a large body of public but partly unpublished data is investigated by appropriate econometric methods, requiring teamwork and the use of high-speed computers. It is indicative of the advance in research technology that ten years ago the use of computers in economics was an innovation, which had to be explained in some detail, whereas now it has become commonplace. Last but not least, the influence of Richard Stone can be traced in both monographs.

We hope that the present work will be of use to economists in business and government as well as to our academic colleagues. Although painfully aware of the weaknesses of our results and the shortcomings of our methods, we believe that many of our demand equations and projections deserve to be taken seriously; whenever we were left dissatisfied with our results, we have said so. At the same time, nothing would please us more than that our work inspires others to do better, whether or not they choose to follow our tracks.

[2] This is not apparent in the earlier study, but see Houthakker and Tobin (1952).

# 1

# *The Economic Background*

The nature of the projection assignment precluded the mechanical extrapolation of past trends in consumption to 1970, even if this were a desirable technique in itself (which it is not). Since projections under alternative assumptions are required, it is necessary to establish how consumer expenditures respond to changes in their main economic determinants (incomes and prices). Hence the appropriate tool of analysis is regression analysis, which permits estimation of the effect of these determinants on the basis of past experience.

The emphasis in the present study has been on time-series analysis, though some use was also made of cross-section data in the early stages of the inquiry. The reasons for relying primarily on time-series analysis were both theoretical and practical. In the first place, cross-section analysis, except under rather heroic assumptions, will not provide information on the influence of prices, which may be of importance in long-term projections. In the second place, some of the notorious difficulties associated with time series can be overcome by the use of recently developed devices, which are more fully explained in Chapter 3. In the third place, the 1950 Household Survey of the Bureau of Labor Statistics on which the cross-section analysis would have had to depend does not provide sufficient commodity detail; it is useful, however, in assessing the possible effect of various demographic factors. Finally, it has been increasingly realized in recent years that the income elasticities provided by cross-section and time-series analyses are conceptually different, and that the latter are probably more suitable for projection over time.[1]

As mentioned already, the 1950 Budget Survey was used in the exploratory stages to gain insight into the mathematical shape of the important relationships and into the possible importance of a number of factors that cannot be readily isolated in time series because of their trendlike behavior. These cross-section results cannot be directly incorporated into the final projections, but they have been useful in the selection of explanatory variables in the time-series analysis.

As a check on the time-series analysis for food and clothing, two of the largest items of expenditure, we have made forecasts for 1960 using 1960 data in functions estimated by other investigators from the 1950 survey. The results of these comparisons are briefly summarized in the third section (note 7) of Chapter 5.

[1] See Meyer and Kuh (1957), Friedman (1957), Modigliani and Brumberg (1954).

The first results of the 1960 Household Survey of the Bureau of Labor Statistics are becoming available at the present time, but it was not possible to use them in the analysis.

## *I. The Time-Series Analysis: General Considerations*

The research strategy followed in the present study was largely determined by practical considerations. Since plausible projections had to be produced within a limited period of time, there was not much opportunity for experimentation with novel ideas and methods. The emphasis had to be on estimation rather than on the testing of hypotheses and the development of new techniques, which are the usual objectives of academic research. It would not have been efficient, however, to concentrate entirely on the routine application of standard methods to the problem at hand, for it is well known that the results thus obtained may be unsatisfactory in important respects. Consequently, we have tried to improve upon these methods without venturing so far into uncharted territory as to endanger the attainment of the ultimate goal.

The standard approach to demand analysis,[2] which was also the starting point of the present study, involves the estimation of the following demand equation:

$$q_{it} = f_i(x_t, p_{it}, z_{1t}, z_{2t}, \ldots, z_{nt}, u_{it}) \tag{1}$$

where $q_{it}$ is per capita consumption of the $i$th commodity in year $t$, $f_i$ is a function whose mathematical form is to be specified later, $x_t$ is a measure of per capita real disposable income, $p_{it}$ is the deflated price of the $i$th commodity, $z_{1t}, z_{2t}, \ldots, z_{nt}$, are any other explanatory variables, and $u_{it}$ is a disturbance term representing both the effect of variables that are not explicitly introduced into the equation and errors of measurement in $q_{it}$. Among the additional predictors, $z_{1t}, z_{2t}, \ldots, z_{nt}$, may be such variables as the price of one or more substitutes or complements of the $i$th commodity, lagged values of $x_t$ or $p_{it}$, a time trend, and many other types. The shortness of economic time series and the lack of independent variation limits the number of predictors that can be usefully introduced. Sometimes even $p_{it}$, or more rarely $x_t$, does not contribute enough to the explanation of $q_{it}$ to be retained as an explicit predictor.

Some of the difficulties associated with this approach are:

(a) The explanatory variables $x_t$ and $p_{it}$ (and possibly some of the $z$'s) are not truly exogenous; at least in theory, they are jointly determined with the $q_{it}$. The demand equation (1) is really only one in a system of equations, which for estimation purposes should be treated as a whole. In particular, it is necessary in principle to specify for each commodity not only a demand equation but a supply equation as well, and to estimate them simultaneously.

[2] Among others, see Wold and Jureen (1953), Stone (1954), Ferber and Verdoorn (1962).

Unfortunately simultaneous-equation techniques have so far only rarely led to convincing results in demand analysis. This appears to be due in large part to the failure of economic theory to formulate an adequate supply equation (except for crops, which are not immediately relevant to the markets for consumer goods). In the absence of such an equation, simultaneous estimation is virtually impossible, and the use of single-equation estimation is unavoidable in demand analysis at the present time. In the discussion of the regression equations for the individual items of expenditure (see Chapter 4), the occurrence of simultaneous-equation bias will be pointed out whenever it appears to have affected the results.

(b) The mathematical form of the demand equation cannot be specified *a priori* in the present state of the art. It is therefore advisable to try out different forms, especially those obtainable by logarithmic transformations of one or more of the variables. The following four forms have been used in connection with nearly all commodities:

linear: $q = \alpha + \beta x + \gamma p$
semi-logarithmic: $q = \alpha + \beta \log x + \gamma \log p$
double-logarithmic: $\log q = \alpha + \beta \log x + \gamma \log p$
inverse semi-logarithmic: $\log q = \alpha + \beta x + \gamma p$

For convenience other variables and subscripts have been suppressed. Other things being equal, the mathematical form giving the best fit to the observations has been retained. For most commodities, however, the dynamic model discussed in the next section was applied and, since this is compatible only with a linear demand equation, there was no possibility of experimenting with transformations of the variables. Experience with the static model suggested that nonlinear equations frequently fit better than the linear one, but that the difference in fit (as measured by the correlation between actual and calculated values of the observations in arithmetic units) was relatively minor. This probably is explained by the fact that in time series (as opposed to cross-section data) the explanatory variables do not vary over a wide range, so that a linear approximation is usually quite satisfactory. Hence the dynamic model does not appear to be seriously weakened by its limitation to the linear form.

(c) The decision as to which predictors are to appear explicitly in a regression equation is also somewhat arbitrary in the absence of a generally agreed criterion. Although the frequently followed rule of regarding a regression coefficient as "insignificant" if it is less than twice its standard error may have some conventional usefulness in the testing of hypotheses, it is irrelevant in a projecting context. The rule followed in the present study is to retain a regression coefficient if it exceeds its standard error, provided its sign is theoretically correct. This is tantamount to minimizing the estimated variance of the projection. If the sign is wrong (in particular a positive own-price elasticity), further efforts to improve the equation are indicated.

As it happens, few instances of unacceptable signs were encountered, though this is not necessarily a reason for self-congratulation; it may be due in part to the way in which the price variables were derived. The undeflated price series for each commodity was the result of dividing expenditure at current prices by expenditure at constant prices. Hence if the constant-price expenditure figure was too high for some reason, the derived price figure would be too low. The correlation between quantity (represented by expenditure at constant prices) and price is therefore biased in the negative direction, and this bias may also have influenced the regression coefficients of prices.

(d) Probably the most serious defect of the standard approach to demand analysis is its static character, which is not essentially changed by the arbitrary inclusion of lagged income or prices as predictors. The effect of a change in, say, income is in general neither immediate nor delayed by a year or some other fixed interval; it is more likely to be spread out over some considerable period of time.[3] Fortunately, methods for dealing with these so-called distributed lags have been developed during the last few years; their economic rationale and application to the present study will be discussed in the next section.

A related difficulty, which also appears to be resolved (or at least mitigated) by these new methods, has to do with the disturbance term $u_{it}$ in equation (1). The residuals in estimated regression equations of this type often show considerable autocorrelation, usually of the positive variety (if the actual observation in year $t$ is higher than predicted, the same tends to be true in year $t + 1$). This does not bias the estimates of the parameters, but it does play havoc with the standard errors that are important for deciding which predictors to include. Autocorrelated residuals also cause problems in projecting; this is discussed more fully in Chapter 3.

## *II. The Time-Series Analysis: A Dynamic Model*

The dynamic model used in this study expresses the generally accepted idea that current decisions are influenced by past behavior. To make this idea operational, a particular type of relationship between the past and the present is postulated. The effect of past behavior is assumed to be represented entirely by the current values of certain "state variables," of which inventories are a concrete (but not the only) example. These state variables themselves are in turn changed by current decisions, and the net result is that of a "distributed lag": current behavior depends on all past values of the predetermined variables, though more on recent values than on very remote ones.

A simple example will illustrate the principles involved. Let $q(t)$ be an

[3] The necessity of a dynamic approach has long been recognized in analyses of the demand for automobiles. Applications to a wider range of commodities were first made by Richard Stone and his associates—for instance, Stone and Croft-Murray (1959). The dynamic model used here differs from Stone's in several respects but is similar to one proposed by Nerlove (1960).

individual's demand for clothing during a very short time interval around $t$, let $x(t)$ be his income during that interval, and let $s(t)$ be his inventory of clothes at time $t$. More exactly, let $q(t)$ be the rate of demand at time $t$ and $x(t)$ be the rate of income at that time. All other variables are ignored for the time being. Then the basic assumption is that

$$q(t) = \alpha + \beta s(t) + \gamma x(t) \tag{2}$$

so that the individual's current demand for clothing depends not only on his current income, but also on his stock of clothing. We may expect that, for a person with given tastes and given income, the more clothes he has to begin with, the fewer he will buy currently. In the case of a durable commodity such as clothing[4] the stock coefficient $\beta$ will therefore be negative, but it will now be shown that equation (2) may also hold for other types of commodities if we allow a more general interpretation of $s(t)$. In fact the equation can represent not only the stock-adjustment behavior just described, but also habit formation or inertia, which is apparently a more widespread phenomenon.

Consider a commodity of which consumers do not normally hold physical inventories of any significance, say tobacco. By all accounts tobacco consumption is habit-forming, which means that it does not adjust immediately to changes in income (or in prices, for that matter) and that current consumption is positively influenced by consumption in the more or less recent past. In this case we can say metaphorically that the consumer has built up a psychological stock of smoking habits. His current consumption will be affected by that stock (or, if one prefers, "state variable") just as it is for clothing, but the sign of $\beta$ will now be positive: the more he has smoked in the past, the more he will smoke currently (tastes and income again being given).

The question arises at once: How can we measure such a psychological stock? It will be shown in a moment that under certain reasonable assumptions there is no need to measure it, because $s(t)$ can be eliminated from the regression equation. Yet it should be stressed first that this difficulty is not peculiar to habit-forming commodities, but arises almost as strongly for durable commodities such as clothing.[5] In the latter case we cannot measure $s(t)$ simply by the number of suits, shirts, and such, for some of these may be worn out and due for replacement; moreover, their heterogeneity also makes direct measurement hard. Clearly some depreciated measure of inventories is needed, but the appropriate depreciation rates are usually not known *a priori* and would have to be either estimated from the data or guessed. Hence even for durables, where the state variable has a concrete interpretation, it is desirable to eliminate it.

[4] The Department of Commerce in its PCE table does not classify clothing as durable because its normal lifetime is not long enough. But for present purposes it may be so regarded, especially in view of our empirical results (item 2.3).

[5] In fact, there is often no *a priori* basis for deciding whether, in the demand for a commodity, habit formation or stock adjustment will predominate.

This can be done in the following manner. First consider the accounting identity

$$\dot{s}(t) \equiv q(t) - w(t) \tag{3}$$

where $\dot{s}(t)$ stands for the rate of change in the (physical or psychological) stock around time $t$ and $w(t)$ stands for the average "using up" or "depreciation" of that stock at the same time. From now on, moreover, we shall assume that

$$w(t) = \delta s(t) \tag{4}$$

where $\delta$ is a constant depreciation rate. Hence the rate of depreciation at any time $t$ is proportional to the stock at that time. The assumption of proportionality corresponds to the "declining balance" method of depreciation, which has been found realistic in many practical situations.[6] Combining (3) and (4) we find that

$$\dot{s}(t) \equiv q(t) - \delta s(t) \tag{5}$$

Next eliminate $s(t)$ from (5) by using (2):

$$s(t) = q(t) - \frac{\delta}{\beta}[q(t) - \alpha - \gamma x(t)]. \tag{6}$$

Now differentiate (2) with respect to time and substitute (6) for $s(t)$:

$$\dot{q}(t) = \beta\left[q(t) - \frac{\delta}{\beta}(q(t) - \alpha - \gamma x(t))\right] + \gamma\dot{x}(t). \tag{7}$$

After simplification this expression becomes

$$\dot{q}(t) = \alpha\delta + (\beta - \delta)q(t) + \gamma\dot{x}(t) + \gamma\delta x(t), \tag{8}$$

which is a first-order differential equation involving only the observable quantities $q$ and $x$.

The short-term derivative of consumption with respect to income is given by $\gamma$, the coefficient of $x(t)$ in (2) and $\dot{x}(t)$ in (8). "Short-term" in this context is taken to mean the instantaneous adjustment in consumption before the state variables have a chance to adjust. It is also possible to calculate a long-term derivative, which is equal to the entire change in demand associated with a once-and-for-all change in income, including any indirect effects through changes in the state variables.

More precisely, we can define a long-term equilibrium in which $q$, $s$, and $x$ all remain constant over time. These long-term levels will be denoted by $\hat{q}$, $\hat{s}$, and $\hat{x}$. Then it follows from (5) that, since $\dot{s}(t) = 0$,

$$\hat{q} = \delta\hat{s}. \tag{9}$$

Substitution into (2) gives

$$\hat{q} = \alpha + \frac{\beta}{\delta}\hat{q} + \gamma\hat{x} \tag{10}$$

[6] In equation (53) of this chapter, an entirely different interpretation of $\delta$ will be given.

and hence, assuming $\beta \neq \delta$,

$$\hat{q} = \frac{\alpha\delta}{\delta - \beta} + \frac{\gamma\delta}{\delta - \beta}\hat{x} \tag{11}$$

The long-run derivative of $q$ with respect to $x$ is given by the coefficient of $\hat{x}$.

Perhaps of greater interest than the above interpretation of the long-term derivative, which in essence takes the dynamic approach of this section to its static limits, is another interpretation in the context of steady (linear) growth defined as a development in which the derivatives of $q$, $s$, and $x$ remain constant over time.[7] In formula:

$$\dot{q}(t) = g_q; \quad \dot{x}(t) = g_x; \quad \dot{s}(t) = g_s \quad \text{for all } t. \tag{12}$$

It then also follows that

$$g_s = q(t) - \delta s(t), \tag{13}$$

which upon differentiating with respect to time yields

$$g_q = \delta g_s, \tag{14}$$

while from (2)

$$g_q = \beta g_s + \gamma g_x. \tag{15}$$

Hence, again assuming $\beta \neq \delta$,

$$g_q - \frac{\gamma}{1 - \frac{\beta}{\delta}} g_x = \frac{\gamma\delta}{\delta - \beta} g_x \tag{16}$$

in agreement with (11). The case $\delta = 0$ will be discussed in Chapter 6.

As indicated above, equation (8) contains only the observable quantities $q$ and $x$. However, in order to estimate the parameters $\alpha$, $\beta$, $\gamma$, and $\delta$ from annual or quarterly observations, the continuous model must be approximated by one involving discrete intervals of time. This is done next.

## *III. A Finite Approximation of the Dynamic Model*

To begin with, we define

$$\bar{q}_{t_0} = \int_{t_0}^{t_0 + \tau} q(t)\, dt. \tag{17}$$

That is, if $q(t)$ is the rate of consumption per unit time, $dt$, then $\bar{q}_{t_0}$ is the

[7] In the theory of economic growth, more emphasis is put on exponential growth, in which the proportional increase per period is constant. Such growth is somewhat harder to fit in with the linear demand function (2), since a linear function of an exponential function is not itself an exponential function. As it happens, linear growth had been postulated by the Bureau of Labor Statistics for the present projection study. Exponential growth is discussed in Chapter 6, under special assumptions.

corresponding average rate of consumption for a longer time interval, $\tau$. Similarly, define

$$(18) \qquad \bar{x}_{t_0} = \int_{t_0}^{t_0+\tau} x(t)\,dt; \qquad \bar{s}_{t_0} = \int_{t_0}^{t_0+\tau} s(t)\,dt$$

However, since $s(t)$ is a stock level at time $t$, the integral $\bar{s}_{t_0}$ is interpreted differently from $\bar{q}_{t_0}$ and $\bar{x}_{t_0}$. In particular, we can interpret $\bar{s}_{t_0}/\tau$ as the average stock level within the time interval $(t_0, t_0 + \tau)$. Finally, the changes in the variables within each period are defined by

$$(19) \qquad \Delta^* q_{t_0} = q(t_0 + \tau) - q(t_0); \qquad \Delta^* s_{t_0} = s(t_0 + \tau) - s(t_0); \text{ etc.}$$

If (2) is integrated over time from $t_0$ to $t_0 + \tau$, the structural equation becomes

$$(20) \qquad \bar{q}_{t_0} = \alpha\tau + \beta\bar{s}_{t_0} + \gamma\bar{x}_{t_0}.$$

Similarly, in period $(t_0 + \tau, t_0 + 2\tau)$,

$$(21) \qquad \bar{q}_{t_0+\tau} = \alpha\tau + \beta\bar{s}_{t_0+\tau} + \gamma\bar{x}_{t_0+\tau}.$$

The within-period change in the level of stock is

$$(22) \qquad \Delta^* s_{t_0} \equiv \bar{q}_{t_0} - \delta\bar{s}_{t_0},$$

and similarly,

$$(23) \qquad \Delta^* s_{t_0+\tau} \equiv \bar{q}_{t_0+\tau} - \delta\bar{s}_{t_0+\tau}.$$

Subtracting (20) from (21) gives

$$(24) \qquad \bar{q}_{t_0+\tau} - \bar{q}_{t_0} = \beta(\bar{s}_{t_0+\tau} - \bar{s}_{t_0}) + \gamma(\bar{x}_{t_0+\tau} - \bar{x}_{t_0}).$$

Moreover, we can infer from (20) and (21):

$$(25) \qquad \bar{s}_{t_0+\tau} = \frac{1}{\beta}(\bar{q}_{t_0+\tau} - \alpha\tau - \gamma\bar{x}_{t_0+\tau});$$

$$(26) \qquad \bar{s}_{t_0} = \frac{1}{\beta}(\bar{q}_{t_0} - \alpha\tau - \gamma\bar{x}_{t_0}).$$

If (25) and (26) are used to replace $\bar{s}_{t_0+\tau}$ and $\bar{s}_{t_0}$ in (22) and (23), we get

$$(27) \qquad \Delta^* s_{t_0+\tau} = \bar{q}_{t_0+\tau} - \frac{\delta}{\beta}(\bar{q}_{t_0+\tau} - \alpha\tau - \gamma\bar{x}_{t_0+\tau});$$

$$(28) \qquad \Delta^* s_{t_0} = \bar{q}_{t_0} - \frac{\delta}{\beta}(\bar{q}_{t_0} - \alpha\tau - \gamma\bar{x}_{t_0}).$$

The difference $\bar{s}_{t_0+\tau} - \bar{s}_{t_0}$ between the two periods may be approximated by

$$(29) \qquad \bar{s}_{t_0+\tau} - \bar{s}_{t_0} \sim \frac{\tau}{2}(\Delta^* s_{t_0+\tau} + \Delta^* s_{t_0}),$$

an approximation that will be more accurate the closer the behavior of the stock variable is linearity within the period. This is illustrated in Figure 1.1.

Figure 1.1

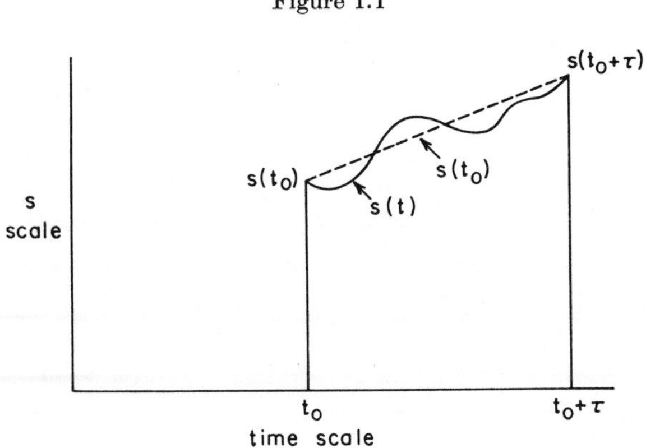


The solid curve represents the actual function, $s(t)$, while the dotted line represents the linear approximation to it. The area under the actual curve is given by

$$\bar{s}_{t_0} = \int_{t_0}^{t_0+\tau} s(t)\,dt, \tag{30}$$

while the area under the linear approximation is equal to

$$\tau s(t_0) + \frac{\tau}{2}[s(t_0+\tau) - s(t_0)] = \frac{\tau}{2}[s(t_0+\tau) + s(t_0)]. \tag{31}$$

Hence the difference $\bar{s}_{t_0+\tau} - \bar{s}_{t_0}$ is approximately equal to

$$\frac{\tau}{2}[s(t_0+2\tau) + s(t_0+\tau) - s(t_0+\tau) - s(t_0)] = \frac{\tau}{2}[\Delta^* s_{t_0+\tau} + \Delta^* s_{t_0}]. \tag{32}$$

Assuming that the approximation is good enough for practical purposes, we can write (24) as

$$\begin{aligned} \bar{q}_{t_0+\tau} - \bar{q}_{t_0} &= \frac{\tau}{2}\beta(\Delta^* s_{t_0+\tau} + \Delta^* s_{t_0}) + \gamma(\bar{x}_{t_0+\tau} - \bar{x}_{t_0}) = \\ &= \frac{\tau}{2}\beta\left[\bar{q}_{t_0+\tau} - \frac{\delta}{\beta}(\bar{q}_{t_0+\tau} - \alpha\tau - \gamma\bar{x}_{t_0+\tau}) \right. \\ &\quad \left. - \frac{\delta}{\beta}(\bar{q}_{t_0} - \alpha\tau - \gamma\bar{x}_{t_0})\right] + \gamma(\bar{x}_{t_0+\tau} - \bar{x}_{t_0}), \end{aligned} \tag{33}$$

which upon simplification and rearrangement becomes

$$(34)\quad \bar{q}_{t_0+\tau} = \frac{\alpha\delta\tau^2}{1 - \frac{\tau}{2}(\beta - \delta)} + \frac{1 + 2(\beta - \delta)}{1 - \frac{\tau}{2}(\beta - \delta)}\bar{q}_{t_0} + \frac{\gamma\left(1 + \frac{\tau\delta}{2}\right)}{1 - \frac{\tau}{2}(\beta - \delta)}\bar{x}_{t_0+\tau} + \frac{\gamma\left(1 - \frac{\tau\delta}{2}\right)}{1 - \frac{\tau}{2}(\beta - \delta)}\bar{x}_{t_0}.$$

Equation (34) is the discrete analogue to equation (8), and once $\tau$ is specified only the observable quantities $q$ and $x$ are involved. If we establish our time scale so that $\tau = 1$ and remove the bars for notational ease, then we have

$$(35)\quad q_t = \frac{\alpha\delta}{1 - \frac{1}{2}(\beta - \delta)} + \frac{1 + \frac{1}{2}(\beta - \delta)}{1 - \frac{1}{2}(\beta - \delta)}q_{t-1} + \frac{\gamma\left(1 + \frac{\beta}{2}\right)}{1 - \frac{1}{2}(\beta - \delta)}x_t + \frac{\gamma\left(1 - \frac{\delta}{2}\right)}{1 - \frac{1}{2}(\beta - \delta)}x_{t-1}.$$

Finally, for computational reasons it is convenient to write $x_t$ as $(x_t - x_{t-1}) + x_{t-1} \equiv \Delta x_t + x_{t-1}$, which transforms (35) into[8]

$$(36)\quad q_t = \frac{\alpha\delta}{1 - \frac{1}{2}(\beta - \delta)} + \frac{1 + \frac{1}{2}(\beta - \delta)}{1 - \frac{1}{2}(\beta - \delta)}q_{t-1} + \frac{\gamma\left(1 + \frac{\delta}{2}\right)}{1 - \frac{1}{2}(\beta - \delta)}\Delta x_t + \frac{\gamma\delta}{1 - \frac{1}{2}(\beta - \delta)}x_{t-1}.$$

This is the equation actually used for estimation.

Equation (36) shows how the parameters $\alpha$, $\beta$, $\gamma$, and $\delta$ of the structural equations enter the estimating equation. These four parameters can in fact be recomputed from the four coefficients of (36), which for convenience we shall rewrite as

$$(37)\qquad q_t = A_0 + A_1 q_{t-1} + A_2 \Delta x_t + A_3 x_{t-1}.$$

It can then be easily verified that (apart from estimating errors)

$$(38)\qquad \alpha = \frac{2A_0(A_2 - \frac{1}{2}A_3)}{A_3(A_1 + 1)};$$

$$(39)\qquad \beta = \frac{2(A_1 - 1)}{A_1 + 1} + \frac{A_3}{A_2 - \frac{1}{2}A_3};$$

[8] Note that the economist's convention of writing $\Delta x_t$ as $x_t - x_{t-1}$ is now being used. The difference $\Delta$ between the means in two periods is not to be confused with the change $\Delta^*$ within a period. From now on $\Delta^*$ will no longer be needed.

(40) $$\gamma = \frac{2(A_2 - \frac{1}{2}A_3)}{A_1 + 1};$$

(41) $$\delta = \frac{A_3}{A_2 - \frac{1}{2}A_3}.$$

Equation (20) shows that the short-term derivative of $q$ with respect to $x$, where "short-term" now means "occurring within the period of observation," is equal to $\gamma$, the same as with the continuous model. From (20) and (22) we see that, when $q$, $s$, and $x$ remain constant over time, the long-term derivative is given by $\gamma\delta/(\delta - \beta)$, again the same as with the continuous model. Similarly, with the case of steady (linear) growth where it is now assumed that $q$, $s$, and $x$ each increase by a constant absolute amount per period, it can easily be shown that

(42) $$g_q = \frac{\gamma\delta}{\delta - \beta} g_x$$

where $g_q = q_t - q_{t-1}$, $g_x = x_t - x_{t-1}$, and $g_s = s_t - s_{t-1} = \Delta s_t$ for all $t$.

The foregoing will be illustrated by two examples, referring to food purchased for home use (excluding alcoholic beverages) and to clothing (including luggage). These are, respectively, items 1.1 and 2.3 in the National Income Accounts. The estimated equation for food is

(43) $$\hat{q}_t = 29.074 + .6044q_{t-1} + .1128\Delta x_t + .0528x_{t-1},$$

where $q$ and $x$ are per capita figures measured in constant (1954) dollars; prices do not appear in this equation since their influence was found to be statistically insignificant. From (38) through (41) it follows that

(44) $$\hat{\alpha} = 59.28; \quad \hat{\beta} = .118; \quad \hat{\gamma} = .108; \quad \hat{\delta} = .614.$$

(The "hats" denote estimates.) It appears therefore, since $\hat{\beta} > 0$, that aggregate food buying is habit-forming (though this conclusion can really be established only by considering the standard error of $\beta$). So there is justification for introducing a "psychological stock of food-buying habits." In the present case this stock depreciates rather rapidly, as can be seen by the large size of $\delta$.

The short-term effect of total consumer expenditure on food expenditure is measured by $\hat{\gamma}$, while the long-term effect is given by

(45) $$\frac{\hat{\gamma}\hat{\delta}}{\hat{\delta} - \hat{\beta}} = \frac{A_3}{1 - A_1} = .13347.$$

A one-dollar increase in total expenditure, therefore, leads to a 10.8 cents increase in food purchases the first year, with a further increase of 2.55 cents in subsequent years ($.108 + .0255 = .1335$). We shall have more to say about (43) in a moment.

The estimated equation for clothing is

(46) $$\hat{q}_t = 17.595 + .6243q_{t-1} + .0763\Delta x_t + .0173x_{t-1},$$

with

(47) $\hat{\alpha} = 84.5902; \quad \hat{\beta} = -.2065; \quad \hat{\gamma} = .0833; \quad \hat{\delta} = .2561$

as the corresponding estimates of the structural coefficients. We see that on balance clothing is subject to an inventory effect ($\hat{\beta} < 0$); hence the earlier discussion treating clothing as a durable good had justification. The estimate of the long-run total-expenditure coefficient is

(48) $$\frac{\hat{\gamma}\hat{\delta}}{\hat{\delta} - \hat{\beta}} = .04605,$$

which is about half the short-run effect. This means that the immediate effect of an increase in total expenditure is to increase the stock of clothing; however, in subsequent periods the higher stock tends to decrease the flow of purchase.

We shall now use the equations for food and clothing to illustrate the behavior over time of our dynamic model. For this purpose we take the actual values of $q_t$ in 1961 (given in Chapter 4) and extrapolate $q_t$ as a function of $x_t$ under four different assumptions (see Table 1.1 and Figure 1.2; the figure also includes housing, which is discussed in section VI).

Figure 1.2a

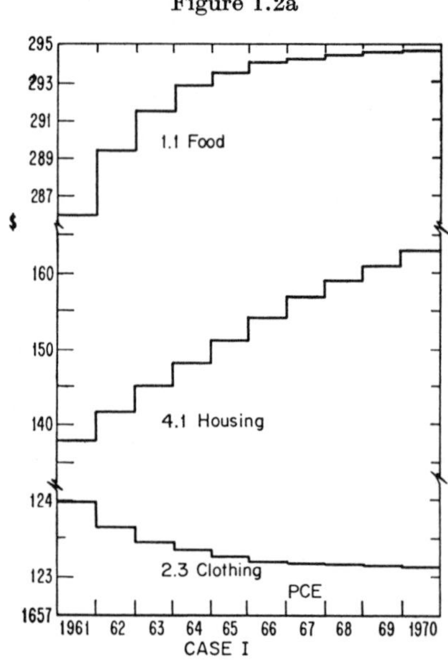


In this table, Case 1 corresponds to a stationary level of total PCE, and thus brings out the approach to a long-run equilibrium of the kind defined by equation (9). We observe that food consumption rises substantially at first, but at a diminishing rate. At the end of the decade it is close to its equilibrium value according to (10), which in this case becomes

(49) $$\hat{q} = 73.49 + .13347\hat{x}.$$

Table 1.1. Equation (37): Behavior of Consumption over Time

| Year | $x_t$ | Item 1.1 (food) $q_t$ | Item 1.1 (food) $\Delta q_t$ | Item 2.3 (clothing) $q_t$ | Item 2.3 (clothing) $\Delta q_t$ |
|---|---|---|---|---|---|
| | | Case 1 | | | |
| 1961 | 1657 | 286.05 | — | 123.98 | — |
| 1962 | 1657 | 289.45 | +3.40 | 123.66 | −0.32 |
| 1963 | 1657 | 291.51 | +2.06 | 123.46 | −0.20 |
| 1964 | 1657 | 292.75 | +1.24 | 123.34 | −0.12 |
| 1965 | 1657 | 293.50 | +0.75 | 123.26 | −0.08 |
| 1966 | 1657 | 293.96 | +0.46 | 123.21 | −0.05 |
| 1967 | 1657 | 294.23 | +0.27 | 123.18 | −0.03 |
| 1968 | 1657 | 294.40 | +0.17 | 123.16 | −0.02 |
| 1969 | 1657 | 294.50 | +0.10 | 123.15 | −0.01 |
| 1970 | 1657 | 294.56 | +0.06 | 123.15 | −0.01 |
| | | Case 2 | | | |
| 1961 | 1657 | 286.05 | — | 123.98 | — |
| 1962 | 1711.22 | 295.57 | +9.52 | 127.80 | +3.82 |
| 1963 | 1765.44 | 304.18 | +8.61 | 131.12 | +3.32 |
| 1964 | 1819.66 | 312.25 | +8.07 | 134.13 | +3.01 |
| 1965 | 1873.88 | 319.99 | +7.74 | 136.94 | +2.81 |
| 1966 | 1928.10 | 327.53 | +7.54 | 139.64 | +2.70 |
| 1967 | 1982.32 | 334.95 | +7.42 | 142.27 | +2.63 |
| 1968 | 2036.55 | 342.30 | +7.35 | 144.85 | +2.58 |
| 1969 | 2090.78 | 349.61 | +7.31 | 147.39 | +2.54 |
| 1970 | 2145 | 356.89 | +7.28 | 149.92 | +2.53 |
| | | Case 3 | | | |
| 1961 | 1657 | 286.05 | — | 123.98 | — |
| 1962 | 1657 | 289.45 | +3.40 | 123.66 | −0.32 |
| 1963 | 1711.22 | 297.62 | +8.17 | 127.60 | +3.94 |
| 1964 | 1711.22 | 299.31 | +1.69 | 126.86 | −0.74 |
| 1965 | 1711.22 | 300.33 | +1.02 | 126.40 | −0.46 |
| 1966 | 1657 | 294.83 | −5.50 | 121.97 | −4.43 |
| 1967 | 1657 | 294.76 | −0.07 | 122.41 | +0.44 |
| | | Case 4 | | | |
| 1961 | 1657 | 286.50 | — | 123.98 | — |
| 1962 | 1711.22 | 295.57 | +9.52 | 127.80 | +3.82 |
| 1963 | 1765.44 | 304.18 | +8.61 | 131.12 | +3.32 |
| 1964 | 1765.44 | 306.14 | +1.96 | 130.00 | −1.12 |
| 1965 | 1711.22 | 301.20 | −4.94 | 125.16 | −4.84 |
| 1966 | 1711.22 | 301.47 | +0.27 | 125.34 | +0.18 |
| 1967 | 1765.44 | 307.75 | +6.28 | 129.59 | +4.25 |
| 1968 | 1819.66 | 314.41 | +6.66 | 133.18 | +3.61 |

For $\hat{x} = 1657$, this gives $\hat{q} = 294.63$. Similarly for clothing,

$$\hat{q} = 46.83 + .04605\hat{x}. \tag{50}$$

For $\hat{x} = 1657$, this gives $\hat{q} = 123.13$; clothing consumption, however, is falling throughout the decade. This means, of course, that in 1961 food consumption was below, and clothing consumption above, its equilibrium level. It will be shown in a moment that these relative positions of the 1961 level are not altogether accidental. Before leaving Case 1 it should be noted that

$$\Delta q_t = A_1 \Delta q_{t-1}, \tag{51}$$

as can easily be proved from equation (37).

Figure 1.2b

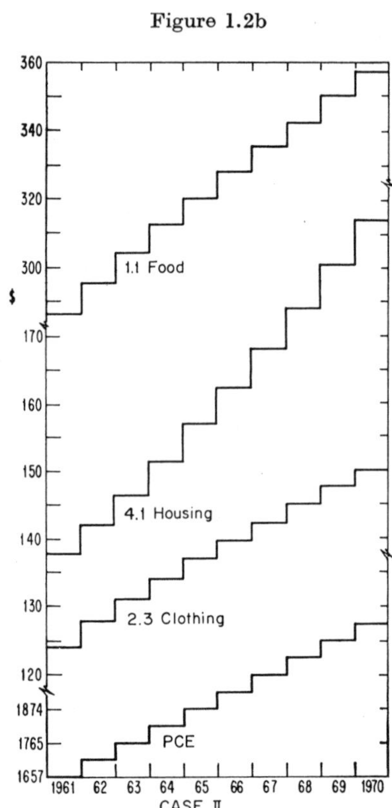


Case 2 represents steady linear growth, equivalent to the average growth rate in aggregate PCE that is used as one assumption in Chapter 4.[9] Each year PCE is increased by about \$54.22 to reach \$2145 in 1970. Both food and clothing consumption increase every year, but at a decreasing rate. At the

[9] The values for $q_t$ in 1970 in Table 1.1 do not agree with those for the same commodities in Chapter 4 because the latter have been adjusted to add up to the given total of PCE in 1970 (see Chapter 3, section V).

end of the period, $\Delta q_t$ is close to the equilibrium growth given by (42), which equals \$7.24 for food and \$2.50 for clothing. The interested reader may like to verify that in Case 2

$$\Delta q_t - \Delta q_{t-1} = A_1(\Delta q_{t-1} - \Delta q_{t-2}), \tag{52}$$

in contrast with (51).

Perhaps the most remarkable feature of Case 2 is that the 1970 values of $q_t$ are not close to the static equilibrium levels $\hat{q}$, given by (49) and (50); the latter, for $x_t = 2145$, are respectively 359.78 and 145.61. The 1970 figure for food falls short of this level; that for clothing exceeds it. Here we can observe the implications of habit formation and stock adjustment: food is below its $\hat{q}$ because PCE is rising and current consumption is held back by the lower levels of the past; but in clothing these lower levels imply that inventories have not reached the currently desired level, so that relatively more has to be bought to bring inventories up to that level. And now it is also clear why in 1961 food consumption was below, and clothing consumption above, the $\hat{q}$ for that year, as we saw in Case 1. One reason (perhaps not the only one) is that per capita PCE had been rising for a few years up to 1961.

Case 2 further suggests that clothing is relatively more responsive to changes in PCE than food. This is also clear from equations (43) and (46): the ratio $A_2/A_3$ is twice as large for clothing as for food.[10] This ratio in turn determines $\delta$, as can be seen if (41) is rearranged to give

$$1/\delta = A_2/A_3 - 1/2. \tag{53}$$

Consequently $\delta$ is smaller the greater the effect of a one-dollar change in PCE compared to that of a dollar's difference in past PCE. This interpretation of $\delta$ is independent of the original one in (4) as the depreciation rate of a physical or psychological stock.

Further evidence on the short-term effects of habit formation and stock adjustment is provided by Cases 3 and 4 of Table 1.1. In Case 3 PCE first remains stationary, then increases by the same amount as in Case 2, remains stationary again, and finally returns to its initial level. Food consumption rises during the first two periods of stationary PCE, when clothing consumption is falling. In the third stationary period, food consumption is higher than in the first, even though PCE is the same, because of the habit-forming effect of higher consumption in the second stationary period. Clothing consumption, on the contrary, is lower finally than initially, because stocks have been built up in the second period. Case 4 represents growth interrupted by a recession. Its analysis is in line with the preceding remarks; we leave it to the interested reader.

It is now time to reintroduce the demand predictors other than $x$ that have

[10] Actually food and clothing are rather moderate examples of habit formation and stock adjustment, respectively. We chose those two, rather than more extreme instances, because they are large items with very simple dynamic equations.

Figure 1.2c

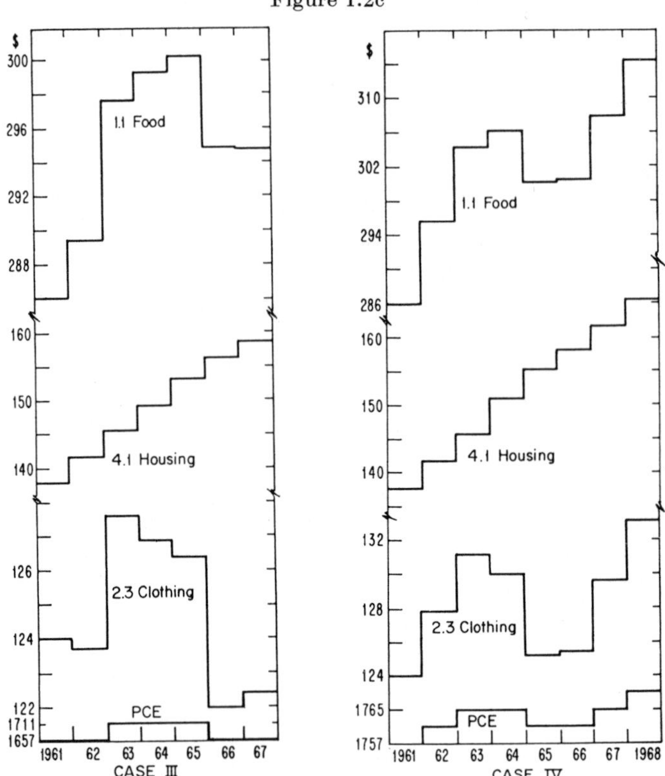


been ignored up to this point. We shall consider only price $p$ and the error term $u$, since the treatment of any additional variables will be clear by analogy.[11]

The basic equation becomes

$$q_t = \alpha + \beta s_t + \gamma x_t + \eta p_t + u_t, \tag{54}$$

while the stock identity remains valid as it stands. The derivation of an estimating equation similar to (36) need not be given in full, for no new questions of principle come up. The result is

$$q_t = A_0 + A_1 q_{t-1} + A_2 \Delta x_t + A_3 x_{t-1} + A_4 \Delta p_t + A_5 p_{t-1} + v_t, \tag{55}$$

where $A_0$, $A_1$, $A_2$, and $A_3$ have the same meaning as before and

$$A_4 = \frac{\eta\left(1 + \frac{\delta}{2}\right)}{1 - \frac{1}{2}(\beta - \delta)}; \tag{56}$$

[11] The single exception to this is the dummy variable $d_t$ introduced to separate the prewar years from the postwar years. (This is discussed in Chapter 2). Since $d_t = d_{t-1}$, the dummy variable enters (55) as $A_6 d_t$, where $A_6 = \xi\delta/[1 - \frac{1}{2}(\beta - \delta)]$ and $\xi$ is the coefficient of $d_t$ in the structural equations.

$$A_5 = \frac{\eta\delta}{1 - \frac{1}{2}(\beta - \delta)}. \tag{57}$$

The $v_t$ is an error term defined by

$$v_t = \frac{\left(1 + \frac{\delta}{2}\right)u_t - \left(1 - \frac{\delta}{2}\right)u_{t-1}}{1 - \frac{1}{2}(\beta - \delta)}. \tag{58}$$

It will be noted that $A_4$ and $A_5$ differ from $A_2$ and $A_3$ only in that $\gamma$ is replaced by $\eta$; this means among other things that, parallel to (11) and (42), the long-term derivative of $q$ with respect to $p$ is given by $\eta\delta/(\delta - \beta)$, so that the lagged effect of a change in any predictor is distributed in the same manner as it is for $x$. Furthermore it also means that two different estimates of $\delta$ can be derived from (53), since in addition to (41) we have (apart from sampling errors):

$$\delta = \frac{A_5}{A_4 - \frac{1}{2}A_5}. \tag{59}$$

These two estimates are not necessarily the same, so that $\delta$ is "overidentified." An iterative technique for arriving at the best single estimate of $\delta$ has therefore been devised and is discussed in the next section.

Also it appears that the error term $v_t$ in (55) is now no longer nonautocorrelated, as is usually assumed for $u_t$ in (54). This has been a long-standing problem with models of the distributed-lag and stock-adjustment types. However, a recently developed technique for dealing with errors distributed as in (58) has been applied in the present investigation; this technique is discussed in Chapter 3.

## *IV. A Problem of Overidentification*

As indicated above, one estimate of $\delta$ can be derived from $\delta/(1 + \delta/2) = A_3/A_2$, while a separate independent estimate can be derived from $\delta/(1 + \delta/2) = A_5/A_4$. For these two estimates of $\delta$ to be consistent, simple algebra shows that the following must hold:

$$A_2 A_5 = A_3 A_4. \tag{60}$$

There are several possible approaches that could be pursued in deriving estimates of the coefficients in (55) under restriction (60). A simple yet effective procedure we have used is to view the estimation problem as one of constrained least squares. Alternatively, this can be seen as an exercise in quadratic programing.

Proceeding formally, we formulate the following expression:

$$\begin{aligned} \phi = \sum (q_t - A_0 - A_1 q_{t-1} - A_2 \Delta x_t - A_3 x_{t-1} - A_4 \Delta p_t - A_5 p_{t-1})^2 \\ - \kappa(A_2 A_5 - A_3 A_4), \end{aligned} \tag{61}$$

where $\kappa$ is a Lagrangian multiplier associated with the restriction on the coefficients. By differentiating (61) partially with respect to each of the parameters, including $\kappa$, a system of seven estimating equations is obtained:

$$(62)\quad \begin{bmatrix} T & q_{-1} & x & x_{-1} & p & p_{-1} \\ q_{-1} & q_{-1}^2 & q_{-1}x & q_{-1}x_{-1} & q_{-1}p & q_{-1}p_{-1} \\ x & q_{-1}x & x^2 & xx_{-1} & xp & xp_{-1} + \frac{\kappa}{2} \\ x_{-1} & q_{-1}x_{-1} & xx_{-1} & x_{-1}^2 & x_{-1}p - \frac{\kappa}{2} & x_{-1}p_{-1} \\ p & q_{-1}p & xp & x_{-1}p - \frac{\kappa}{2} & p^2 & pp_{-1} \\ p_{-1} & q_{-1}p_{-1} & xp_{-1} + \frac{\kappa}{2} & x_{-1}p_{-1} & pp_{-1} & p_{-1}^2 \end{bmatrix} \begin{bmatrix} A_0 \\ A_1 \\ A_2 \\ A_3 \\ A_4 \\ A_5 \end{bmatrix} = \begin{bmatrix} q \\ qq_{-1} \\ qx \\ qx_{-1} \\ qp \\ qp_{-1} \end{bmatrix}$$

$$A_2A_5 - A_3A_4 = 0$$

(The summation signs and the subscript $t$ have been dropped for convenience; $T$ is the number of observations.)

We see $\kappa$ enters four of the first six equations as either an addition or a subtraction to the cross-products between the total expenditure and price terms. A nonzero value of $\kappa$ amounts to adjusting the covariance, and hence the correlation, between total expenditure and price. Note that once a value for $\kappa$ is specified, the first six equations are linear in the regression coefficients.

If the first six equations are solved for $A_0, \ldots, A_5$ in terms of $\kappa$, it is possible to define a function

$$(63)\quad \theta(\kappa) = A_2A_5 - A_3A_4.$$

The object is to find a solution for $\theta(\kappa) = 0$. Unfortunately, the functional form of $\theta$ is both unknown and nonlinear, so that an immediate solution of $\theta(\kappa) = 0$ is not evident. As a result, the procedure we follow is to approximate $\theta(\kappa)$ by a linear function, $\theta^*(\kappa)$, by solving the first six equations for two arbitrary values of $\kappa$, $\kappa_1$, and $\kappa_2$, and then evaluating $\theta(\kappa_1)$ and $\theta(\kappa_2)$. Given these two values of $\theta$, $\kappa_3$ for $\theta^*(\kappa_3) = 0$ is evaluated. Again $\kappa_3$ is used to solve the first six equations for new values of $A_0, \ldots, A_5$. Then $A_2$, $A_3$, $A_4$, and $A_5$ are substituted in (63) to see if in fact $\theta(\kappa_3)$ does equal $\theta^*(\kappa)$. In other words, we have

(64) $$\theta(\kappa_1) = \theta^*(\kappa_1) \quad \text{and} \quad \theta(\kappa_2) = \theta^*(\kappa_2),$$

so that the objective is to have

(65) $$\theta(\kappa_3) = \theta^*(\kappa_3) = 0.$$

If equality is not attained, the entire procedure is repeated using the value of $\kappa$ suggested by the first iteration, and so on.

The mechanics of the technique are illustrated graphically in Figure 1.3, where it is assumed that the correct value of $\kappa$ is reached in two iterations. The solid line is the true $\theta$, while the hatched line is $\theta_1^*$ and the dotted line is $\theta_2^*$. (Note: the shape of the "true" $\theta$ in this diagram is completely arbitrary and is used only for illustrative purposes.)

Figure 1.3

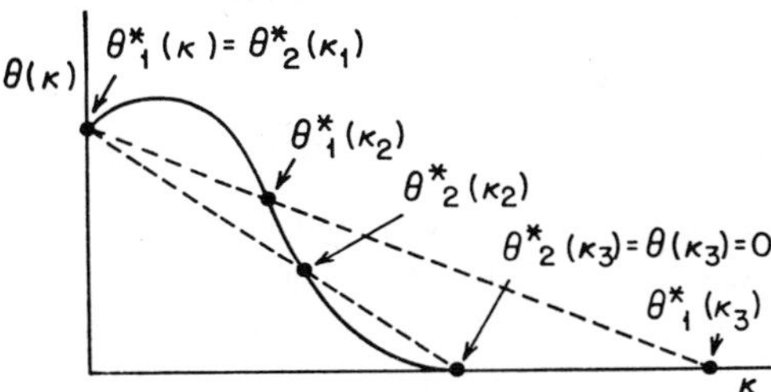


The validity of the method depends, of course, upon the eventual converging of the process. Although there is no guarantee of convergence, our experience suggests that a fairly rapid one can be expected, usually after three or four iterations. Moreover, multiple roots are possible, in which case the root which gives the highest $R^2$ should be used (assuming, of course, that the corresponding estimates of the coefficients are acceptable).

The size of $\kappa$ is of particular interest, for in a sense it can be interpreted as a measure of the compatibility of the model and the data. A small value for $\kappa$ is to be preferred, for this means that the data are nearly consistent (in the sense of identifiability) with the model as they stand. A large value of $\kappa$ indicates the opposite. Among other things, this means that the empirical covariance between total expenditure and prices must be altered considerably.[12] In fact, since $\kappa$ enters (62) in only the off-diagonal terms, it is possible for the value of $\kappa$ to be so large that the moment matrix in (62) becomes negative-definite, a result that has no meaning in classical statistical theory. This actually happened in several instances, one of which is presented below.

[12] This creates the problem of deciding when $\kappa$ is to be considered "small." One possibility is to look at the size of $\kappa$ relative to some measure of the "size" of the matrix in (62), say the trace. However, we have not pursued this beyond looking at the absolute value of $\kappa$.

Of the 72 dynamic models estimated in the study, 23 of them include prices and have been estimated using constrained least squares. In order further to illustrate the method, the equations for item 8.1a (new cars and net purchases of used cars) are presented and briefly discussed here. (Note: $\kappa = 0$ corresponds to ignoring the identifying restriction.)

$\kappa = 0$ (ordinary least squares)

$$q_t = \underset{(.0980)}{.5193q_{t-1}} + \underset{(.02591)}{.15460\Delta x_t} + \underset{(.00880)}{.01506x_{t-1}} - \underset{(.1995)}{.4774\Delta p_t} - \underset{(.1426)}{.0498p_{t-1}} + \underset{(3.578)}{14.115d_t} \tag{66}$$

$$\delta_1 = .1024 \qquad \delta_2 = .1101 \qquad R^2 = .958 \qquad D.W. = 1.97$$

$\kappa = 99.7052$ (constrained least squares)

$$\hat{q}_t = \underset{(.0908)}{.5183q_{t-1}} + \underset{(.025894)}{.154442\Delta x_t} + \underset{(.007803)}{.014852x_{t-1}} - \underset{(.1999)}{.4749\Delta p_t} - \underset{(.1427)}{.0457p_{t-1}} + \underset{(3.579)}{14.073d_t} \tag{67}$$

$$\delta = .1010 \qquad R^2 = .958 \qquad D.W. = 1.95$$

(The symbols and notations are explained at the beginning of Chapter 4.)

These equations, selected deliberately because the value of $\kappa$ for this item is the smallest of the 23 categories, show that the data are nearly consistent with the identifying restriction as they stand. In particular, the two estimates of $\delta$ for $\kappa = 0$ are .1024 and .1101, respectively, which are close indeed. Ideally one would like to have the variances and covariances of the two $\delta$'s so that a test of the null hypothesis $\delta_1 = \delta_2$ could be performed. Unfortunately these statistics can be derived only with considerable effort; however, tests of $A_3 \neq 0$ and $A_5 \neq 0$ are tests of $\delta_1 \neq 0$ and $\delta_2 \neq 0$, so that in equation (66) above we can conclude that $\delta_2$ does not differ significantly from zero.

It was mentioned earlier that it is possible for $\kappa$ to become so large that the estimating moment matrix becomes negative-definite. The equations for 8.2a (street and electric railway and local bus), one of the several categories for which this actually occurred, follow:

$\kappa = 0$ (ordinary least squares)

$$\hat{q}_t = \underset{(.0129)}{.9135q_{t-1}} + \underset{(.001364)}{.005126x_t} + \underset{(.000573)}{.000978x_{t-1}} - \underset{(.012930)}{.074162p_t} - \underset{(.004911)}{.001524p_{t-1}} - \underset{(.3363)}{.1647d_t} \tag{68}$$

$$\delta_1 = .2109 \qquad \delta_2 = .0229 \qquad R^2 = .996 \qquad D.W. = 1.91$$

$\kappa = 66{,}524$ (constrained least squares)

$$\hat{q}_t = .9669q_{t-1} + .006939x_t + .000023x_t - .062206p_t - .000890p_{t-1} - .5309d_t \tag{69}$$

$$\delta_1 = .0034 \qquad \delta_2 = .0014 \qquad R^2 = .990 \qquad D.W. = .94$$

Standard errors are not included in (69) because one variance was negative due to the negative definiteness of the estimating matrix. The category was finally estimated under the assumption $\delta = 0$. This special assumption, along with several others, is discussed in the next section.

## *V. Special Cases of the Dynamic Model*

In the course of estimating equation (55) for the several commodities, four special cases emerged that we shall now discuss separately. With a few commodities $A_1$ was found to be close to one, thereby implying that $\beta$ is close to $\delta$. In this case the equation can be simplified by putting $A_1 = 1$ and transferring the second term to the left-hand side so that the equation becomes

$$(70) \qquad q_t - q_{t-1} = A_0 + A_2 \Delta x_t + A_3 x_{t-1} + A_4 \Delta p_t + A_5 p_{t-1} + v_t.$$

Note that in this situation the long-term interpretation of the model breaks down because of the required division by $\delta - \beta$ (compare equations [11] and [42]). This is elaborated further below.

The second special case occurs when $A_2$ and $A_4$ do not differ significantly from $A_3$ and $A_5$, respectively. This implies that $\delta = 2$ and means that equation (55) becomes

$$(71) \qquad q_t = A_0 + A_1 q_{t-1} + A_2 x_t + A_4 p_t + v_t,$$

which includes only the current levels of total expenditure and prices. The case $\delta = 2$ appears to be of some importance as a special limiting case. As can be seen from (9), in long-term equilibrium $\delta$ can be interpreted as a consumption-inventory ratio. Then $\delta = 2$ would arise with a commodity with a lifetime of one year that is bought once a year. Admittedly, this is a polar example and would be unlikely to occur with broadly defined consumption categories. Indeed, when habit formation is permitted this interpretation loses much of its force; a more plausible interpretation is given below.

The third special case of the dynamic model arises when $A_3$ and $A_5$ do not differ significantly from zero, but when $A_2$ and $A_4$ do. This implies that $\delta$ is close to zero. Assuming that $\delta$ is in fact zero involves eliminating the intercept $x_{t-1}$ and $p_{t-1}$ from (55)—that is, $A_0$, $A_3$, and $A_5$ are assumed to equal zero. The long-run interpretation of the model becomes implausible with this case, for in long-run equilibrium $\delta = 0$ implies $\hat{q} = 0$ (compare [9]), a result that would be reasonable only with a markedly inferior good; moreover, as can be seen from (38), $\alpha$ becomes indeterminate. Consequently an alternative interpretation of this case is in order (see section III of Chapter 6).

The last special case of the dynamic model is a rather peculiar one and may possess only limited economic interest. It is conceivable that a commodity will have a zero or even a negative short-run income coefficient, but nevertheless a positive one in the long run. This case arises when $A_3$ is large relative to $A_2$, and where $A_2$ may even be negative. If $A_2$ does not differ from zero, the elimination of $x_t$ from the model involves assuming $\delta = -2$. However, as was the case of $\delta = 2$, the interpretation of $\beta$ and $\delta$ is not clear in this situation.

Note that the four special cases have in common the fact that a particular value of $\delta$ is involved; moreover, for each of these values of $\delta$, the interpretation of the model is strained. In particular, the long-run interpretation of the model breaks down completely with case one and becomes implausible with case two, while the interpretation of $\delta$ becomes hazy with cases three and four. These observations suggest that an alternative formulation of the set of underlying structural equations might be in order.

This is possible in cases two and four, $\delta = 2$ and $\delta = -2$. The differential equations corresponding to these two cases have been elusive, but to recast the equations in the framework of a meaningful discrete process is a straightforward exercise.

The case $\delta = 2$ corresponds to the classical geometric distributed-lag model as formulated by Koyck (1954) and others. We formulate the model as a single equation:

$$q_t = \alpha + \beta \sum_{i=0}^{\infty} \lambda^i x_{t-i}. \tag{72}$$

We now subtract

$$\lambda q_{t-1} = \lambda\alpha + \beta(\lambda x_{t-1} + \lambda^2 x_{t-2} + \cdots) \tag{73}$$

from (72):

$$q_t - \lambda q_{t-1} = (1 - \lambda)\alpha + \beta x_t, \tag{74}$$

or

$$q_t = (1 - \lambda)\alpha + \lambda q_{t-1} + \beta x_t, \tag{75}$$

which conforms to equation (71), with prices and the error term omitted (see also section III of Chapter 6).

Similarly, the case $\delta = -2$ corresponds to a geometric distributed-lag model with a complete lapse of one time period; that is, the structural equation is

$$q_t = \alpha + \beta \sum_{i=1}^{\infty} \lambda^{i-1} x_{t-i}. \tag{76}$$

If we apply the "Koyck transformation" in the same manner as above, we obtain

$$q_t = (1 - \lambda)\alpha + \lambda q_{t-1} + \beta x_{t-1}, \tag{77}$$

which corresponds to the basic equation with $A_2 = 0$ (again with prices and the error term omitted).

It is apparent from previous considerations that prices are treated in a manner parallel to income, so that their inclusion does not create any problem. Similarly the addition of the error term does not raise any new questions of principle.

To recapitulate, we have found in the empirical part of the study that there are four values of $\delta$ which have particular significance. These are $\beta = \delta$ and $\delta = 2$, 0, and $-2$, respectively, which in turn corresponds to $A_1 = 1$, $A_2 = A_3$ (and $A_4 = A_5$), $A_3 = 0$ (and $A_5 = 0$) and $A_2 = 0$ (and $A_4 = 0$). At this point we abandoned the original interpretation of the set of structural equations and reformulated them in order to provide a more plausible interpretation of two of the special cases. In the empirical work in Chapter IV these cases will be noted as they occur.

## *VI. An Alternative Dynamic Model*

In several of the habit-forming commodities analyzed in Chapter 4, our basic dynamic equation (37) implies values of the depreciation rate $\delta$ that at first sight seemed implausibly high.[13] This gave rise to the suspicion that we might be estimating something that is indeterminate because the basic equation does not hold even approximately for certain commodities. An alternative dynamic model has therefore been considered, which was suggested to us by A. R. Bergstrom of the London School of Economics.

In the "Bergstrom model" the state variables do not appear. Rather than as a process of adjustment in physical or psychological stocks, the dynamics of consumption is viewed as an attempt on the part of consumers to bring their actual consumption closer to some desired level, which is determined by PCE (and possibly by other variables as well). In its continuous form the model consists of

$$\dot{q} = \theta(\hat{q} - q); \tag{78}$$

$$\hat{q} = \xi + \mu x. \tag{79}$$

Again $\dot{q}$ is the rate of change of consumption over time, and $q$ is the desired level of consumption.

With our usual approximation,

$$q_t - q_{t-1} = \tfrac{1}{2}(\Delta^* q_t + \Delta^* q_{t-1}), \tag{80}$$

the estimating equation becomes

$$q_t = A_0^* + A_1^* q_{t-1} + A_2^*(x_t + x_{t-1}). \tag{81}$$

[13] They seemed high in comparison with the depreciation rates for durables, but we do not yet know what values of $\delta$ are plausible in the case of habit formation. The alternative interpretation in equation (53) above, which makes high values more plausible, is an afterthought and the results in Chapter 4 have been evaluated without its benefit.

In this case

$$A_0^* = \frac{\theta\xi}{1 + \frac{1}{2}\theta}; \tag{82}$$

$$A_1^* = \frac{1 - \frac{1}{2}\theta}{1 + \frac{1}{2}\theta}; \tag{83}$$

$$A_2^* = \frac{\theta\mu}{1 + \frac{1}{2}\theta}; \tag{84}$$

$$\theta = \frac{2(1 - A_1^*)}{1 + A_1^*}; \tag{85}$$

$$\xi = \frac{A_0^*}{1 - A_1^*}; \tag{86}$$

$$\mu = \frac{2A_2^*}{1 - A_1^*}. \tag{87}$$

Table 1.2. Equation (81): Behavior of Consumption over Time

Item 4.1: owner-occupied housing

| | Case 1 | | | Case 2 | | |
|---|---|---|---|---|---|---|
| Year | $x_t$ | $q_t$ | $\Delta q_t$ | $x_t$ | $q_t$ | $\Delta q_t$ |
| 1961 | 1657 | 137.84 | – | 1657 | 137.84 | – |
| 1962 | 1657 | 141.73 | +3.89 | 1711.22 | 142.08 | +4.24 |
| 1963 | 1657 | 145.31 | +3.58 | 1765.44 | 146.70 | +4.62 |
| 1964 | 1657 | 148.60 | +3.29 | 1819.66 | 151.66 | +4.96 |
| 1965 | 1657 | 151.63 | +3.03 | 1873.88 | 156.94 | +5.28 |
| 1966 | 1657 | 154.42 | +2.79 | 1928.10 | 162.51 | +5.57 |
| 1967 | 1657 | 156.99 | +2.57 | 1982.32 | 168.35 | +5.84 |
| 1968 | 1657 | 159.35 | +2.36 | 2036.55 | 174.44 | +6.09 |
| 1969 | 1657 | 161.53 | +2.18 | 2090.78 | 180.76 | +6.32 |
| 1970 | 1657 | 163.53 | +2.00 | 2145 | 187.29 | +6.53 |
| | Case 3 | | | Case 4 | | |
| 1961 | 1657 | 137.84 | – | 1657 | 137.84 | – |
| 1962 | 1657 | 141.73 | +3.89 | 1711.22 | 142.08 | +4.24 |
| 1963 | 1711.22 | 145.66 | +3.87 | 1765.44 | 146.70 | +4.62 |
| 1964 | 1711.22 | 149.64 | +3.98 | 1765.44 | 151.31 | +4.61 |
| 1965 | 1711.22 | 153.30 | +3.66 | 1711.22 | 155.19 | +3.88 |
| 1966 | 1657 | 156.31 | +3.01 | 1711.22 | 158.41 | +3.22 |
| 1967 | 1657 | 158.73 | +2.42 | 1765.44 | 161.73 | +3.32 |
| 1968 | – | – | – | 1819.66 | 165.50 | +3.77 |

In terms of the basic equation (37) the Bergstrom model corresponds to $A_2 = 2A_3$, so that $\delta$ is indeterminate according to (53). The Bergstrom model was used for three commodities, namely 4.1 (space rental value of owner-occupied dwellings), 4.4 (other housing), and 5.8b (gas). It was tried without success for several other items.

As a numerical example similar to those in Table 1.1, we shall take 4.1 (owner-occupied housing), even though it is a somewhat extreme case of habit formation. However, 4.1 is not only a large item and a suitable counterpart to 1.1 and 2.3, but it also possesses some very interesting features (see Table 1.2 and Figure 1.2). The four cases considered are the same as in Table 1.1. The equation for 4.1 used is

$$q_t = -6.9625 + .9205q_{t-1} + .00658(x_t + x_{t-1}), \tag{88}$$

where the terms with $d_t$ and $z_t$ given in Chapter 4 have been absorbed into the intercept (with $d_t = 1$ and $z_t$ equal to its historical mean, given in Table 4.3). The corresponding equation for desired consumption is

$$\hat{q} = -87.58 + .1655x, \tag{89}$$

which for 1961 ($x = 1657$) gives $\hat{q} = 186.65$.

The most striking pattern of all four cases in Table 1.2 is the rise in consumption in every year without exception. This is, of course, due mostly to the large shortfall of actual compared to desired consumption in 1961, which cannot be made up quickly because of the slow adjustment ($\mu = .0828$). In the ten years covered by Case 1 only a little more than half of this shortfall is made good. Indeed, in the earlier years of Case 2 the rise in consumption is not much greater than in Case 1, though later on Case 2 shows a more rapid rise. In 1970, however, actual consumption at \$187.29 is still very much below the desired level of \$267.42 at a PCE of \$2145; the shortfall is even greater than in 1961, both in dollars and in percentage terms.

The fluctuations in PCE of Cases 3 and 4 have almost no effect on housing consumption, which rises inexorably. Even the annual increase is only slightly affected by the changes in PCE. If these results can be taken seriously,[14] owner-occupied housing promises to be a tower of strength in the American economy for many years to come!

[14] It is worth noting that the alternative dynamic model for item 4.1 given in Chapter 4 leads to very similar conclusions. In the case of rental housing (item 4.2), 1961 consumption was close to its equilibrium level.

# 2

# *Data and Variables*

The principal source of data was the United States Department of Commerce, which has published annual data on 84 different categories of personal consumption expenditures (PCE) from 1929 to date. These published data are in current dollars; constant-dollar figures (in prices of 1954) are not published in the same detail, because they are not considered as reliable, but they were made available by the Office of Business Economics in the form of worksheets. In a few instances the unpublished data gave more commodity detail than is published.

All calculations reported in this study are in terms of constant dollars, both for the dependent variables and for total expenditure. The current-dollar figures have been used only to obtain price indices (base 1954) for each category of expenditures by dividing the constant-dollar amount into the current-dollar amount. These price indices are therefore so-called implicit deflators which means that (unlike the Consumer Price Index) the weights of the various components of each category shift over time. The individual price series were deflated by the price index for total PCE derived in the same manner, thus giving a set of relative price indices.

The Department of Commerce data have been taken as they came, without any attempt at adjustment.[1] The projections presented in Chapters 4 and 5 are therefore directly comparable with the actual data that will be published in 1970, except for changes in Commerce Department estimating procedures between now and 1970 and for revisions in already published data. In particular it appears that Commerce Department data on consumption are less accurate after 1954 than before, since the 1954 Census of Manufactures is the most recent one used for deriving these data. Consequently considerable revisions in the figures for 1955–1961 are expected when the data using the 1958 Census become available. The bulk of the empirical work in this study was completed by August 1963.

It may be appropriate at this point to insert some comments on the quality of the Commerce Department data for PCE. Since for most commodities they are the only figures available, there is no basis for discussing their accuracy without a great deal of additional research. It is clear that some series are more reliable than others, but no attempt has been made to

[1] There is one difference from the published classification. Alcohol had been separated out from items 1.1 and 1.2 and is treated here as a distinct category, which we have numbered 1.0.

classify the series by accuracy, for such an attempt would not have improved the projection exercise. There is always a temptation to attribute unsatisfactory regression results to defects in the data, though it is equally conceivable that crude data give higher correlations: everything depends on how the data were derived. Indeed, it should be emphasized that many of the data series are themselves the result of more or less indirect estimating procedures, and that regression analysis on such series may on occasion amount to nothing more than an ex-post reconstruction of these procedures.[2]

Some of the PCE series are greatly influenced by the bookkeeping conventions on which the United States National Accounts are based, so that their interpretation in terms of actual transactions is often difficult. One important example is the space rental value of owner-occupied dwellings, not to be confused with the housing expenditure of homeowners;[3] another is the "expense of handling life insurance," which represents expenditures by life insurance companies rather than by households.[4] Perhaps the most debatable item of this type is "services furnished without payment by financial intermediaries other than life insurance companies," amounting to well over $5 billion in 1961, which is merely a bookkeeping entry designed to offset an anomaly in the treatment of interest elsewhere in the accounts.[5] It is wholly out of line with any realistic estimate of the net cost of handling checks for nonbusiness accounts; indeed, it exceeds the total operating cost (excluding interest) of all commercial banks by a considerable margin. For projection purposes, however, any doubts about the meaning of the consumption categories have been rigorously suppressed.

Another factor limiting the usefulness of the Commerce Department data is the uneven fineness with which expenditures are broken down. Huge undivided aggregates such as "food purchased for off-premise consumption," amounting to $61 billion in 1961, contrast with such minute items as "purchased intercity transportation other than by rail, bus or air," amounting to $22 million. These are admittedly extreme examples; most of the individual items are between $1 and $5 billion, which is a reasonable range. However, a further breakdown of the food item and a few others would greatly increase the value of the published PCE table. To conclude these critical remarks, however, we wish to put on record our conviction that the Commerce Department data, for all their weaknesses, are derived with unusual conceptual clarity, painstaking care, and keen critical judgment. We certainly do not wish to leave the impression that our work is built on sand.

Some remarks about the period of observation underlying the regressions are in order here. Except for the two cases noted in our footnote, this was

[2] A general ex-ante description of these procedures may be found on pp. 103–122 of *National Income*, 1954 ed. (a supplement to the *Survey of Current Business*), but it usually does not give enough detail to permit an independent derivation of the individual series, which no doubt also reflect a certain amount of expert judgment.

[3] *National Income*, p. 46.

[4] *Ibid.*, p. 48.

[5] *Ibid.*, pp. 46–47.

1929–1961 excluding the war years 1942–1945, leaving 29 years in all (in the dynamic models discussed in Chapter 1 the observations for 1929 and 1946 are lost by differencing).[6] The reasons for omitting the war years are obvious, but it is possible to question the inclusion of the prewar period on the grounds that it is too remote. The main advantage of including this period is that it nearly doubles the number of observations, which are always at a premium in time-series analysis.[7] It also increases the range of variation of the predictors and thus increases the confidence with which the regression coefficients can be used for projection. Furthermore, as indicated, the PCE data from 1955 on are subject to revision and therefore should not be given undue weight.

Moreover, there is another reason for keeping the prewar years, which has to do with our extensive use of the dynamic model in the study. The dynamic model, it will be recalled, is basically a process whereby physical and psychological stocks are adjusted to income. In the postwar period, the dependent variables, as well as income, in many instances have been dominated by strong trends so that an equilibrium between stocks and income may never have been reached. In particular this would be true if, over a considerable portion of the period, there was for some reason or another a constraint upon supply. Since we are ignoring supply in our analyses, it becomes mandatory, if the dynamic model is to be valid for projection, that somewhere in the experience used to estimate the model there should exist an equilibrium between stocks and income. This is where the experience of the 1930s comes to the fore: at the low (relative) levels of income prevailing in the early thirties, the existing levels of stocks probably came close in many instances to being equilibrium amounts.

On the other hand, it is conceivable that consumers' tastes changed markedly as a result of World War II, which would render the prewar experience irrelevant. There is no convincing indication that any major change has occurred, but in the regressions this possibility was allowed for to some extent by the introduction of a "dummy variable," which permits demand to have a different level (but not a different response to income or price changes) in the postwar years compared to the prewar years. For many commodities this dummy variable turned out to be insignificant, even under the rather generous criteria adopted in this study (see section I of Chapter 1).

## I. *Variables Used in the Analyses*

The usual approach in demand analysis is to set out a relationship between quantity consumed and prices, with disposable income as the relevant budget

[6] The exceptions are alcoholic beverages, for which there were no data prior to 1933 since the Commerce Department figures do not cover illicit transactions, and the space rental of farmhouses which are analyzed only from 1946 on since there was no farm-income series for earlier years.

[7] A fresh reading of Yule's classic paper (1926) on spurious correlation and the dangers inherent in using short time series will help to bring home the points of this paragraph.

variable. However, rather than using disposable income we have used total consumption expenditure as the independent variable. This is in keeping with the end objective of the investigation, which is to take a given level of total PCE in 1970 and allocate it optimally among its components. In the early days of demand analysis, particularly in budget inquiries, investigators often had to use total expenditure rather than income because typically income information was not given, nor could it be derived.[8] Hence the use of total expenditure is not novel.

There is, moreover, a more sophisticated reason for using total expenditure, even in the face of availability of income data. This is the argument that, at least over short periods of time, consumers have more control over their expenditures than over their receipts of income, so that total expenditure is a better measure of the "true" income of the consumer. It is an easy extension to interpret this argument as a variant of the permanent-income hypothesis made popular in recent years by Modigliani and Brumberg (1954), Friedman (1957), and their followers. We postpone further discussion of this topic until Chapter 6 where a permanent-income hypothesis is incorporated into the dynamic model. We mention it here only to point out that the use of total expenditure is in keeping with such a hypothesis.

For prices, with two exceptions, we have used the implicit deflators derived in the manner described in Chapter 1. The exceptions are items 8.1a (new cars and net purchases of used cars) and 5.8a (electricity). For 8.1a we used the deflated average price paid for new cars in each year—that is, total expenditure in current prices was divided by the number of new cars sold (adjusted for imports) and this figure divided by the total PCE deflator. For 5.8a we used a deflated marginal price.

Two stock variables have been used frequently in various forms of the static model.[9] These are the stocks of automobiles per capita (as measured by car registrations), which appears in several categories of Group VIII (transportation expenditures), and the stocks of television sets per capita, which is in a few equations of Group IX (recreation expenditures). In preliminary work these two variables, as well as certain predictors other than total PCE and relative prices, were occasionally used in the dynamic model. However, of the 72 categories with the dynamic model only in item 5.10 (domestic services) does a predictor other than total PCE and price appear in the final equation.[10]

A distribution-of-income variable, derived from unpublished data provided by the Bureau of Labor Statistics, has been used frequently and appears in several of the equations. This variable has been constructed from graphical interpolation on double logarithmic paper, and is designed to allow for different marginal propensities to consume between the top fifth and the bottom

[8] See, among others, Allen and Bowley (1935) and Prais and Houthakker (1955).

[9] These are not to be confused with the (theoretical) state variables that characterize the dynamic model of Chapter 1.

[10] This predictor is the distribution of income and is discussed in the next paragraph.

four fifths of the income groups.[11] The measure is defined as the difference between 1/5 times the mean income of the top group and 4/5 times the mean income in the bottom group. With this definition, the different marginal propensities to consume are derived as follows:

> Let $x_1$ be the mean income for the top group, and $x_2$ the mean income for the bottom group. Then the overall mean is $(x_1 + 4x_2)/5$, while by definition the income distribution measure is $(x_1 - 4x_2)/5$. Hence in the regression
>
> $$y = a + b\left(\frac{x_1 + 4x_2}{5}\right) + c\left(\frac{x_1 - 4x_2}{5}\right)$$
>
> the MPC of the upper group is $(b + c)/5$, while it is $4(b - c)/5$ for the lower group.

The intercepts of the regression equations have been estimated as the coefficients of a dummy variable that takes the value 1 for all observations. This allows the intercept to be treated like any other explanatory variable in an equation. Accordingly, the intercept has been suppressed whenever it did not exceed its standard error.

Finally, there remain only the predictors that have been used in isolated instances. These are treated in Chapter 4 when the equations in which they appear are discussed. The historical series for these variables, as well as for the variables discussed above, are given in the data appendix.

## *II. Use of Per Capita Figures*

In the calculations reported in this book—except for certain derived projections in Chapter 4 and 5 and for the analysis at the end of Chapter 6—consumption, total PCE, and similar variables are expressed in per capita terms. This is necessary partly because the underlying theory of consumer choice refers primarily to individuals, and partly because per capita relationships are likely to be more meaningful and stable than relationships between aggregates. Thus the fact that aggregate PCE has risen by 5 percent does not lead to any conclusions about, say, food consumption unless we know how much of the rise is due to population growth and how much to an increase in per capita PCE. To take two polar cases, if all the aggregate increase reflects population growth, food consumption may be expected to rise by the same 5 percent, but if population remains constant the rise in food consumption is determined by its elasticity with respect to per capita PCE, so that it may be no more than about 3 percent. The use of aggregate PCE in static models is legitimate only if the elasticity of the item considered is close to one.

The use of per capita figures raises two difficulties, however. In the first

[11] It is well known that redistribution of income has no effect on total demand unless there is a difference in the MPC's of different income groups.

place, it is not strictly correct to give all persons equal weight irrespective of age and sex; as is well known, in principle one should use a different scale of weights (or "equivalent adult scale") for each commodity, with a "general scale" for PCE. But the limited evidence there is on these scales (see Prais and Houthakker, 1955) suggests that equal-weight scales do not produce too much distortion; moreover, the age and sex distribution of the population is fairly stable. For the few commodities where the problem appeared to be more serious, we have special demographic variables to achieve the desired correction (for instance, the percentage of the population over eighteen or on farms).

The second difficulty is connected with the dynamic model developed in Chapter 1. The basic behavior equation (1.2) is unaffected, but the accounting identity (1.3) holds only if population is constant. If it is not, the per capita stocks will be affected also by population changes. To see more clearly how this works out, let us put $S$ for the aggregate stock and $\pi$ for population, so that

$$S = \pi s. \tag{1}$$

Also writing $Q$ for aggregate consumption and $W$ for aggregate "using up," it is still true that

$$\dot{S} = Q - W. \tag{2}$$

But differentiation of (1) gives

$$\dot{S} = \dot{\pi}s + \pi\dot{s}, \tag{3}$$

and by virtue of (1.2) and the definitions of $S$, $Q$, and $W$ we get

$$\pi\dot{s} = Q - W - \dot{\pi}s; \tag{4}$$

hence

$$\dot{s} = q - w - \frac{\dot{\pi}}{\pi}s. \tag{5}$$

Now we introduce two special assumptions. The first is identical with (1.4), which defines the depreciation rate. The second lets population grow at a constant percentage rate $\psi$:

$$\pi(t) = \pi_0 e^{\psi t}, \tag{6}$$

where $\pi_0 = \pi(0)$. Consequently

$$\frac{\dot{\pi}}{\pi} = \psi \tag{7}$$

and (5) become

$$\dot{s} = q - \delta s - \psi s. \tag{8}$$

The effect of exponential population growth, then, is to replace (1.5) by

$$\dot{s} = q - (\delta + \psi)s. \tag{9}$$

Since $\delta$ does not appear anywhere else in the basic equation, this means we have to replace it by $(\delta + \psi)$ in all subsequent formulas of Chapter 1.

Fortunately the difference between $\delta$ and $(\delta + \psi)$ is quite small. The average rate of population growth was 1.3 percent from 1929 to 1961, so that all estimated $\delta$'s in Chapters 4 and 6 should really be increased by about .013. For most items $\delta$ is much larger than this, and the correction is negligible compared to the errors in the estimation of $\delta$; we have therefore not made it. However, in two important cases where the estimated $\delta$ is small (namely automobiles and savings), we have noted this "population effect," and in section IV of Chapter 6 we have analyzed it explicitly. The results of that section do not suggest that the population effect is of much quantitative importance.

# 3

# *Problems of Estimation and Projection*

The discussion up to this point has centered largely on the models and the data. Since the objective of the investigation was to provide a set of projections for 1970 of the components of PCE, the methods employed and some problems encountered in preparing the projections will be discussed in this chapter. The projections themselves will be discussed in Chapter 5.

Projection with the static model is essentially a trivial exercise, for the value of the predictors (or their logarithms, as the case may be) have only to be substituted into the equation. Since the estimating form of the dynamic model is a first-order difference equation, either the projection must be built up year by year from some initial conditions, or else a solution must be obtained for the difference equation and the projection made from the solved equation. Though these procedures are in principle equivalent, projecting from the solved equation is likely to involve more rounding error. Hence we have chosen to build up the projections year by year. We shall have occasion later to use the solution of the dynamic model. It is given by

$$(1)\quad q_{1970} = [A_0 + A_6 + A_2 q + A_3(x_{1961} + 8q) + A_4 h + A_5(p_{1961} + 8h)] \times \left[\frac{1 - A_1^9}{1 - A_1}\right] + \frac{9A_1^9}{1 - A_1} - \frac{A_1(1 - A_1^9)}{(1 - A_1)^2}(A_3 q + A_5 h) + A_1^9 q_{1961} + \sum_{i=1}^{q} A_1^{9-i} v_{1961+i},$$

where $q = \Delta x_i$ and $h = \Delta p_i$ for all $i$, and $A_6$ is the coefficient of the war-dummy variable.

Since 1961 is the most recent experience in the model, the 1961 values have been used for initial conditions; among other things, to use an earlier year would imply a higher variance, about which more will be said below. The only point at issue is how to treat the error in the dependent variable for 1961. Clearly it should be taken into account, for to ignore it by using the regression value for 1961 would amount to throwing away valuable information. We could force the 1961 value to lie on the regression line by incorporating the 1961 error into the intercept. However, since the data for the years after 1954 are subject to considerable revision, the last few years should not be given undue weight. Hence we have used the actual 1961 value of the dependent variable as an initial condition and have not altered the intercept of the estimated equation. Other than for those equations without intercepts, this means that the projections are tied to the means of the historical period.

The sequence of topics in this chapter is as follows. The impossibility of providing a classical measure of the efficiency of the projections from the dynamic model and the problem of autocorrelated residuals are discussed in sections I and II. A difficulty encountered in projecting from the three-pass equations is treated in section III, while the results of a Monte Carlo experiment designed to resolve this difficulty are presented in section IV. Section V discusses the adding-up problem, and a final problem is noted at the end.

## I. The Projecting Variance

Except for the special case where $\beta = \delta$ is assumed, it is not possible to provide an estimate of the standard error of the projection with the dynamic model. This problem is not peculiar to our dynamic model, but rather is a general problem with all such models. We can use the following simple dynamic equation to illustrate the problem:

$$y_{t+1} = \xi + \lambda y_t + \kappa x_{t+1} + u_{t+1}. \tag{2}$$

If we assume $x_{t+1} = x_t + h$ for all $t$, the general solution for (2) can be written

$$\begin{aligned} y_{t+n} = {} & \xi(1 + \lambda + \lambda^2 + \cdots + \lambda^n) + \lambda^n y_t \\ & + \kappa(\lambda^n + 2\lambda^{n-1} + 3\lambda^{n-2} + \cdots + (n-1)\lambda + n)hx_t \\ & + \sum_{i=1}^{n} \lambda^{n-i} u_{t+i}. \end{aligned} \tag{3}$$

The projection for $y_{t+n}$ will be

$$\begin{aligned} \hat{y}_{t+n} = {} & a(1 + b + b^2 + \cdots + b^n) + b^n y_t \\ & + c(b^n + 2b^{n-1} + \cdots + (n-1)b + n)hx_t, \end{aligned} \tag{4}$$

and the variance of the projection is

$$\begin{aligned} E(y_{t+n} - \hat{y}_{t+n})^2 = {} & E[(a - \xi)^2 + (ab - \xi\lambda)^2 + \cdots + (ab^n - \xi\lambda^n)^2 \\ & + (b^n - \lambda^n)^2]y_t^2 + [n^2(c - \kappa)^2 + c^2(b^n - \lambda^n)^2 \\ & + 4c^2(b^{n-1} - \lambda^{n-1})^2 + \cdots \\ & + (n-1)^2c^2(b - \lambda)^2]h^2x_t^2 \\ & + \left[\sum_{i=1}^{n} \lambda^{n-1} u_{t+i}\right]^2 + \text{cross product terms}. \end{aligned} \tag{5}$$

It is seen immediately that the terms involving powers of the coefficients are not estimatible from the data in the usual manner. Indeed it is not clear that they can even be estimated in principle.

The problem disappears if it is assumed that $\lambda = 1$; that is, if $y_t$ is moved to the left-hand side in (2). The solution becomes

$$y_{t+n} = n\xi + y_t + \kappa x_t + \frac{n(n-1)}{2}\kappa h + \sum_{i=1}^{n} u_{t+i}, \tag{6}$$

with

$$(7) \qquad \hat{y}_{t+n} = na + y_t + cx_t + \frac{n(n-1)}{2} ch$$

as the corresponding projection. Hence

$$(8) \qquad E(y_{t+n} - \hat{y}_{t+n})^2 = n^2 \text{ var } a + x_t^2 \text{ var } b + h^2 \frac{(n(n-1))^2}{4} \text{ var } c + n\sigma^2 + \text{covariance terms},$$

where $\sigma^2$ is the variance of $u$. Each of these variances and covariances can be estimated directly from the data. This case has practical interest also for the dynamic model when $\beta = \delta$ fits the hypothesis of (6). Accordingly, it is possible to provide standard errors for the projections from the equations in this category. Unfortunately, these are the only dynamic equations for which this can be done.

Nonetheless, it is possible to offer several remarks of a qualitative nature regarding the projecting variance of the other dynamic models. First, Stone and Prais (1953) have pointed out that, as long as the coefficient of the lagged dependent variable is positive but less than one, the resulting contribution of the stochastic element in the projecting variance is considerably lessened. To see this, we note that the contribution of the error term in (5) if $\lambda = 1$ is $n\sigma^2$, while it is

$$[(1 - \lambda^{2n})/(1 - \lambda^2)]\sigma^2 < n\sigma^2 \text{ if } 0 \leqslant \lambda < 1.$$

Next, $\lambda = 1$ is ordinarily only an assumption. As a result, (8) is correspondingly understated because $\lambda$ has a variance that is not taken into account. Theil (1961), among others, has suggested a method whereby an *a priori* distribution on $\lambda$ can be used in estimation. However, this has not been tried here.[1] These two observations suggest that the projecting variance for the dynamic models in which $\lambda = 1$ is not assumed is probably smaller, other things being equal, than for those in which $\lambda = 1$ is assumed.

Third, the projecting variance foı the dynamic model is much more sensitive to the length of the projection period than for a corresponding static model. This is because of the accumulating effect of the errors in the dynamic model, which is not present in the static model. The result is that, for a given $R^2$, the projecting variance of the static model is likely to be smaller than it is for the dynamic model. However, it must be remembered that one of the other major sources of error in a projection is not being measured. The error that results from the inadequacy of the assumed model does not enter the classical measure of the projecting variance. The classical formula only measures the errors of estimation on the hypothesis that the specified relationship is correct. There is considerable reason to believe

[1] In a recent demand study, Barten (1964) has made considerable use of *a priori* information in the form of restrictions on own- and cross-price and income elasticities.

on both the theoretical and the empirical level, that the dynamic model is a more adequate representation of reality than is the static model. Indeed, much of this monograph provides evidence to this effect. Hence, for a given $R^2$, the "true" projecting variance of the static model is understated relative to the dynamic model.

Finally, there is the problem of autocorrelation, which merits a section of its own.

## *II. The Problem of Autocorrelation*

It is an established fact that autocorrelation in the error term leads to an underestimate of $\sigma^2$ when the method of least squares is used to estimate the parameters. Correspondingly, the classical formula will understate the true projecting variance, and this will be so regardless of whether the static or the dynamic model is being used. Malinvaud (1961), in an important recent Monte Carlo study of forecasts made from distributed-lag models, found that the forecasting variance increased sharply upon the introduction of autocorrelation in the error term, with the increase being more marked the longer the forecast interval. Hence the presence of autocorrelation not only leads to an underestimate of the true forecasting variance, but to an increase in this variance as well.

Autocorrelation has been detected much less with the dynamic model than with the static model. This is primarily because the dynamic model is a more adequate specification, and because the three-pass method used to estimate the dynamic model is designed to greatly reduce autocorrelation. As a result, because of the lack of autocorrelation, the dynamic model will give more efficient projections than the static model.

Autocorrelation in the error term may imply bias in the projection as well as inefficiency. This is true for two reasons, both of which arise because of the presence of the lagged value of the dependent variables as a predictor. The first of these is that autocorrelation leads to a biased estimate of $A_1$ in equation (1.54),[2] which if there are no offsetting biases in the other coefficients is sufficient to give a biased projection. The second reason is that, with the effect of errors being spread out over succeeding periods, an error in period $t$ affects the level of the dependent variable in $t + 1$ directly as well as through the level of the dependent variable in $t$. If a large error (or errors) should occur in the early part of the projection period, a projection based on the assumption that the errors are identically zero during the projection period could be either seriously overstated or understated.

It was indicated in Chapter 1 that, even if $u_t$ in (1.54) is nonautocorrelated, $v_t$ in (1.58) will be autocorrelated. To see this, we note that the asymptotic covariance of $v_t$ and $v_{t-1}$ is given by

[2] This is discussed in detail in the next section. References such as (1.54) are to equations in another Chapter, in this case Chapter 1, equation (54).

$$(9) \quad E(v_t v_{t-1}) = \frac{\left(1+\frac{\delta}{2}\right)u_t - \left(1-\frac{\delta}{2}\right)u_{t-1}}{1-\frac{1}{2}(\beta-\delta)} \cdot \frac{\left(1+\frac{\delta}{2}\right)u_{t-1} - \left(1-\frac{\delta}{2}\right)u_{t-2}}{1-\frac{1}{2}(\beta-\delta)}$$

$$= \frac{\left(\left[\frac{\delta}{2}\right]^2 - 1\right)\sigma^2}{(1-\frac{1}{2}[\beta-\delta])^2} \neq 0 \text{ unless } \delta = 2.$$

With the case of first order autocorrelation in $u$, we have

$$(10) \quad E(v_t v_{t-1}) = \frac{2(1+\delta^2/4)\sigma_{tt-1}}{(1-\frac{1}{2}[\beta-\delta])^2} + \frac{\left(\left[\frac{\delta}{2}\right]^2 - 1\right)\sigma^2}{(1-\frac{1}{2}[\beta-\delta])^2}$$

$$\neq 0 \text{ unless } \frac{2(1+\delta^2/4)\sigma_{tt-1}}{(1-\frac{1}{2}[\beta-\delta])^2} = \frac{-\left(\left[\frac{\delta}{2}\right]^2 - 1\right)\sigma^2}{(1-\frac{1}{2}[\beta-\delta])^2}$$

where $\sigma_{tt-1}$ is the covariance between $u_t$ and $u_{t-1}$.
We assume, of course, that $1 - \frac{1}{2}(\beta - \delta) \neq 0$ in both (9) and (10).

In terms of the Durbin–Watson statistic,

$$D.W. = \frac{\sum (\hat{v}_{t-1} - \hat{v}_t)^2}{\sum \hat{v}_t^2}$$

(assuming $(T - 1)/T \cong 1$ where $T$ is the number of observations)

$$(11) \quad E(D.W.) \cong 2 - \frac{\left(\frac{\delta}{2}\right)^2 - 1}{(1+\delta^2)/4}$$

in the nonautocorrelated case, and

$$(12) \quad E(D.W.) \cong 2 + \frac{(1+\delta^2/4)\sigma_{tt-1} - (1-\delta^2/4)\sigma^2}{(1-\delta^2/4)\sigma_{tt-1} + (1+\delta^2/4)\sigma^2}$$

in the autocorrelated case.

Unfortunately, a direct test for autocorrelation in $u_t$ is not possible, for a direct estimate of $u_t$ is not obtained; but an indirect test is possible. When $u_t$ is nonautocorrelated, the autoregression coefficient of $v_t$ is not a free parameter, but depends upon $\beta$ and $\delta$. Given the estimates of $\beta$ and $\delta$, the Durbin–Watson coefficient can be adjusted and used as a crude test for autocorrelation on $u_t$. Suppose that $\beta = .14$ and $\delta = .30$, then the expected value of the $D.W.$, assuming no autocorrelation in $u_i$, should be

$$(13) \quad E(D.W.) \cong 2 - \frac{.3^2/4 - 1}{.3^2/4 + 1} \cong 2.96.$$

Hence if $u_t$ is not autocorrelated, the adjusted $D.W.$ should be in the neighborhood of 2.96.

Further experiment with combinations of $\beta$ and $\delta$ on the assumption of zero autocorrelation in $u_t$ indicates that the expected value of the *D.W.* ranges between 2.6 and 3.0. Moreover, it can be shown without difficulty that $\sigma_{tt-1} > 0$ (positive first-order autocorrelation in $u_t$) implies a lower value for the *D.W.*, while $\sigma_{tt-1} < 0$ implies a higher value than these limits.[3] Thus values of the *D.W.* either near or below two indicates presence of positive autocorrelation in $u_t$. The fact that so many of our dynamic equations had *D.W.*'s in either the "acceptable" range or below suggests that the assumption of zero autocorrelation in $u_t$ is generally untenable. Yet this test should be taken with a grain of salt, for a number of reasons. The two most important are: (1) the autoregressive parameters of $v_t$ adds a further restriction on the estimates of $\beta$ and $\delta$, which is not taken into account, and (2) the distribution of the "adjusted" *D.W.* is unknown. In fact, the significance limits of the *D.W.* corresponding to $v_t$ tabulated by Durbin and Watson (1951) are inappropriate because of the presence of $q_{t-1}$ as a predictor.[4]

We have indicated that the three-pass method used to estimate the dynamic model is designed to eliminate the autocorrelation in $v_t$, so that in principle the adverse effects of autocorrelation on the projections are overcome. As is often the case, however, with the solving of one problem another appears: how does one treat the three-pass variable in the projection period? Since this question is not dealt with in the Taylor–Wilson paper (1964), it will be discussed in detail later. But first we shall outline the three-pass estimation method.

## III. *Projection by the Three-Pass Method*

With least squares, it is a well-known result that the presence of autocorrelation in the error term of a model containing a lagged value of the dependent variable as a predictor leads to an inconsistent estimate of the coefficient of the lagged value.[5] This arises because the composite error term of the model is necessarily correlated with the lagged dependent variable, thereby violating one of the basic assumptions of least squares.

Let the model under consideration be

$$y_t = ay_{t-1} + bx_t + cx_{t-1} + u_t, \tag{14}$$

where

$$u_t = du_{t-1} + \epsilon_t. \tag{15}$$

For convenience, $y$ and $x$ are assumed to be measured from their means so that the intercept disappears; $\epsilon_t$ is assumed to be a random error term with a constant variance for all $t$. If $u_t$ were a known variable, (14) and (15) could be combined and

$$y_t = ay_{t-1} + bx_t + cx_{t-1} + du_{t-1} + \epsilon_t \tag{16}$$

[3] Assuming $\delta > 0$.

[4] We have used the range 1.6 to 2.4 as the "acceptable" region as a rough rule of thumb.

[5] See, for instance, Klein (1958).

estimated directly with no problem of inconsistent estimates; but $u_t$ is unknown so that this is not possible. Still it is possible to get an estimate of $u_{t-1}$ which under certain conditions[6] converges stochastically to $u_{t-1}$, and a consistent estimate of $a$ can be obtained. We shall now show how such an estimate of $u_{t-1}$ can be derived.

*Pass 1.* Equation (14) is estimated by least squares ignoring the autocorrelated error term

$$y_t = a_1 y_{t-1} + b_1 x_t + c_1 x_{t-1} + r_t, \tag{17}$$

where $r_t$ is the calculated residual. If we treat $u_{t-1}$ as an omitted variable and take the probability limit[7] of $r_t$, we get

$$\begin{aligned} \text{plim } r_t &= y_t - \text{plim } a_1 y_{t-1} - \text{plim } b_1 x_t - \text{plim } c_1 x_{t-1} \\ &= y_t - (a + dg)y_{t-1} - bx_t - (c + dh)x_{t-1}, \end{aligned} \tag{18}$$

where $g$ and $h$ are the partial regression coefficients of $y_{t-1}$ and $x_{t-1}$ in the "auxiliary" regression of $u_{t-1}$, the omitted variable, on $y_{t-1}$, $x_t$, and $x_{t-1}$.[8]

If (18) is subtracted from (14), we obtain after rearrangement

$$u_t = \text{plim } r_t + dgy_{t-1} + dhx_{t-1}. \tag{19}$$

Upon substitution of (19) for $u_t$ in (16), the "true" model becomes

$$y_t = ay_{t-1} + bx_t + cx_{t-1} + d \text{ plim } r_{t-1} + d^2 gy_{t-2} + d^2 hx_{t-2} + \epsilon_t. \tag{20}$$

*Pass 2.* Largely for reasons of reducing multicollinearity, we now subtract from $y_t$ the $b_1 x_t$ and $c_1 x_{t-1}$, where $b_1$ and $c_1$ are the estimates of $b$ and $c$ from pass 1, and estimate the following equation by least squares:

$$y_t - b_1 x_t - c_1 x_{t-1} = a^* y_{t-1} + d^* r_{t-1} + (d^2 g)^* y_{t-2} + \epsilon_t^*. \tag{21}$$

Note from (18) that $b_1$ is a consistent estimate of $b$; the same is not true for $c_1$. Asymptotically, (21) can be written as

$$y_t - bx_t - cx_{t-1} = a^* y_{t-1} + d^* \text{ plim } r_{t-1} + (d^2 g)^* y_{t-2} + dhx_{t-1} + \epsilon_t^*. \tag{22}$$

[6] These conditions are that $x_t$ must be nonautocorrelated and that $x_{t-1}$ must be excluded from (14). It is an interesting result that, if $x_{t-1}$ is included in the model, even when $x$ is nonautocorrelated the estimates of $a$ and $c$ will be inconsistent. For additional discussion see Taylor and Wilson (1964).

With economic time series, the usual situation is that $x_t$ is autocorrelated. We assume this to be the case in what follows. Also, because the estimating equation of the dynamic model includes $x_{t-1}$, we keep $x_{t-1}$ in (14). This means that the three-pass estimates of $a$ and $c$ are still inconsistent. However, Monte Carlo studies indicate that the bias is moderate. (The results that follow are stated without proof, which can be found in Taylor and Wilson.)

[7] The probability limit of a random variable $z$ is defined as the value to which $z$ converges with probability one as the number of observations becomes indefinitely large. We assume that these probability limits exist.

[8] The theorem being used here relates to the impact of an omitted variable (or variables, as the case may be) on the estimated coefficients of explanatory variables included in the regression. A full discussion of the theorem is found in Theil (1961, pp. 326–327). A statement and proof of the theorem can also be found in Griliches (1961).

(21) will be the same equation asymptotically as (20) only if

$$\epsilon_t^* = d^2hx_{t-2} - dhx_{t-1} + \epsilon_t.$$

Hence two relevant variables, $x_{t-1}$ and $x_{t-2}$, have been omitted from (21). As a result, the probability limit of the estimate of $a^*$ is

(23) $$\text{plim } a_2 = a - dhm + d^2hn,$$

where $m$ and $n$ are the partial regression coefficients of $y_{t-1}$ in the "auxiliary" regressions of $x_{t-1}$ and $x_{t-2}$, the omitted variables, on $y_{t-1}$, $r_{t-1}$, and $y_{t-2}$.

We now take $b_1$ and $c_1$ together with $a_2$ and compute

(24) $$\hat{u}_t = y_t - a_2y_{t-1} - b_1x_t - c_1x_{t-1},$$

which is an estimate of $u_t$ in (14).

*Pass 3.* If $\hat{u}_t$ is lagged one period and substituted for $u_{t-1}$ in (16), we have

(25) $$y_t = ay_{t-1} + bx_t + cx_{t-1} + d^{**}u_{t-1} + \epsilon_t^{**},$$

which is the equation estimated in pass 3. If $\hat{u}_{t-1}$ were to converge stochastically to $u_{t-1}$, thereby implying $\epsilon_t^{**} \rightarrow \epsilon_t$, the least squares estimates of all the coefficients in (25) would be consistent. But due to the asymptotic expression for $\epsilon_t^{**}$ involving $y_{t-2}$ and $x_{t-2}$, only the estimate of $b$ is consistent.

It can be shown that the asymptotic expression for $\hat{u}_{t-1}$ is

(26) $$\text{plim } \hat{u}_{t-1} = u_{t-1} - (d^2hn - dhm)y_{t-2} - dhx_{t-2}$$

which means that the probability limit of the pass 3 estimate of $a_3$ is

(27) $$\text{plim } a_3 = a + (d^3hn - d^2hm)e + dhf,$$

where $e$ and $f$ are the partial regression coefficients of $y_{t-1}$ in the "auxiliary" regressions of $y_{t-2}$ and $x_{t-2}$ (the variables omitted from [25]) on $y_{t-1}$, $x_t$, $x_{t-1}$, and $\hat{u}_{t-1}$. The Taylor–Wilson Monte Carlo experiments indicate that the bias in $a_3$ is slight, thereby indicating that the three-pass method is appropriate for estimating the dynamic model.

At the same time, it is evident that the use of the method poses a problem when it comes to projecting from the estimated equation: except for the historical period, $\hat{u}_{t-1}$ is an unknown quantity.[9] The question emerges of how to project this unknown quantity. One impulse is to say assume $z_t$ to be identically zero in the projection period. However, asymptotic theory tells us that this is clearly an inappropriate assumption because the expected value of $z_t$, assuming $E(u) = 0$, is

(28) $$E(z_t) = (dhm - d^2hn)E(y) - dhE(x),$$

which in general is different from zero.

While this possibility is quickly dismissed, at least four other alternatives require more detailed examination. These include: (1) assume that $z$ takes on its historical mean in the projection period; (2) compute $z$ year by year in the

[9] Hereafter $\hat{u}_{t-1}$ will be referred to as $z_t$.

projection period according to its asymptotic formula; (3) use the least-squares equation; (4) abandon the idea of making the projection from the estimating equation by instead building up the implicit "stocks" and returning to the original structural equation to make the projection.

Unfortunately, existing theory is a poor guide in assessing these alternatives; moreover, there is no body of accumulated experience to draw upon in making a choice. So it seemed prudent to take an empirical approach to the problem by running several Monte Carlo experiments using the alternatives, and then choosing the projection form of the equation on the basis of the Monte Carlo results. The experiments and results are described in the next section.

## IV. Monte Carlo Forecasting Experiments

The following model has been used in the Monte Carlo experiments:

$$q_t = 25 + .14s_t + .10x_t + \epsilon_t; \tag{29}$$

$$\dot{s}_t = q_t - .30s_t. \tag{30}$$

Of 50 observations per sample, 52 samples were generated using a Gaussian random-number generator. In order to give the model some economic flavor, a long historical series for national income of the United Kingdom[10] that begins at 1870 was used for the $x$ series. This series was, of course, fixed in repeated samples.

The stock series was constructed observation by observation, using the approximation for $s_t - s_{t-1}$ assumed in (1.29) above; that is, we used

$$s_t - s_{t-1} = \tfrac{1}{2}(q_t - .30s_t + q_{t-1} - .30s_{t-1}). \tag{31}$$

The first two samples were discarded, as were the first nine observations of each sample, in order to remove the possible effects of atypical initial conditions for $q$ and $s$. Observations 11–40, with observation 10 as the initial value, have been used to estimate the coefficients in

$$q_t = A_0 + A_1q_{t-1} + A_2x_t + A_3x_{t-1} + u_t, \tag{32}$$

by both ordinary least squares (OLS) and the three-pass method (3PLS). The estimated equation, in one form or another, has then been used to forecast observations 41–49; these correspond to the nine years between 1961 and 1970 over which the actual projections will be made.

The results of the four Monte Carlo experiments performed are summarized in Tables 3.1, 3.2, and 3.3. Table 3.1 indicates the bias in the mean values of the coefficients, while Table 3.3 gives the mean values of the forecasts for each of the nine periods in the forecast interval for the alternative experiments.

Experiment 1 uses the estimating equation of the model to make the

[10] The source is Prest (1948).

forecasts—that is, (32). The "actual" value of $z$, computed from the last observation of the historical period, has been used for $z$ in the first forecast, while the historical mean of $z$ computed from the sample is used thereafter.

Experiment 2 also uses the estimating equation to make the forecasts. However, after using the computed value of $z$ for the first forecast, values of $z$ computed according to the asymptotic (28) are used thereafter.

Experiment 3 uses the structural equation with estimates of the structural coefficients computed from estimates of $A_0, \ldots, A_3$ to make the forecasts. The implicit stocks are built up by an observation at a time, using the estimated depreciation rate and the actual values of $q$. For the initial value of $s$, it is assumed that there is no error in the first observation.[11]

Experiment 4 also uses the structural equation for making the forecasts; the structural coefficients are re-estimated directly by using the computed stocks in the structural equation.

Table 3.1. Estimates of the Coefficients of the Estimating Equation

| Coefficient | Actual | OLS | $\sigma_A$ | 3PLS | $\sigma_A$ |
|---|---|---|---|---|---|
| $A_0$ | 6.9444 | 11.7225 | 4.8179 | 10.1389 | 4.575 |
| $A_1$ | 0.8519 | 0.8366 | 0.0181 | 0.8468 | 0.0518 |
| $A_2$ | 0.1065 | 0.1033 | 0.0176 | 0.1050 | 0.0161 |
| $A_3$ | −0.0787 | −0.0751 | 0.0177 | −0.0770 | 0.0175 |
| $A_4$ | – | – | – | −0.4638 | 0.1384 |
| $R^2$ | – | 0.9685 | – | 0.9740 | – |
| $D.W.$ | – | 2.8095 | – | 2.3105 | – |

*Note.* The OLS and the 3PLS estimates are the means of the 50 samples. The "actual" values are computed from $\alpha$, $\beta$, $\gamma$, and $\delta$ using formulas (1.38)–(1.41). $A_4$ is the coefficient of $z_t$. The $\sigma_A$'s are empirical standard errors computed from the 50 samples.

As is to be expected, the bias in the estimates of the coefficients are smaller with 3PLS than with OLS. However, with exception of the intercept that may appear to be an anomaly, the biases, even for OLS, are small. The large bias in the estimates of the intercept can be traced to the fact that although the bias in the other coefficients is slight, the mean values of $q$ and $x$ are not. This results in a considerable bias in the estimates of the intercept.

Since $\epsilon_t$ is nonautocorrelated, the error term of the estimating equation will have negative autocorrelation. The mean value of 2.8095 for the OLS $D.W.$ agrees quite well with its expected value of 2.96 (see equation [13] above), though there is a downward bias. This bias is no doubt due to the presence of $q_{t-1}$ as a predictor.

Table 3.2 gives the estimates in terms of the structural coefficients. The numbers in columns two and three are derived from the information in

[11] It would be more in keeping with the theory of least squares if the initial value were chosen so that the mean came out without error. But it is impossible to pinpoint a particular year with this assumption.

columns three and four of Table 3.1, using formulas of Chapter 1. The numbers in columns four and five are direct estimates of the structural coefficients

Table 3.2. Estimates of the Coefficients of the Structural Model

| | | Indirect | | Direct | |
|---|---|---|---|---|---|
| Coefficient | Actual | OLS | 3PLS | OLS | 3PLS |
| $\alpha$ | 25.00 | 39.8934 | 2.9873 | 32.5617 | 23.2514 |
| $\beta$ | 0.14 | 0.1510 | 0.1527 | 0.1411 | 0.1447 |
| $\gamma$ | 0.10 | 0.0972 | 0.0984 | 0.0975 | 0.0956 |
| $\delta$ | 0.30 | 0.3292 | 0.3203 | 0.3292 | 0.3203 |
| | | *Standard errors* | | | |
| $\alpha$ | | 18.0970 | 0.6908 | 44.4183 | 53.3986 |
| $\beta$ | | 0.0722 | 0.0605 | 0.0160 | 0.1931 |
| $\gamma$ | | 0.0192 | 0.0168 | 0.0043 | 0.0108 |
| $\delta$ | | 0.0742 | 0.0780 | 0.0742 | 0.0780 |

*Note.* The entries in this table are means of the 50 samples. The estimates in column 5 are obtained by using the 3PLS estimates of the estimating equation in building up the stocks. The standard errors are empirical standard errors computed from the 50 samples. $\delta$ is not re-estimated when the structural equation is estimated directly.

obtained from building up the implicit stocks and then re-estimating equation (29) directly. The formula used to build up the stocks is

$$(33) \qquad s_t = \frac{1}{2\left(1 + \frac{\hat{\delta}}{2}\right)}(q_t + q_{t-1}) + \frac{\left(1 - \frac{\hat{\delta}}{2}\right)}{\left(1 + \frac{\hat{\delta}}{2}\right)} s_{t-1},$$

where $\hat{\delta}$ is the derived estimate of $\delta$. This formula is obtained from (31).

We see from Table 3.2 that, of the estimates derived from the coefficients of the estimating equation (columns two and three), the largest bias is in the estimate of $\alpha$ and that the estimates of $\beta$ and $\delta$ are obviously biased upward. 3PLS slightly reduces the bias in the estimates of $\gamma$ and $\delta$, but increases it slightly in the estimate of $\beta$. The estimate of $\delta$ is of central importance, since it is used directly in building up the stocks.

When the structural coefficients are estimated directly by using the built-up stocks in the structural equation (columns four and five), the bias in both the 3PLS and OLS estimates of $\gamma$ is reduced.[12] Indeed it practically disappears in the OLS estimate. On the whole, when standard errors are considered, the results indicate that the OLS estimates are better than those of 3PLS when the structural equation is re-estimated directly. Table 3.3 presents the forecasts from the various experiments.

[12] The 3PLS estimates in this case refer to using the stocks computed with the 3PLS estimates from Table 3.1.

Table 3.3. Forecasts

| Forecast number | Actual | Experiment 1 OLS | 1 3PLS | 2 3PLS | 3 OLS | 3 3PLS | 4 OLS | 4 3PLS |
|---|---|---|---|---|---|---|---|---|
| 1 | 419.93 | 419.40 | 420.02 | 420.02 | 447.01 | 428.38 | 445.71 | 447.19 |
| 2 | 431.95 | 430.05 | 431.24 | 465.46 | 464.93 | 444.57 | 462.29 | 464.40 |
| 3 | 451.01 | 446.94 | 448.92 | 514.07 | 487.21 | 466.67 | 483.63 | 486.27 |
| 4 | 466.53 | 462.04 | 464.92 | 570.24 | 507.54 | 487.59 | 503.27 | 506.57 |
| 5 | 459.30 | 455.14 | 458.69 | 611.48 | 505.43 | 486.34 | 500.59 | 505.06 |
| 6 | 497.37 | 492.00 | 496.90 | 705.14 | 545.36 | 528.13 | 540.28 | 545.17 |
| 7 | 555.44 | 547.69 | 554.51 | 824.64 | 606.33 | 592.05 | 601.45 | 606.58 |
| 8 | 628.08 | 617.79 | 627.16 | 971.57 | 683.13 | 672.81 | 678.71 | 684.06 |
| 9 | 723.94 | 711.34 | 724.13 | 1157.63 | 784.67 | 779.52 | 780.99 | 786.45 |

*Note.* The forecasts are the means of the 50 samples. The different experiments are described above. The least-squares forecasts for 2 are the same as for 1.

A careful look at Table 3.3 shows three major results: (1) the forecasts from the structural equation (experiments 3 and 4) have a considerable upward bias; (2) an even larger upward bias is evident in the 3PLS forecasts of experiment 2, thereby implying that computing $z$ according to its asymptotic formula is unadvisable; and (3) the 3PLS forecasts of experiment 1 are practically unbiased. At the same time, the OLS forecasts of this experiment possess a bias of less than 2 percent in the final period, a fact that precludes summary rejection of the OLS equation for projection. It is clear, therefore, that we can confine our attention to experiment 1 in what follows.

Table 3.4. Forecast Variances and Mean-Square Errors for Experiment 1

| Forecast number | Variance OLS | Variance 3PLS | Mean-square error OLS | Mean-square error 3PLS |
|---|---|---|---|---|
| 1 | 43.6060 | 30.8228 | 21.2419 | 12.7102 |
| 2 | 37.2938 | 37.4843 | 28.6574 | 26.5668 |
| 3 | 69.8600 | 91.3961 | 53.2950 | 65.0194 |
| 4 | 77.7388 | 133.0116 | 68.0292 | 117.8909 |
| 5 | 55.4643 | 163.4204 | 54.9008 | 154.6348 |
| 6 | 118.0343 | 280.5748 | 109.3807 | 295.1619 |
| 7 | 267.3773 | 582.9199 | 283.7307 | 614.8230 |
| 8 | 605.0296 | 1230.9009 | 598.4442 | 1206.5326 |
| 9 | 1126.3272 | 2273.4368 | 1155.3163 | 3209.4873 |

*Note.* The variance is defined as $\sum (p_i - a_i)^2/50$ where $p_i$ is the predicted and $a_i$ is the actual value. The mean-square error is defined as $\sum (p_i - a)^2/50$ where $a$ is the mean of the actual values for the 50 samples. That the mean-square error on occasion is smaller than the variance is because of our somewhat different definition of the variance.

The forecasting variances and mean-square errors for experiment 1 are tabulated in Table 3.4. The OLS forecasts are more efficient on the whole than the 3PLS forecasts, both in terms of a smaller variance and a smaller mean-square error. The 3PLS forecasts are more efficient for the first two periods, a result that is of particular interest for short-term forecasting, but the 3PLS variances are about double the OLS variances in the final four periods. It should be noted that for both methods the variances roughly double from one period to the next from the sixth period on. The increase in the variance for the 3PLS forecasts over the first five periods is in rough agreement with the results of Malinvaud (1961) for models without autocorrelation in the error term.[13]

Further insight can be gained into our model by breaking the forecasting variance down into the part due to the error term of the true model and the part due to the errors of estimation. This can be done as follows. If the true coefficients were used in the forecasting equation, the forecasting variance would be due entirely to the random term of the model, which from equation (1) would be equal to

$$(34)\qquad E\left[\sum_{i=1}^{T} A_i^{T-i}V_i\right]^2 = \sigma^2(1 + A_1^2 + A_1^4 + \cdots + A_1^{2T-2})$$

for $T = 1, 2, \ldots, 9$. Now:

$$(35)\qquad \sigma^2 = E(v_t^2) = E\left[\frac{\left(1 + \frac{\delta}{2}\right)u_t - \left(1 - \frac{\delta}{2}\right)u_{t-1}}{1 - \frac{1}{2}(\beta - \delta)}\right]^2$$

$$= \frac{\left(1 + \frac{\delta}{2}\right)^2 + \left(1 - \frac{\delta}{2}\right)^2}{(1 - \frac{1}{2}(\beta - \delta))^2}\,\sigma_\varepsilon^2.$$

In generating the samples, $\sigma_\varepsilon^2 = 16$; hence with $A_1 = .8519$, $\beta = .14$ and $\delta = .30$, we have $\sigma^2 = 28.05$. If we subtract (34) from the forecasting variance for each $T$, we are left with the part of the variance due to the errors in estimating the coefficients. This breakdown is given in Table 3.5.

We see that for 3PLS forecasts the errors of estimation dominate the forecasting variance from the sixth period on, and from the seventh period on for OLS. The "negative" contribution of the errors of estimation in two of the first four periods may be attributed to any one or all of three reasons: (1) negative covariances between the estimates of the regression coefficients;

[13] It is somewhat surprising, in view of Malinvaud's results, to find that the variances of the OLS forecasts for the first five periods are so small. Malinvaud found that the variances increase significantly when the error term is autocorrelated. However, his results are for a model with positive autocorrelation, while our model, since we have assumed $\epsilon_t$ to be nonautocorrelated, has negative autocorrelation. Although it may sound paradoxical, negative autocorrelation may lead to a reduced forecasting variance in some instances. We have not looked into this possibility, even though it would be worthwhile to do so.

Table 3.5. Breakdown of Forecasting Variances for Experiment 1

| Variances | Forecast number | | | | | | | | |
|---|---|---|---|---|---|---|---|---|---|
| | 1 | 2 | 3 | 4 | 5 | 6 | 7 | 8 | 9 |
| OLS | 42.61 | 37.29 | 69.86 | 77.74 | 55.46 | 118.03 | 267.38 | 605.03 | 1126.33 |
| 3PLS | 30.82 | 37.48 | 91.40 | 133.01 | 163.42 | 280.57 | 582.92 | 1230.90 | 2273.44 |
| Variance due to true model | 28.05 | 48.41 | 62.42 | 73.14 | 80.92 | 86.57 | 90.66 | 93.64 | 95.79 |
| Variance due to errors of estimation | | | | | | | | | |
| OLS | 15.56 | −13.12 | 7.44 | 4.60 | −25.46 | 31.46 | 176.72 | 511.39 | 1030.54 |
| 3PLS | 2.77 | −12.93 | 28.98 | 59.87 | 82.50 | 194.00 | 492.16 | 1237.16 | 2177.65 |

*Note*. The variances are the same as in Table 3.4. The variance due to the true model is calculated according to formula (35) with $A_1 = .8519$ and $\sigma^2 = 28.05$. The variance due to the errors of estimation is then obtained as a residual.

(2) negative autocorrelation in the error term (especially for the OLS forecasts); or (3) an unusual drawing of actual error terms.

Table 3.6 presents the Theil $U$ for each of the individual samples in experiment 1. The Theil $U$ is a statistic that measures the goodness of fit of a set of forecasts with the actual values and is defined as

$$U = \frac{[\sum (P_i - A_i)^2]^{1/2}}{\sqrt{\sum P_i^2} + \sqrt{\sum A_i^2}}, \tag{36}$$

where $P$ is the predicted value and $A$ is the actual value. $U$ must lie between zero and one. A value of zero denotes a perfect forecast, while one denotes the other extreme.[14]

In general the individual forecasts are very good, for with the exception of the 3PLS forecasts for number 46, the values of $U$ are all less than .04. The mean values are .0133 and .0172 for OLS and 3PLS, respectively. The larger value of $U$ for the 3PLS forecasts corresponds to their larger forecasting variance, which we had noted earlier.

At this point it will be useful to summarize the results thus far:

1. We have found that the estimating equation is the best form of the model for making the projections.

2. The best way to project the $z$ variable is to use its value computed from the last observation of the historical period for the first forecast, and its historical mean thereafter.

3. The forecasts from the 3PLS equation are essentially unbiased, while the OLS forecasts are biased downward.

4. The 3PLS forecasts are less efficient than those of OLS, although for both the forecasting variance increases sharply from the sixth period on.

Our remaining task is to choose between the 3PLS and OLS equations for making the projections. On a criterion of unbiasedness 3PLS is the choice.

[14] For an extensive discussion of $U$, see Theil (1961, pp. 31–42).

Table 3.6. Theil $U$ for Experiment 1

| Forecast number | OLS | 3PLS | Forecast number | OLS | 3PLS |
|---|---|---|---|---|---|
| 1 | .0087 | .0042 | 26 | .0280 | .0287 |
| 2 | .0050 | .0198 | 27 | .0057 | .0218 |
| 3 | .0261 | .0149 | 28 | .0173 | .0272 |
| 4 | .0202 | .0039 | 29 | .0046 | .0107 |
| 5 | .0193 | .0225 | 30 | .0254 | .0206 |
| 6 | .0131 | .0303 | 31 | .0104 | .0061 |
| 7 | .0128 | .0267 | 32 | .0050 | .0048 |
| 8 | .0315 | .0123 | 33 | .0182 | .0115 |
| 9 | .0077 | .0050 | 34 | .0112 | .0090 |
| 10 | .0143 | .0277 | 35 | .0086 | .0097 |
| 11 | .0076 | .0333 | 36 | .0051 | .0233 |
| 12 | .0029 | .0044 | 37 | .0160 | .0373 |
| 13 | .0115 | .0066 | 38 | .0268 | .0298 |
| 14 | .0015 | .0061 | 39 | .308 | .0181 |
| 15 | .0095 | .0079 | 40 | .0135 | .0150 |
| 16 | .0126 | .0214 | 41 | .0254 | .0223 |
| 17 | .0222 | .0173 | 42 | .0060 | .0078 |
| 18 | .0049 | .0107 | 43 | .0055 | .0050 |
| 19 | .0044 | .0141 | 44 | .0118 | .0109 |
| 20 | .0149 | .0166 | 45 | .0207 | .0284 |
| 21 | .0123 | .0233 | 46 | .0260 | .0829 |
| 22 | .0114 | .0246 | 47 | .0153 | .0134 |
| 23 | .0094 | .0067 | 48 | .0138 | .0188 |
| 24 | .0019 | .0034 | 49 | .0132 | .0036 |
| 25 | .0117 | .0074 | 50 | .0100 | .0203 |

while on a criterion of efficiency we would use OLS. Which criterion do we use in choosing? To make the choice properly, we actually need more information; we need, among other things, to know how and under what circumstances the projections are to be used. Ideally we should know the utility function of the user (or users) of the projections, from which we could derive the trade-off between smaller variance and increased bias. Given this knowledge we could then choose the method of projection that maximized the user's utility.

Since the projections were prepared for a government agency for inclusion in a comprehensive economy-wide model intended for a variety of uses, it is not possible to be very specific about the disutilities associated with increased variance and increased bias. However, in a context where considerable experimentation and simulation is to take place and where a large number of projections are involved, it would appear that being correct on the average (unbiasedness) is more important than a smaller variance (but with bias) or even a smaller mean-square error.[15]

[15] These last two paragraphs have only touched upon a very difficult and complex topic. The reader is urged to consult Theil (1961, chaps. 7–9), Meyer and Glauber (1964, chap. 10), and Christ (1956).

Although this does not provide a rigorous justification for use 3PLS, it does provide some. Moreover, since up to now 3PLS has been tested only by Monte Carlo techniques, this creates a good chance to try the method in the real world, particularly since little will be lost by doing so. Hence we have used 3PLS to project 23 of the 84 consumption categories. The OLS equations have been used wherever the *D.W.* coefficient was initially in the "acceptable" range.[16]

## *V. The Adding-Up Problem*

At this point we should recall that the independent variable in the analysis is total consumption expenditure rather than disposable income. The single exception to this is in category 4.3 (space rental value of farm housing), for which disposable farm income is used in place of total PCE. Since total expenditure in 1970 is taken as given, the projection exercise is to allocate the aggregate among the components, rather than to project the aggregate itself. As a result, care must be taken to ensure that we do not allocate either more or less than what we have at the start: the individual items should add up to the total. If each equation were static and linear and had the same set of predictors, then additivity would be assured and there would be no problem.[17] But several of the categories are nonlinear; 72 are dynamic; and, with 84 categories and only 29 observations, it is impossible that all the equations will include the same set of predictors. Hence our set of demand functions is not forcibly additive.

Fortunately, additivity has not been much of a problem. It was decided before we started that, if the discrepancy were on the order of 4 percent or less, the projections would be adjusted in order to give additivity. The only question at issue was whether the dependent variables (the projections) would be adjusted directly, or whether the independent variable (PCE) would be adjusted. The former would be quicker and easier, but the latter is more correct in principle.[18] If all elasticities with respect to total expenditure were unity, the two methods would be equivalent. However, if an

[16] It should be noted that in principle the projections from the OLS equations could be adjusted upward so as to overcome the downward bias. However, this would require the perhaps dubious assumption that the bias in the real world is in the same direction as in our Monte Carlo model.

[17] This is, of course, only one of the possible functional forms that possesses the adding-up property. See Nicholson (1949), Prais (1952), Stone (1954), Prais and Houthakker (1955), and Leser (1963) for discussions of other functional forms that satisfy the criterion, as well as the criterion itself.

[18] In principle, it is the marginal utility of income that would be adjusted, for it is this that ensures consistency when a set of demand functions are derived from an ordinal utility function. When the consumer is in equilibrium, we have $MU_i/P_i = \xi\mu_x$ for all $i$, where $\mu_x$ is the marginal utility of income. If expenditure for the individual items should add up to more than the total, this means, assuming the second-order conditions hold, that $\xi\mu_x$ is too low. If we also assume a diminishing marginal utility of income, $\xi$ can be effectively increased by reducing income. In other words, we increase the marginal utility of income in the eyes of the consumer by reducing (in effect) the amount of income he sees.

elasticity were two, say, and the discrepancy were 3 percent, then it would be a difference between 3 percent and 6 percent in consumption for the item. The procedure adopted was to adjust the independent variable (total PCE) until the projections added up to the original unadjusted PCE. The process converged rapidly, usually after three iterations.

Since the relative prices are, by construction, the ratio of the individual implicit deflators to the aggregate deflator, an aggregate deflator for 1970 is implied by projecting the relative prices to 1970. Although not enough information is given to derive the general price level for 1970, it is possible to derive an expression for the projections in 1970 dollars deflated by the aggregate deflator for 1970 (with 1954 = 100). This is done simply by multiplying the projections by their respective relative prices. The question emerges: should these projections also add up?

The answer is that they indeed must add up—but they add up to the constant dollar total rather than to the current dollar total. We can see this as follows. The projection for 1970 for each category is

$$q_{1970} \cdot p_{1954}. \tag{37}$$

Summed over all categories, these projections have been made to add up to the independently projected total PCE, which we denote by

$$\sum q_{1970} \cdot p_{1954} = Q^*_{1970}. \tag{38}$$

If the projection is multiplied by its relative price, we have

$$\frac{q_{1970} p_{1954}}{1} \cdot \frac{p_{1970}/p_{1954}}{\sum q_{1970} \cdot p_{1970}/Q^*_{1970}} = \frac{q_{1970} \cdot p_{1970}}{\sum q_{1970} p_{1970}/Q^*_{1970}}, \tag{39}$$

so that when (39) is summed over all categories, we have

$$\frac{\sum q_{1970} \cdot p_{1970}}{\sum q_{1970} \cdot p_{1970}/Q^*_{1970}} = Q^*_{1970}. \tag{40}$$

A much more interesting question in many ways is whether, once a separate projection of the general price level has been made, the projections that have been made to add up in constant will also add up in current dollars. As the following simple illustration will show, the general answer to this is no.

Assume that there are only two commodities, $q_1$ and $q_2$. Denote the constant dollar PCE by $x$ and let $\delta_1 x$ be the adjustment made in $x$ so that the estimates of $q_1$ and $q_2$, $\hat{q}_1$, and $\hat{q}_2$, add up to $x$: $p_{11}\hat{q}_1 + p_{21}\hat{q}_2 = x$, where $p_{11}$ is the price of $q_1$ in the base period, etc. In other words, we have

$$p_{11}\hat{q}_1 = a_1 + b_1(x + \delta_1 x) + c_1 p_1, \tag{41}$$

$$p_{21}\hat{q}_2 = a_2 + b_2(x + \delta_1 x) + c_2 p_2, \tag{42}$$

---

The correct way, of course, would be to increase $\xi\mu_x$ directly. If we were to assume a quadratic utility function with independent marginal utilities, then it is possible by an iterative scheme to increase $\xi$ directly. R. Robert Russell has looked into the static form of this model in his dissertation (Harvard), but we have not had time to pursue the dynamic form. It does look promising, however.

where

$$p_1 = \frac{p_{12}}{p_{11}} \Big/ \frac{p_{12}q_1 + p_{22}q_2}{p_{11}q_1 + p_{21}q_2} \quad \text{and} \quad p_2 = \frac{p_{22}}{p_{21}} \Big/ \frac{p_{12}q_1 + p_{22}q_2}{p_{11}q_1 + p_{21}q_2}.$$

If we let $b_1 + b_2 = \kappa$ where $\kappa \neq 0$, it then follows, since $p_{11}\hat{q}_1 + p_{21}\hat{q}_2 = x$, that

$$(43) \qquad \delta_1 = \frac{(1-\kappa)x - a_1 - a_2 - c_1p_1 - c_2p_2}{\kappa x} =$$

$$= \frac{(1-\kappa)x - a_1 - a_2 - c_1\left(\frac{p_{12}}{p_{11}} \Big/ \frac{p_{12}q_1 + p_{22}q_2}{p_{11}q_1 + p_{21}q_2}\right) - c_2\left(\frac{p_{22}}{p_{21}} \Big/ \frac{p_{12}q_1 + p_{22}q_2}{p_{11}q_1 + p_{21}q_2}\right)}{\kappa x} =$$

$$= \frac{1-\kappa}{\kappa} - c_1\left(\frac{p_{12}}{p_{11}} \Big/ p_{12}q_1 + p_{22}q_2\right) - c_2\left(\frac{p_{22}}{p_{21}} \Big/ p_{12}q_1 + p_{22}q_2\right) - \frac{a_1 + a_2}{\kappa x}.$$

Similarly, in terms of the prices of period two:

$$(44) \qquad p_{12}\hat{q}_1 = a_1 + b_1(x^* + \delta_2 x^*) + c_1p_1^*;$$

$$(45) \qquad p_{22}\hat{q}_2 = a_2 + b_2(x^* + \delta_2 x^*) + c_2p_2^*;$$

$$x^* = p_{12}q_1 + p_{22}q_2, \qquad p_1^* = p_2^* = 1;$$

$$(46) \quad \delta_2 = \frac{(1-\kappa)x^* - a_1 - a_2 - c_1 - c_2}{\kappa x^*} = \frac{1-\kappa}{\kappa} - \frac{a_1 + a_2 + c_1 + c_2}{\kappa(p_{12}q_1 + p_{22}q_2)},$$

where $\delta_2$ has been chosen so that

$$p_{12}\hat{q}_1 + p_{22}\hat{q}_2 = x^*.$$

The relevant question becomes, does $\delta_1$ equal $\delta_2$? Careful study of (43) and (46) shows that $\delta_1$ does not equal $\delta_2$ identically, for an arbitrary shift in the relative prices from periods one to two does not leave $\delta_1$ unaffected. Indeed, it does not even hold for a proportional increase in all prices, which leaves relative prices unchanged.[19]

Yet the situation would be different if all prices were included in each equation:

$$(47) \qquad p_{11}q_1 = a_1 + b_1(x + \delta x) + c_1p_1 + d_1p_2;$$

$$(48) \qquad p_{21}q_2 = a_2 + b_2(x + \delta x) + c_2p_2 + d_2p_1.$$

In this case $\delta$ would be zero, for if least squares were used to estimate the coefficients, we would have $a_1 + a_2 = 0$, $c_1 + d_2 = 0$, $c_2 + d_1 = 0$, and $b_1 + b_2 = 1$.[20] Hence the equations would be additive in either constant or current dollars.

One final item of interest before we close this chapter concerns the use of the

[19] It should be noted that this result is dependent upon the particular form of relative price index used.

[20] For a statement and proof of this theorem, see Nicholson (1949) and Prais and Houthakker (1955, pp. 84–85).

inverse semi-logarithmic form of the static model. This form has been used to project three of the categories and earlier had been used in several additional categories. However, in these latter categories the resulting projections were clearly too high. Unfortunately, this seems to be a serious drawback of the inverse semi-logarithmic function. It often gives the best historical fit, but its use in forecasting is limited because of this mechanical defect.

At this point, the moral of the projection exercise should be clear. The final equations were not chosen completely *a priori*; nor were they chosen completely on statistical grounds. Rather they were chosen on criteria involving a rather complex mixture of *a priori* and statistical grounds and independent notions about what a reasonable projection should be. But among these criteria, the most weight was nearly always given to plausibility of the estimated parameters and goodness of fit during the period of observation.

# 4

# *Demand Equations and Projections for Detailed Items of Expenditure*

This chapter contains the empirical results obtained from applying our theory and methods to 84 categories of personal consumption expenditure. The results for the categories are presented individually here, while a more analytical discussion is found in Chapter 5. Included among the diverse results in this chapter are the regression equation used in making the projections, the projections, and usually an alternative equation. Occasionally, the alternative equation is truly alternative in the sense that it could have been used in projection; more often, though, the alternative is either an earlier false start or the static equation if the dynamic model is being used, or conversely. In addition, the total expenditure and price elasticities are given. The elasticities, except for the double-logarithmic static equation, have been computed at the means of the respective variables. For the dynamic equations, the coefficients of the structural equation have also been computed.

The projections, though also presented here, are discussed more fully in the next chapter. Four sets of projections have been made. These correspond to two alternative projections of the relative prices in 1970 under, first, a 4 percent and, then, a 5 percent full-employment equilibrium rate of growth in aggregate GNP between 1961 and 1970. The first set of projections of the relative prices is essentially an extrapolation of trends of the five years preceding 1961, although there are numerous exceptions to this. The other set assumes that relative prices in 1970 will be the same as they were in 1961. These two sets of relative prices are given in Table 4.1. The projections for the other predictors, including total PCE, are given in Table 4.2. Finally, the values of the $z$ variable for 1962 and its historical mean are tabulated in Table 4.3.

The projections have been multiplied by the projected population for 1970 to give the aggregate expenditure for the commodities in 1954 dollars. Standard errors of the projections, which are provided for all of the static equations and the special case of the dynamic model where $\beta = \delta(A_1 = 1)$ is assumed, have been calculated for the first set of prices and the 4 percent growth rate.

For convenience the following symbols and notation are used throughout.

$q_t$ per capita personal consumption expenditure of the good in question in year $t$ (1954 dollars)

| | |
|---|---|
| $\Delta q_t$ | $q_t - q_{t-1}$ |
| $x_t$ | total per capita personal consumption expenditure in year $t$ (1954 dollars) |
| $\Delta x_t$ | $x_t - x_{t-1}$ |
| $p_t$ | relative price in year $t$ of the good in question (1954 = 100) |
| $\Delta p_t$ | $p_t - p_{t-1}$ |
| $d_t$ | dummy variable used to separate the pre-World War II years from those following; takes the value 0 for 1929–1941 and 1 for 1946–1961 |
| $z_t$ | 3-pass variable (only in connection with 3PLS, see below) |
| $R^2$ | coefficient of multiple determination, defined as the square of the correlation between the actual and predicted values in their original units (i.e., in 1954 dollars) |
| *D.W.* | Durbin–Watson coefficient |
| $s_p$ | standard error of the projection |

Other variables are defined as they appear. The parameters of the dynamic model are defined as follows:

| | |
|---|---|
| $\alpha$ | intercept |
| $\beta$ | stock coefficient |
| $\gamma$ | short-run total expenditure coefficient |
| $\gamma'$ | long-run total expenditure coefficient |
| $\eta$ | short-run total expenditure elasticity |
| $\eta'$ | long-run total expenditure elasticity |
| $\lambda$ | short-run relative price coefficient |
| $\lambda'$ | long-run relative price coefficient |
| $\sigma$ | short-run relative price elasticity |
| $\sigma'$ | long-run relative price elasticity |
| $\delta$ | depreciation rate |
| $\xi$ | intercept in Bergstrom model |
| $\theta$ | adjustment coefficient in Bergstrom model |
| $\mu$ | total expenditure coefficient in Bergstrom model |

For the dynamic models, the estimation method is indicated by OLS (ordinary least squares) or 3PLS (three-pass least squares).

Graphs of actual and computed values for each of the 84 items of expenditures accompany the discussion. The key to these graphs is as follows:

| | |
|---|---|
| ———————— | actual |
| ----------- | calculated |
| —·—·— | actual and calculated (if identical) |
| ........................ | link to 1970 (does not represent projection for intervening years) |

Tables 4.1, 4.2, and 4.3, presenting summaries of the projections and values, follow below.

Table 4.1. Projected Relative Prices, 1970

| Item | Set I | Set II | Item | Set I | Set II |
|---|---|---|---|---|---|
| 1.0 | 87.8 | 95.0 | 7.1 | 176.1 | 159.6 |
| 1.1 | 92.1 | 95.0 | 7.2 | 133.7 | 123.1 |
| 1.2 | 112.3 | 103.3 | 7.3 | 141.6 | 116.5 |
| 1.3 | 78.5 | 82.5 | 7.4 | 122.6 | 111.7 |
| 1.4 | 76.4 | 89.0 | 7.5 | 99.9 | 127.4 |
| 1.5 | 108.3 | 103.9 | 7.6 | 107.8 | 99.5 |
| 2.1 | 113.6 | 108.6 | 7.7 | 108.9 | 105.3 |
| 2.2 | 124.0 | 114.8 | 8.1a | 72.7 | 101.2 |
| 2.3 | 88.0 | 95.2 | 8.1b | 72.7 | 84.0 |
| 2.4 | 86.3 | 93.4 | 8.1c | 112.1 | 107.5 |
| 2.5 | 105.8 | 103.7 | 8.1d | 98.4 | 99.7 |
| 2.6 | 121.9 | 111.5 | 8.1e | 77.8 | 90.0 |
| 2.7 | 65.0 | 80.6 | 8.1f | 109.4 | 108.7 |
| 2.8 | 99.7 | 100.9 | 8.2a | 130.0 | 118.9 |
| 3.1 | 100.0 | 100.4 | 8.2b | 11.9 | 108.8 |
| 3.2 | 122.3 | 112.7 | 8.2c | 1170.0 | 108.8 |
| 4.1 | 99.1 | 100.6 | 8.3a | 110.0 | 105.4 |
| 4.2 | 99.1 | 100.6 | 8.3b | 133.6 | 118.6 |
| 4.3 | 86.9 | 91.6 | 8.3c | 105.0 | 102.8 |
| 4.4 | 115.0 | 110.2 | 8.3d | 85.0 | 90.0 |
| 5.1 | 89.0 | 93.6 | 9.1 | 128.2 | 112.7 |
| 5.2 | 80.0 | 86.2 | 9.2 | 128.1 | 112.7 |
| 5.3 | 120.4 | 113.7 | 9.3 | 90.7 | 95.9 |
| 5.4 | 97.0 | 98.1 | 9.4 | 91.4 | 94.0 |
| 5.5 | 85.4 | 93.4 | 9.5 | 88.1 | 90.8 |
| 5.6 | 100.2 | 99.0 | 9.6 | 127.0 | 113.1 |
| 5.7 | 111.4 | 108.1 | 9.7 | 80.0 | 87.7 |
| 5.8a | 70.0 | 81.7 | 9.8a | 138.5 | 121.6 |
| 5.8b | 105.4 | 103.0 | 9.8b | 130.0 | 117.7 |
| 5.8c | 136.5 | 119.5 | 9.8c | 95.5 | 98.8 |
| 5.8d | 99.0 | 100.4 | 9.9 | 113.3 | 107.3 |
| 5.9 | 98.0 | 94.2 | 9.10 | 137.3 | 118.5 |
| 5.10 | 123.3 | 110.4 | 9.11 | 112.0 | 105.8 |
| 5.11 | 111.4 | 105.7 | 9.12 | 119.1 | 109.9 |
| 6.1 | 101.5 | 99.5 | 10.1 | 135.3 | 118.2 |
| 6.2 | 102.5 | 104.1 | 10.2 | 158.1 | 127.9 |
| 6.3 | 127.4 | 114.9 | 10.3 | 122.7 | 110.7 |
| 6.4 | 110.1 | 105.0 | 11.0 | 108.6 | 104.8 |
| 6.5 | 120.0 | 112.5 | 12.1 | 85.2 | 91.5 |
| 6.6 | 128.1 | 114.2 | 12.2 | 85.0 | 92.3 |
| 6.7 | 60.0 | 73.0 | 12.3 | 95.0 | 97.6 |
| 6.8 | 127.1 | 117.6 | 12.4 | 88.0 | 88.3 |

*Source.* Set I, Bureau of Labor Statistics. Set II, 1961 relative prices.

Table 4.2. Values of the Predictors

| Predictor | 1961 | 1970 | |
|---|---|---|---|
| | | 4% growth | 5% growth |
| Total personal consumption expenditures (per capita) | $1657 | $2038 | $2145 |
| Farm income (per farm capita) | $1194 | $1492 | $1525 |
| Income distribution (in dollars) | −210.00 | −291.77 | −310.53 |
| Farm population as percent of total population | 8.1 | 5.5 | 5.5 |
| Stocks of cars (per capita) | 0.3457 | 0.4013 | 0.4116 |
| Stocks of television sets (per capita) | 0.2592 | 0.2714 | 0.2800 |
| Number of shares sold on New York Stock Exchange (per capita) | 5.55 | 6.53 | 7.28 |
| Labor union membership (percent of total population) | 9.86 | 10.09 | 10.09 |
| Population over 18 (percent of total population) | 64.1 | 63.8 | 63.8 |
| Nonimmigrant aliens admitted (per capita) | 0.0066 | 0.0115 | 0.0115 |
| Population foreign-born (percent of total population) | 5.25 | 4.20 | 4.20 |

For definitions of the variables and sources of data, see the section entitled "Data Sources" at the end of the volume.

Table 4.3. Values of the $z$ Variable: 1962 and the Historical Mean

| Item | 1962 | Mean | Item | 1962 | Mean |
|---|---|---|---|---|---|
| 1.3 | −2.21 | −1.43 | 7.2 | 0.32 | 0.17 |
| 1.5 | −5.62 | −5.03 | 7.3 | 2.12 | 0.62 |
| 2.2 | 0.06 | 0.02 | 8.2c | −0.08 | −0.12 |
| 3.2 | −3.13 | −2.98 | 8.3c | 0.61 | 0.21 |
| 4.1 | 0.15 | −1.10 | 9.1 | 1.65 | 0.63 |
| 4.2 | 1.74 | 2.03 | 9.3 | 1.81 | 1.00 |
| 4.4 | −2.17 | −1.57 | 9.4 | −0.39 | −0.25 |
| 5.5 | 5.55 | 4.09 | 9.10 | 0.22 | 0.22 |
| 5.8c | −1.31 | −1.24 | 9.11 | −0.08 | −0.03 |
| 5.8d | −7.63 | −8.97 | 12.1 | −3.21 | −1.40 |
| 6.2 | 0.92 | 0.57 | 12.2 | −0.68 | −0.25 |
| 6.4 | 1.79 | 1.31 | | | |

## 1.0 ALCOHOLIC BEVERAGES

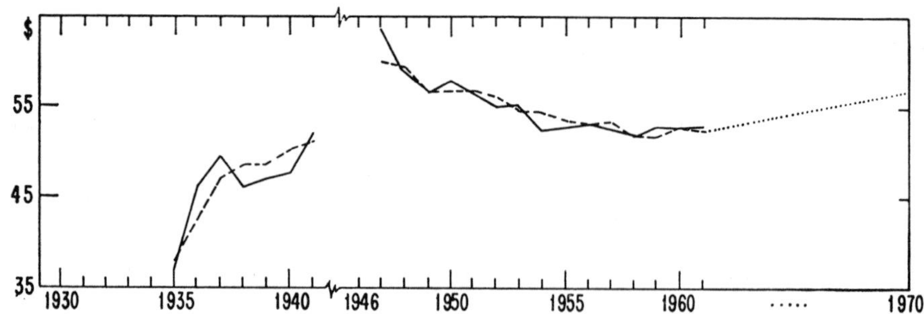


Dynamic model
OLS $\delta = 2$

$$q_t = -68.672 + .3731\ q_{t-1} + .0129\ x_t + 1.2489\ (\%\ \text{pop. over } 18)_t$$
$$\quad (38.141) \quad (.1228) \quad (.0054) \quad (.5449)$$

$R^2 = .916 \qquad D.W. = 1.85$

$\alpha = -50.001 \qquad \beta = 1.0869 \qquad \gamma = .0094 \qquad \gamma' = .0205$

$\kappa = .2430 \qquad \kappa' = .5323 \qquad \delta = 2$

| | 1961 level | 1970 projections | | | |
|---|---|---|---|---|---|
| | | 4% | | 5% | |
| | | I | II | I | II |
| per capita | \$53.24 | \$57.59 | \$57.90 | \$59.84 | \$60.06 |
| aggregate (billions) | | \$12.05 | \$12.10 | \$12.50 | \$12.55 |

In the basic data made available to us, alcoholic beverages had been separated out of items 1.1 and 1.2 in the published PCE table. We first estimated this equation using the population over age 18 as the deflator rather than total population. The $R^2$ was higher and we did not need to restrict $\delta$. However, this procedure posed a serious problem in the interpretation of total PCE (we should have PCE just for those over 18), so it was dropped. The "Bergstrom" model was also tried, but without success.

With the static model, the fit was poor; the residuals were autocorrelated; and the own-price elasticity was positive. The price of 1.2 was tried, but its coefficient was positive, indicating that restaurant food and drink are substitutes. While perhaps a case can be made for this, it was decided not to pursue the issue. Income distribution was also tried, but without success. The static model, with total expenditure, the relative price of alcohol, and the war dummy, is given below.

$$q_t = -537.00 + 35.874 \ln x_t + 70.521 \ln p_t + 5.5139\ d_t$$
$$\quad (183.96) \quad (14.669) \quad (22.593) \quad (5.1781)$$

$R^2 = .687 \qquad D.W. = .67$

## 1.1 FOOD PURCHASED FOR OFF-PREMISE CONSUMPTION (EXCLUDING ALCOHOLIC BEVERAGES)[1]

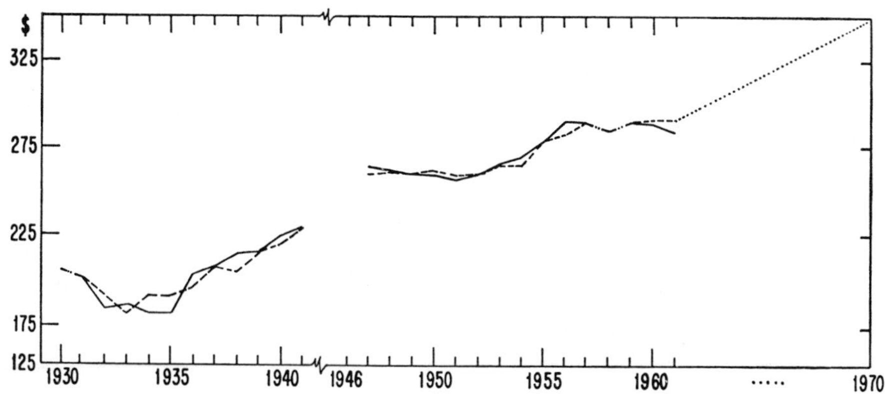


Dynamic model
OLS

$$q_t = 29.074 + .6044\, q_{t-1} + .1128\, \Delta x_t + .0528\, x_{t-1}$$
$$\quad (11.727) \quad (.1586) \qquad (.0208) \qquad (.0221)$$

$R^2 = .988 \qquad D.W. = 1.85$

$\alpha = 59.2774 \qquad \beta = .1182 \qquad \gamma = .1077 \qquad \gamma' = .1135$

$\eta = .5551 \qquad \eta' = .6882 \qquad \delta = .6114$

| | 1961 level | 1970 projections 4% | | 5% | |
|---|---|---|---|---|---|
| | | I | II | I | II |
| per capita | $286.05 | $334.87 | $332.62 | $349.20 | $346.93 |
| aggregate (billions) | | $69.96 | $69.49 | $72.96 | $72.48 |

As was indicated above, alcoholic beverages have been excluded from this category. The relative price was dropped from the dynamic model when the own-price elasticity turned out to be positive. Food consumed in the home is seen to be subject to some habit formation ($\beta > 0$), although the habit wears off quite rapidly, as evidenced by the rather large value of $\delta$. The total expenditure elasticities are consistent with those obtained in other studies, both for the United States and for other countries.[2]

A negative own-price elasticity was obtained in the semi-logarithmic form of the static model. While the fit of this model, given below, is about the same as with the dynamic model above, the residuals have positive autocorrelation.

$$q_t = -830.41 + 178.85 \ln x_t - 43.719 \ln p_t - .9431\, d_t$$
$$\quad (61.69) \quad (7.40) \qquad (20.381) \qquad (.6117)$$

$R^2 = .985 \qquad D.W. = 1.20$

[1] For a discussion of this equation, see also section III of Chapter 1.
[2] See, for instance, Crockett (1960).

## 1.2 PURCHASED MEALS (EXCLUDING ALCOHOLIC BEVERAGES)

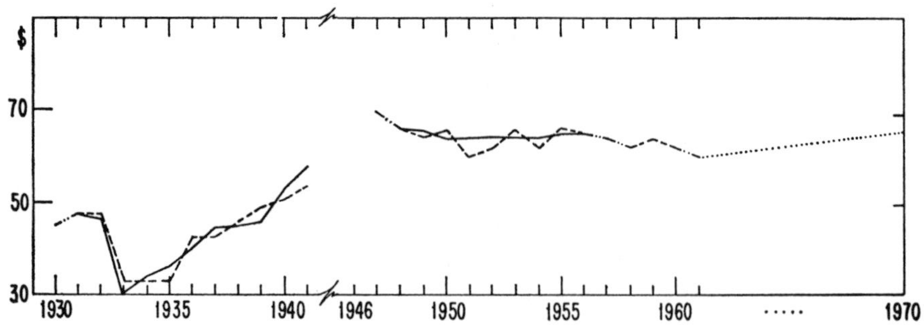


**Dynamic model**

OLS

$$q_t = 20.963 + .7159\, q_{t-1} + .0621\, \Delta x_t + .0097\, x_{t-1}$$
$$(10.984) \quad (.0681) \qquad (.0151) \qquad (.0034)$$
$$- 1.2311\, \Delta p_t - .1922\, p_{t-1}$$
$$(.1806) \qquad (.1572)$$

$R^2 = .974 \qquad D.W. = 2.30$

$\alpha = 144.325 \qquad \beta = .1618 \qquad \gamma = .0668 \qquad \gamma' = .0341$

$\lambda = -1.3229 \qquad \lambda' = -.6763 \qquad \eta = 1.5172 \qquad \eta' = .7757$

$\sigma = -2.2995 \qquad \sigma' = -1.1756 \qquad \delta = .1693$

| | 1961 level | 1970 forecasts | | | |
|---|---|---|---|---|---|
| | | 4% | | 5% | |
| | | I | II | I | II |
| per capita | \$59.77 | \$66.55 | \$73.11 | \$71.55 | \$78.70 |
| aggregate (billions) | | \$13.90 | \$15.40 | \$14.95 | \$16.44 |

This category has one of the highest short-run own-price elasticities of all the categories in the study; the long-run price elasticity is also considerable—hence the large difference in the forecasts for price sets I and II. As was the case with 1.1, meals purchased in restaurants are subject to habit formation, but here the habit wears off much more slowly.

The relative price of 1.1 was tried with the static model. The coefficient was positive, confirming the obvious substitution effect, but the fit of this model, given below, was poor and the residuals had strong positive autocorrelation.

$$\ln q_t = 3.4714 + .00046\, x_t - .0144\, p_t + .0128\, (\text{price of } 1.1)_t + .2013\, d_t$$
$$(.6587) \quad (.00025) \qquad (.0092) \qquad (.0084) \qquad\qquad (.1544)$$

$R^2 = .722 \qquad D.W. = .55$

## 1.3 FOOD FURNISHED GOVERNMENT (INCLUDING MILITARY) AND COMMERCIAL EMPLOYEES

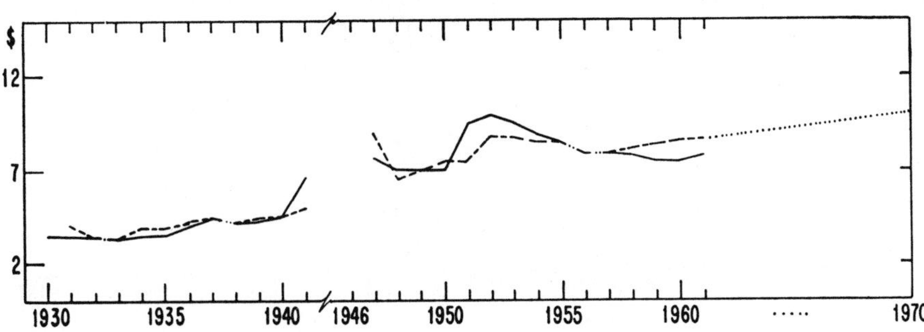


**Dynamic model**

**3PLS**

$$q_t = .2070\, q_{t-1} + .0055\, \Delta x_t + .0037\, x_{t-1} + 1.3498\, d_t + .3498\, z_t$$
$$\quad (.2017) \qquad (.0040) \qquad (.0010) \qquad (.7097) \qquad (.2677)$$

$R^2 = .892 \qquad D.W. = 1.81$

$\alpha = 0 \qquad \beta = -.2718 \qquad \gamma = .0059 \qquad \gamma' = .0047$

$\eta = 1.1625 \qquad \eta' = .9221 \qquad \delta = 1.0422$

| | 1961 level | 1970 projections I | | II | |
|---|---|---|---|---|---|
| | | 4% | 5% | 4% | 5% |
| per capita | \$7.71 | \$10.31 | \$10.23 | \$10.85 | \$10.76 |
| aggregate (billions) | | \$2.15 | \$2.14 | \$2.27 | \$2.25 |

When the own relative price was included in the dynamic model, the coefficients were both positive, so prices were deleted. This equation should be interpreted with due regard for the peculiar nature of the commodity; the item does not reflect the decisions of private households, but of employers.

The fit of the static model, given below, is poorer than the above model; the residuals are positively autocorrelated; and the own-price elasticity is positive.

$$q_t = -4.9092 + .0041\, x_t + .0531\, p_t + 1.8888\, d_t$$
$$\quad (4.1695) \quad (.0025) \qquad (.0246) \qquad (1.4429)$$

$R^2 = .819 \qquad D.W. = 1.08$

## 1.4 FOOD PRODUCED AND CONSUMED ON FARMS

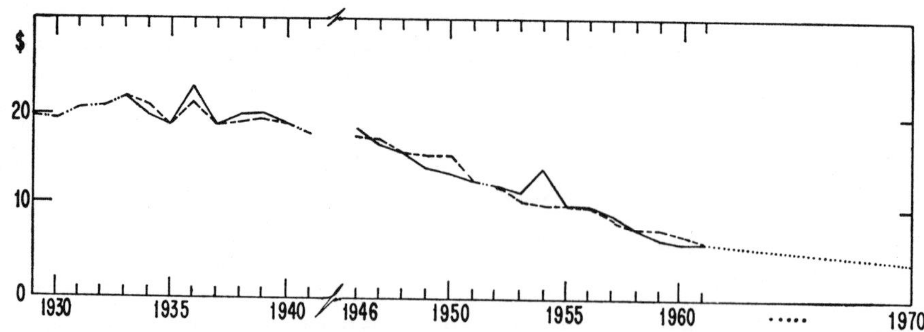


Static model
double-logarithmic

$$\ln q_t = \underset{(2.2203)}{-3.0435} + \underset{(.3231)}{.4016} \ln x_t - \underset{(.2092)}{.3965} \ln p_t$$
$$+ \underset{(.2019)}{1.5834} \ln (\text{farm pop. as \% of total pop.})_t + \underset{(.1016)}{.3949}\, d_t$$

$R^2 = .965 \qquad D.W. = 1.50$

$\eta = .4016 \qquad \sigma = -.3965 \qquad s_p = 1.11$

| | 1961 level | 1970 forecasts | | | |
|---|---|---|---|---|---|
| | | 4% | | 5% | |
| | | I | II | I | II |
| per capita | \$6.10 | \$4.01 | \$3.76 | \$4.10 | \$3.85 |
| aggregate (billions) | | \$.84 | \$.79 | \$.86 | \$.80 |

Farm population should have been used as the deflator for this item rather than the total population. But to do this would have required the use of some measure of farm income as the explanatory variable. Unfortunately, total consumption expenditure is not broken down into farm and nonfarm; nor are disposable farm-income data available on a yearly basis prior to 1946. An equation was fitted to the period 1946–1961, using the farm population as the deflator, with disposable farm income as the independent variable, but results were very unsatisfactory. Hence it was decided to use the total population as the deflator and to introduce the farm population as a percentage of the total. The 1946–1961 equation is given below.

$$q_t = \underset{(105.95)}{260.37} - \underset{(.0307)}{.0735} (\text{disp. farm income})_t + \underset{(.4217)}{3.3623}\, p_t$$

$R^2 = .831 \qquad D.W. = 1.37$

## 1.5 TOBACCO PRODUCTS

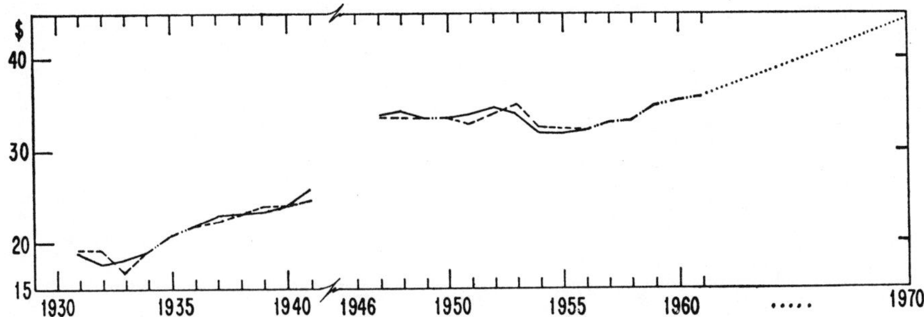


Dynamic model
3PLS

$$q_t = \underset{(.6899)}{1.0236} + \underset{(.0763)}{.8426}\, q_{t-1} + \underset{(.0037)}{.0140}\, \Delta x_t + \underset{(.0020)}{.0041}\, x_{t-1} + \underset{(.1670)}{.3350}\, z_t$$

$R^2 = .989 \qquad D.W. = 1.99$

$\alpha = 3.2190 \qquad \beta = .1743 \qquad \gamma = .0130 \qquad \gamma' = .0262$

$\kappa = .5770 \qquad \kappa' = 1.1517 \qquad \delta = .3452$

| | 1961 level | 1970 projections 4% | | 5% | |
|---|---|---|---|---|---|
| | | I | II | I | II |
| per capita | $35.89 | $44.47 | $44.12 | $46.64 | $46.29 |
| aggregate (billions) | | $9.29 | $9.22 | $ 9.74 | $9.67 |

When the own relative price was included in the dynamic model, the depreciation rate converged to a negative value. While this in itself might not be unreasonable, it also implied a negative stock coefficient which, given the nature of the commodity, was felt to be unreasonable. Hence prices were deleted.

The static model, given below, gave a poorer fit and had strong positive autocorrelation in the residuals.

$$q_t = \underset{(5.798)}{22.077} + \underset{(.0026)}{.0116}\, x_t - \underset{(.0485)}{.1047}\, p_t + \underset{(1.6905)}{4.8228}\, d_t$$

$R^2 = .957 \qquad D.W. = .38$

## 2.1 SHOES AND OTHER FOOTWEAR

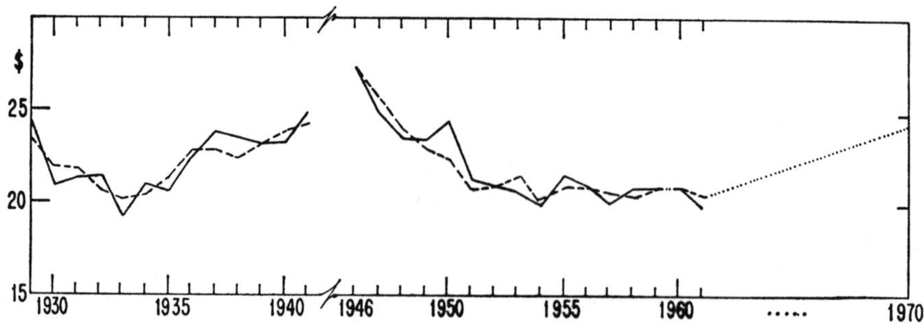


Static model
linear

$$q_t = \underset{(4.163)}{19.575} + \underset{(.0032)}{.0298\, x_t} - \underset{(.0522)}{.0923\, p_t} - \underset{(10.061)}{99.568\, (\text{car stocks per cap.})_t} - \underset{(1.1634)}{4.0663\, d_t}$$

$R^2 = .857 \qquad D.W. = 1.86$

$\kappa = 1.6944 \qquad \sigma = -.3878 \qquad s_p = 1.15$

| | 1961 level | 1970 projections 4% I | 4% II | 5% I | 5% II |
|---|---|---|---|---|---|
| per capita | $19.99 | $23.98 | $23.91 | $27.32 | $27.25 |
| aggregate (billions) | | $5.01 | $5.00 | $5.71 | $5.69 |

This was a very troublesome category. The dynamic model gave very poor results, even when the per capita stock of automobiles was included as a predictor. It was thought at one time that the percentage of the labor force accounted for by women would be relevant. Reliable estimates of this proportion are available only from 1946 on, so only a postwar regression could be used to test the hypothesis. Yet the results indicated that, although the coefficient of the variable was positive, the female percentage of the labor force is not important.

Except for the lower $R^2$ than might be desired, the above equation is quite satisfactory. Total expenditure and automobile stocks per capita are the most important explanatory variables, and there is a significant difference between levels of the prewar and postwar periods. While the equation projects a level in 1970 that reverses the postwar trend, this does not seem unreasonable.

The dynamic equation which included auto stocks per capita is given below.

$$q_t = \underset{(5.087)}{22.723} + \underset{(.1576)}{.1436\, q_{t-1}} + \underset{(.0059)}{.0238\, x_t} - \underset{(.0657)}{.1582\, p_t} - \underset{(23.528)}{73.455}\, (\text{car stocks per cap.})_t$$

$R^2 = .805 \qquad D.W. = 2.09$

It might appear anomalous that this equation, which is almost the same equation as the static equation above, has a lower $R^2$. This is because, with the inclusion of $q_{t-1}$, the first observation is lost.

## 2.2 SHOE CLEANING AND REPAIRS

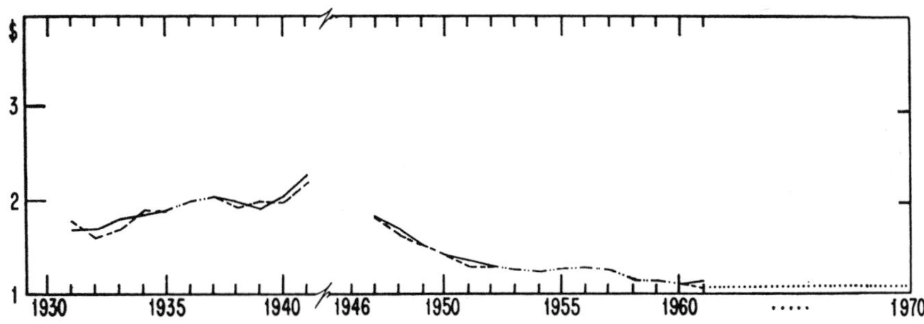


Dynamic model
3PLS

$$q_t = \underset{(.4476)}{1.2321} + \underset{(.0690)}{.6315}\, q_{t-1} + \underset{(.00034)}{.00067}\, \Delta x_t + \underset{(.00015)}{.00033}\, x_{t-1} - \underset{(.0063)}{.0185}\, \Delta p_t - \underset{(.0035)}{.0090}\, p_{t-1} + \underset{(.2680)}{.2621}\, z_t$$

$R^2 = .981 \qquad D.W. = 1.96$

$\alpha = 2.3456 \qquad \beta = .1923 \qquad \gamma = .0006 \qquad \gamma' = .0009$

$\lambda = -.0171 \qquad \lambda' = -.0244 \qquad \sigma = -1.0692 \qquad \sigma' = 1.5244$

$\kappa = .4949 \qquad \kappa' = .7055 \qquad \delta = .6439$

| | 1961 level | 1970 projections 4% | | 5% | |
|---|---|---|---|---|---|
| | | I | II | I | II |
| per capita | $1.13 | $1.11 | $1.30 | $1.20 | $1.40 |
| aggregate (billions) | | $.23 | $.27 | $.25 | $.29 |

As with 2.1, there is evidence from the static model that the stock of automobiles has had an important influence on this item. The fit of the static model was only slightly poorer than the dynamic, particularly the double-logarithmic version, given below, and there is little autocorrelation in the residuals. However, the total expenditure elasticity of 2.02 seems quite high. Note that the price elasticity is high enough to cause a considerable difference between the two projections based on different assumptions about 1970 relative prices; this is only rarely the case.

$$\ln q_t = -\underset{(1.545)}{12.755} + \underset{(.1491)}{2.0222} \ln x_t - \underset{(.1462)}{.7500} \ln p_t - \underset{(.0960)}{1.7373} \ln (\text{car stocks per cap.})_t - \underset{(.0419)}{.4281}\, d_t$$

$R^2 = .977 \qquad D.W. = 1.86$

## 2.3 CLOTHING, INCLUDING LUGGAGE[3]

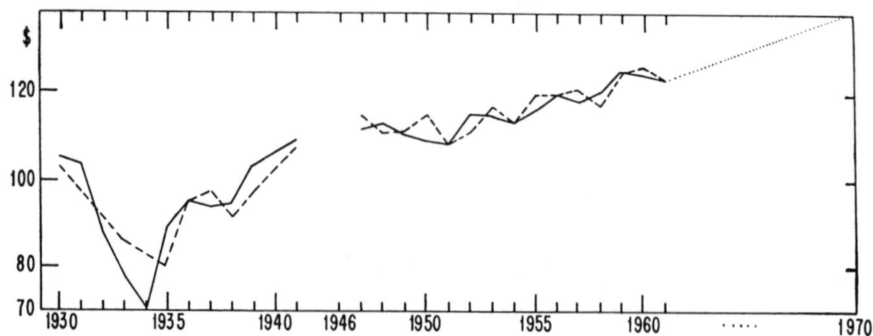


Dynamic model

OLS

$$q_t = 17.595 + .6243\, q_{t-1} + .0763\, \Delta x_t + .0173\, x_{t-1}$$
$$(8.905) \quad (.1479) \qquad (.0242) \qquad (.0074)$$

$R^2 = .904 \qquad D.W. = 2.03$

$\alpha = 84.590 \qquad \beta = -.2065 \qquad \gamma = .0833 \qquad \gamma' = .0461$

$\kappa = .9670 \qquad \kappa' = .5353 \qquad \delta = .2561$

| | 1961 level | 1970 projections 4% I | 4% II | 5% I | 5% II |
|---|---|---|---|---|---|
| per capita | $123.98 | $140.46 | $139.49 | $146.62 | $145.64 |
| aggregate (billions) | | $29.35 | $29.14 | $30.63 | $30.43 |

A considerable amount of time and energy was spent in getting a satisfactory equation for this large item. Equations were first estimated for the components, which are 2.3a (men's clothing) and 2.3b (women's clothing). However, because of the difficulty of separating out the luggage component and because little could apparently be gained from estimating the components, it was decided to use the aggregate.

When the relative price was included in the dynamic model, the coefficient of $\Delta p_t$ was negative, but was positive for $p_{t-1}$. When the identifying restriction on $\delta$ was taken into account, the estimates converged to unreasonable values, so prices were deleted.

Various static models tried gave less favorable results than the dynamic model. The own-price elasticity always had the wrong sign; the fits were poor; and the residuals were always positively autocorrelated. The distribution of income appeared to be of some importance, but not enough to make the static model acceptable. In addition, the derived marginal propensity to consume of the income group receiving the bottom four fifths of income was negative, which clearly is unreasonable.

Dynamic equations for the components, 2.3a and 2.3b, and the static equation for the aggregate with the distribution of income are given below.

[3] For a discussion of this equation, see also section III of Chapter 1.

2.3a *Men's Clothing*[4]

Dynamic model

3PLS

$$\begin{aligned} q_t = & -6.8350 + .4659\, q_{t-1} + .0566\, \Delta x_t + .0297\, x_{t-1} - .7077\, \Delta p_t \\ & \quad (14.643) \quad (.1603) \quad (.0156) \quad (.0100) \quad (.1854) \\ & + .0806\, p_{t-1} - 9.8203\, d_t - .5313\, z_t \\ & \quad (.1111) \quad (5.0948) \quad (.2707) \end{aligned}$$

$R^2 = .961 \qquad D.W. = 2.00$

2.3b *Women's clothing*

Dynamic model

3PLS

$$\begin{aligned} q_t = & -7.9723 + .5673\, q_{t-1} + .0386\, \Delta x_t + .0117\, x_{t-1} + .0342\, \Delta p_t \\ & \quad (8.3544) \quad (.2501) \quad (.0052) \quad (.0071) \quad (.0859) \\ & + .1439\, p_{t-1} - 6.2174\, d_t - .4709\, z_t \\ & \quad (.1061) \quad (3.8459) \quad (.3198) \end{aligned}$$

$R^2 = .963 \qquad D.W. = 2.32$

2.3 *Clothing, including luggage* [static model]

$$\begin{aligned} q_t = & \ 11.664 + .0848\, x_t + .0967\, (\text{income distribution})_t - 1.4199\, d_t \\ & \ (15.237) \quad (.0147) \quad (.0242) \quad (8.0375) \end{aligned}$$

$R^2 = .815 \qquad D.W. = .88$

## 2.4 STANDARD CLOTHING ISSUED TO MILITARY PERSONNEL

Owing to the peculiar nature of this commodity, no regression equation was estimated. Instead, the mean value of consumption of this item for 1955–1961 has been used for the projection for 1970. The projections are:

| | 1961 level | 1970 projections | | | |
|---|---|---|---|---|---|
| | | 4% | | 5% | |
| per capita | $.28 | $.24 | $.24 | $.24 | $.24 |
| aggregate (billions) | | $.05 | $.05 | $.05 | $.05 |

[4] The identifying restriction on δ has been ignored with these two equations; also the relative prices include the luggage component, while the dependent variables do not.

## 2.5 CLEANING, DYEING, PRESSING, ETC.

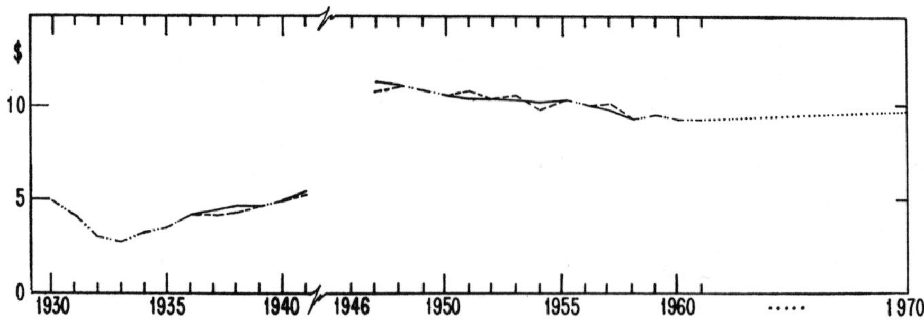


Dynamic model
OLS $\delta = 0$

$$q_t = .9817\, q_{t-1} + .0056\, \Delta x_t - .0303\, \Delta p_t$$
$$\quad (.0047) \qquad (.0010) \qquad (.0069)$$

$R^2 = .997$ $D.W. = 2.13$

$\alpha = 0$ $\beta = .0185$ $\gamma = .0056$ $\lambda = -.0306$

$\kappa = .9303$ $\sigma = -.4543$ $\delta = 0$

| | 1961 level | 1970 projections 4% | | 5% | |
|---|---|---|---|---|---|
| | | I | II | I | II |
| per capita | \$9.54 | \$9.66 | \$9.63 | \$10.25 | \$10.21 |
| aggregate (billions) | | \$2.01 | \$2.01 | \$2.14 | \$2.13 |

Note that $\delta = 0$ is assumed in this equation, and hence there is no long-run interpretation. We see that the dynamic effect is small, for $\beta$ is close to zero; it is positive, though, indicating slight habit formation.

The stock of washing machines per capita was important in the static model, along with total expenditure and the own relative price. The fit of this model, given below, is good, but the residuals have high positive autocorrelation.

$$q_t = 11.680 + .0026\, x_t - .0696\, p_t$$
$$\quad (2.690) \quad (.0015) \quad (.0140)$$
$$- 11.229 \text{ (washing machines per cap.)}_t + 3.9114\, d_t$$
$$\quad (3.617) \qquad\qquad\qquad (.4589)$$

$R^2 = .986$ $D.W. = .79$

## 2.6 LAUNDERING IN ESTABLISHMENTS

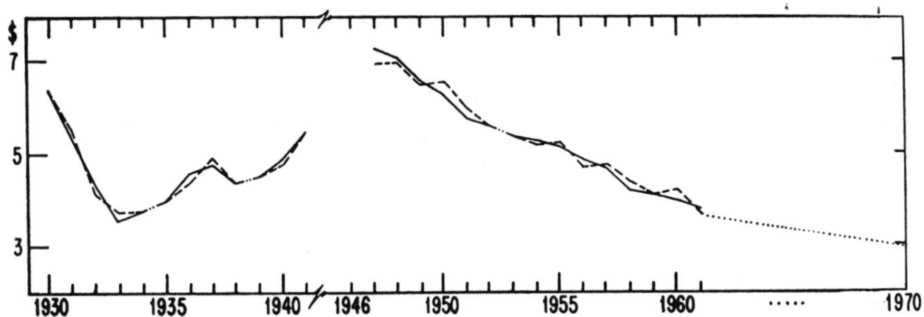


Dynamic model
OLS $\beta = \delta$

$$q_t - q_{t-1} = \underset{(.4352)}{.5048} + \underset{(.0007)}{.0042\Delta\, x_t} + \underset{(.0003)}{.0012\, x_{t-1}} - \underset{(.0076)}{.0577\Delta\, p_t}$$
$$- \underset{(.0038)}{.0167\, p_{t-1}} - \underset{(.1584)}{.9049\, d_t}$$

$R^2 = .916$ $D.W. = 2.33$

$\alpha = 1.4938$ $\beta = \delta = .3380$ $\gamma = .0036$ $\kappa = .9139$

$\lambda = -.0493$ $\sigma = -1.0180$

| | 1961 level | 1970 projections | | | |
|---|---|---|---|---|---|
| | | 4% | | 5% | |
| | | I | II | I | II |
| per capita | \$3.84 | \$2.92 | \$4.06 | \$3.93 | \$5.07 |
| aggregate (billions) | | \$.61 | \$.85 | \$.82 | \$1.06 |

The fit of this equation is quite remarkable in view of the fact that the dependent variable is a first difference; but it should be recalled that the long-run interpretation breaks down with this case. Note the substantial effect of prices on the projections.

With the static model, total PCE was insignificant; the fit was poor; and there was the usual positive autocorrelation in the residuals. The stock of washing machines per capita and prices were the most important predictors in the static model. The double-logarithmic version is given below.

$$\ln q_t = \underset{(3.4091)}{9.0918} + \underset{(.3037)}{.1531 \ln x_t} - \underset{(.3078)}{1.9707 \ln p_t}$$
$$- \underset{(.1055)}{.2426 \ln (\text{washing machines per cap.})_t} + \underset{(.0809)}{.1056\, d_t}$$

$R^2 = .895$ $D.W. = .78$

## 2.7 JEWELRY AND WATCHES

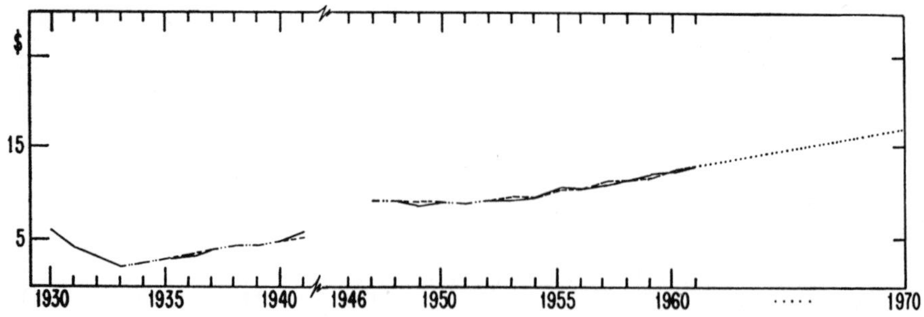


Dynamic model
OLS

$$q_t = .5375\,q_{t-1} + .0075\,\Delta x_t + .0049\,x_{t-1} - .0364\,\Delta p_t - .0241\,p_{t-1}$$
$$\quad (.0086) \qquad (.0018) \qquad (.0009) \qquad (.0120) \qquad (.0045)$$

$R^2 = .991 \qquad D.W. = 2.50$

$\alpha = 0 \qquad \beta = .3888 \qquad \gamma = .0065 \qquad \gamma' = .0107$

$\lambda = -.0316 \qquad \lambda' = -.0521 \qquad \sigma = -.4392 \qquad \sigma' = -.7231$

$\kappa = 1.0278 \qquad \kappa' = 1.6920 \qquad \delta = .9903$

| | 1961 level | 1970 projections 4% | | 5% | |
|---|---|---|---|---|---|
| | | I | II | I | II |
| per capita | \$13.24 | \$17.22 | \$16.29 | \$18.32 | \$17.40 |
| aggregate (billions) | | \$3.59 | \$3.40 | \$3.83 | \$3.64 |

$\beta > 0$ might appear to be inappropriate; however, though jewelry and watches are durables in the physical sense, it is possible for their ownership to be habit-forming. In the short run, an increase in income may lead to repair of the existing stock, while the long-run effect is to purchase new and more expensive items. Moreover, this is consistent with the results obtained with item 2.8, which includes a substantial amount of jewelry and watch repair. (Ideally 2.7 and 2.8 should be estimated simultaneously; an effort is made to do so with 2.8, discussed below.) Yet the large value of $\delta$ indicates that the habit wears off rapidly.

The static model for this item had a poorer fit, and the residuals had positive autocorrelation.[5] The static model, with total expenditures, the own relative price, and the war dummy, is given below.

$$q_t = -51.016 + 10.430\,x_t - 3.4198\,p_t + 1.4511\,d_t$$
$$\quad (23.474) \qquad (2.375) \qquad (1.8781) \qquad (.8545)$$

$R^2 = .957 \qquad D.W. = .70$

[5] The residuals in the above dynamic model became negatively autocorrelated when the identifying restriction of $\delta$ was taken into account.

## 2.8 OTHER CLOTHING, ACCESSORIES, ETC.[6]

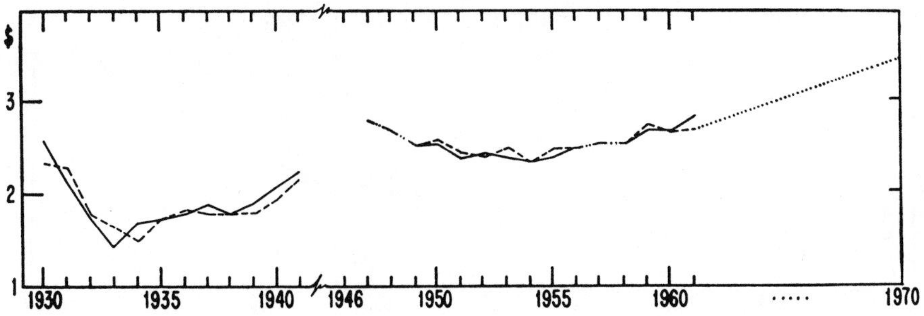


Dynamic model
OLS

$$q_t = .7704\, q_{t-1} + .00216\, \Delta x_t + .00037\, x_{t-1}$$
$$(.0622) \qquad (.00050) \qquad (.00012)$$

$R^2 = .944 \qquad D.W. = 1.94$

$\alpha = 0 \qquad \beta = -.0706 \qquad \gamma = .0022 \qquad \gamma' = .0016$

$\kappa = 1.2393 \qquad \kappa' = .9012 \qquad \delta = .1888$

| | 1961 level | 1970 projections | | | |
|---|---|---|---|---|---|
| | | 4% | | 5% | |
| | | I | II | I | II |
| per capita | \$2.83 | \$3.49 | \$3.46 | \$3.71 | \$3.68 |
| aggregate (billions) | | \$.73 | \$.72 | \$.78 | \$.77 |

When prices were included in the dynamic model, both coefficients were negative but smaller than their respective standard errors. Since watch and jewelry repair is a major item in this category, the negative stock coefficient is consistent with the positive stock coefficient in 2.7 (jewelry and watches). We made an effort to estimate 2.7 and 2.8 simultaneously, but muticollinearity precluded success.

The static model was disappointing. Though there was a significant price elasticity, the $R^2$ was low and the residuals had high positive autocorrelation. The double-logarithmic static model follows.

$$q_t = -2.0569 + 1.2109 \ln x_t - 1.3065 \ln p_t + .1464\, d_t$$
$$(2.2953) \qquad (.4994) \qquad (1.0181) \qquad (.1692)$$

$R^2 = .609 \qquad D.W. = .42$

[6] Comprises watch, clock, and jewelry repairs, dressmakers and seamstresses not in shops, costumes and dress-suit rental, and miscellaneous personal services related to clothing.

## 3.1 TOILET ARTICLES AND PREPARATIONS

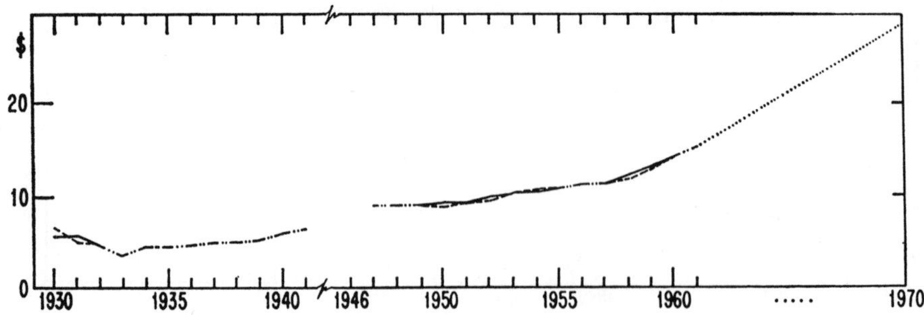


Dynamic model

OLS

$$q_t = 2.9116 + 1.1117\, q_{t-1} - .0707\, \Delta p_t - .0252\, p_{t-1} - 1.1418\, d_t$$
$$\quad (1.7751) \quad (.0585) \quad (.0130) \quad (.0120) \quad (.4307)$$

$R^2 = .990 \qquad D.W. = 2.13$

$\alpha = 6.3743 \qquad \beta = .5384 \qquad \lambda = -.0551 \qquad \lambda' = .2252$

$\sigma = -.7672 \qquad \sigma' = 3.1375 \qquad \delta = .4326$

| | 1961 level | 1970 projections 4% | | 5% | |
|---|---|---|---|---|---|
| | | I | II | I | II |
| per capita | \$15.31 | \$28.93 | \$28.83 | \$28.93 | \$28.83 |
| aggregate (billions) | | \$6.04 | \$6.02 | \$6.04 | \$6.02 |

It seems strange that total expenditure is not important for this commodity. Somewhat paradoxically, the static model showed it to be important, but not the own relative price. The explanation for the former no doubt lies in the very large coefficient for lagged consumption; the model is essentially indicating a strong trend, which swamps the effect of total expenditure, with short-term aberrations explained largely by prices. Also, the commodity is subject to strong habit formation, which may account for the absence of an independent influence of total expenditure. The positive long-run price elasticity reflects the greater-than-unity coefficient for lagged consumption.

The inverse semi-logarithmic form of the static model, with total expenditure, price, and the war dummy, is given below.

$$\ln q_t = .3934 + .00145\, x_t - .00125\, p_t - .0256\, d_t$$
$$\quad (.4417) \quad (.00016) \quad (.00234) \quad (.0703)$$

$R^2 = .977 \qquad D.W. = 1.21$

## 3.2 BARBERSHOPS, BEAUTY PARLORS, AND BATHS

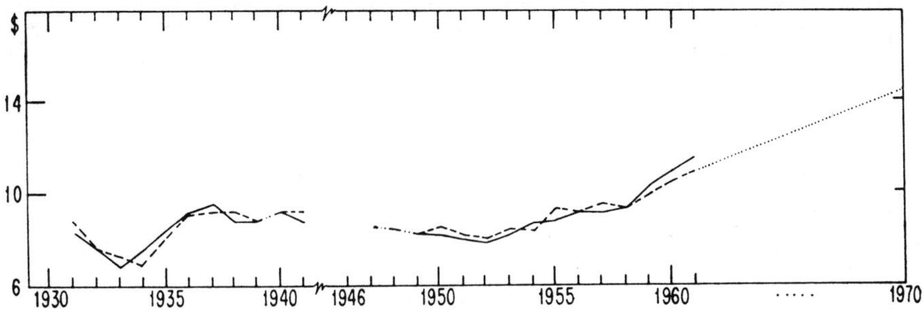


Dynamic model
3PLS

$$q_t = \underset{(.1462)}{.7703\, q_{t-1}} + \underset{(.0019)}{.0065\, \Delta x_t} + \underset{(.0014)}{.0028\, x_{t-1}} - \underset{(.6825)}{1.1317\, d_t} + \underset{(.1656)}{.2829\, z_t}$$

$R^2 = .892$ $D.W. = 1.99$

$\alpha = 0$ $\beta = .2819$ $\gamma = .0057$ $\gamma' = .0120$

$\kappa = .8212$ $\kappa' = 1.7136$ $\delta = .5414$

| | 1961 level | 1970 projections 4% | | 5% | |
|---|---|---|---|---|---|
| | | I | II | I | II |
| per capita | \$11.53 | \$14.66 | \$14.49 | \$15.75 | \$15.58 |
| aggregate (billions) | | \$3.06 | \$3.03 | \$3.29 | \$3.26 |

When the relative price was included in the dynamic model, both price coefficients were negative, but less than their standard errors. As was the case with 3.1, this item is subject to strong habit-formation, although it wears off more quickly than with 3.1.

The static model was generally disappointing for this category: the fit was poor; the own-price elasticity was usually positive; and the residuals had positive autocorrelation. The linear static model with PCE, prices, and the war dummy is given below.

$$q_t = \underset{(1.5638)}{1.3100} + \underset{(.0014)}{.0072\, x_t} + \underset{(.0023)}{.0027\, p_t} - \underset{(.5866)}{3.2865\, d_t}$$

$R^2 = .675$ $D.W. = .84$

## 4.1 SPACE RENTAL VALUE OF OWNER-OCCUPIED HOUSING[7]

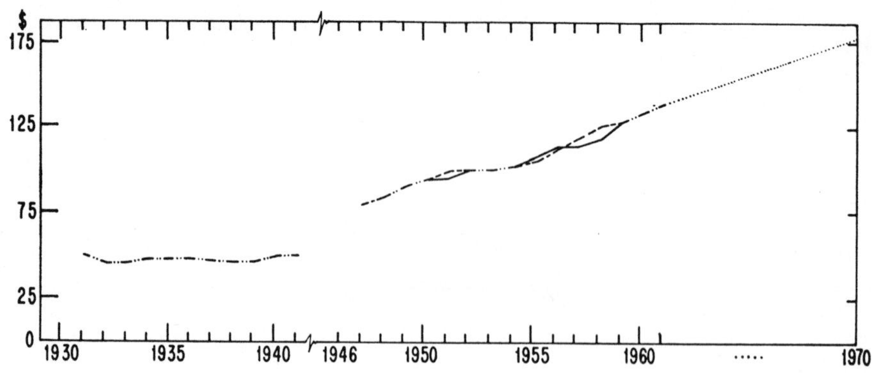


Dynamic model
3PLS/Bergstrom model

$$q_t = -8.2292 + .9205\, q_{t-1} + .00658\, (x_t + x_{t-1}) + 1.9410\, d_t + .6130\, z_t$$
$$(2.7328) \quad (.0260) \qquad (.00185) \qquad\qquad (1.3043) \quad (.1571)$$

$R^2 = .999 \qquad D.W. = 1.46$

$\xi = -103.51 \qquad \theta = .0828 \qquad \mu = .1655 \qquad \kappa = 2.4615$

| | 1961 level | 1970 projections 4% | | 5% | |
|---|---|---|---|---|---|
| per capita | $137.84 | $178.42 | $177.56 | $183.89 | $183.02 |
| aggregate (billions) | | $37.28 | $37.10 | $38.42 | $38.24 |

This is the first of three Bergstrom models. The adjustment coefficient of .0828 is smaller than might be expected; conceivably this could reflect a supply constraint at some time during the period, say following the war and lasting until 1957 or 1958. Whether or not such a constraint was in operation is a question of fact, and one that our model cannot answer in its present form. Our results do suggest the possibility, however.

Some preliminary projections were made from the dynamic model, with $\delta$ assumed equal to two:

$$q_t = .9306\, q_{t-1} + .0100\, x_t - .0495\, p_t + .6249\, z_t$$
$$(.0216) \qquad (.0018) \qquad (.0070) \qquad (.1725)$$

$R^2 = .999 \quad D.W. = 1.40$

$\alpha = 0 \qquad \beta = 1.9281 \qquad \gamma = .0052 \qquad \gamma' = .1441 \qquad \kappa = .0802$

$\kappa' = 2.2313 \qquad \lambda = -.0286 \qquad \lambda' = -.7133 \qquad \sigma = -.0354 \qquad \sigma' = -.9837$

$\delta = 2$

The projections from this equation are several dollars lower than from the Bergstrom equation, probably as a result of the presence of prices. (The price elasticity was positive in the Bergstrom model.) The large positive stock coefficient may again reflect a supply constraint.

[7] For a discussion of this equation, see also section VI of Chapter 1.

The distribution of income was important in the static model; the marginal propensity to consume of the upper income group (top one fifth) is about 2½ times its value for the lower income groups. The own price elasticity was positive with the static model and the fit was poorer than for the dynamic model. Moreover, the residuals had very high positive autocorrelation.[8] The static model, with PCE, income distribution, and the war dummy, is given below.[9]

$$q_t = -84.659 + .1328\, x_t + .1046\, ID_t + 13.118\, d_t$$
$$\quad (22.289) \quad (.0215) \quad (.0621) \quad (11.758)$$

MPC (upper) = .0488 MPC (lower) = .0173

$R^2 = .929$ $D.W. = .40$

[8] Though positive autocorrelation is usual with the static model, it is interesting to note that the OLS *D.W.* was .70 with the Bergstrom equation. The OLS *D.W.* was also very low with the dynamic model for item 4.2. These low *D.W.*'s could reflect the method used by the Commerce Department to estimate these series.

[9] See footnote 16 below for the adjustment factor used in deriving these estimates.

## 4.2 SPACE RENTAL VALUE OF TENANT-OCCUPIED HOUSING

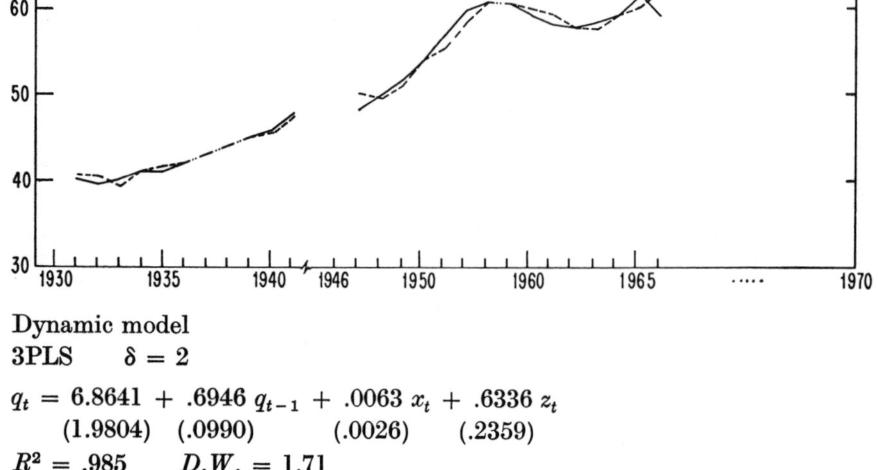


Dynamic model
3PLS $\delta = 2$

$$q_t = \underset{(1.9804)}{6.8641} + \underset{(.0990)}{.6946}\, q_{t-1} + \underset{(.0026)}{.0063}\, x_t + \underset{(.2359)}{.6336}\, z_t$$

$R^2 = .985$ $D.W. = 1.71$

$\alpha = 4.0506$ $\beta = 1.6396$ $\gamma = .0037$ $\gamma' = .0206$

$\kappa = .0925$ $\kappa' = .5131$ $\delta = 2$

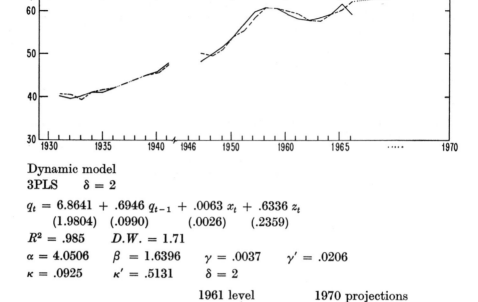

| | 1961 level | 1970 projections 4% | | 5% | |
|---|---|---|---|---|---|
| | | I | II | I | II |
| per capita | \$59.27 | \$65.76 | \$65.48 | \$67.51 | \$67.23 |
| aggregate (billions) | | \$13.74 | \$13.68 | \$14.10 | \$14.05 |

The depreciation rate converged to a high positive value when the identifying restriction on $\delta$ was taken into account. This suggested trying the Bergstrom model, but the coefficient of $q_{t-1}$ was significantly greater than one. Since the price coefficients, though negative, were insignificant in the dynamic model, they were excluded when we finally estimated the equation with $\delta = 2$. Possible reasons for the large values of $\beta$ and $\delta$ were discussed for 4.1 and need not be gone into again.

Results from the static model indicate the distribution of income to be important for tenant rental housing also; the MPC for the lower-income groups is considerably higher than for the upper income group. In fact the derived value is negative for the upper group, a result which must be viewed with some suspicion, though it might be explained by the higher MPC on owner-occupied dwellings for this group. The own price had the wrong sign in the static model, and the residuals had high positive autocorrelation. One of the static models is given below.[10]

$$q_t = \underset{(6.159)}{18.415} + \underset{(.0048)}{.0081}\, x_t + \underset{(.0466)}{.1325}\, p_t - \underset{(.0151)}{.0825}\,(\text{income dist.})_t - \underset{(2.6793)}{3.2096}\, d_t$$

MPC (upper) $= -.0156$ MPC (lower) $= .0767$

$R^2 = .954$ $D.W. = .95$

[10] We may note in passing that it is impossible to test for a price substitution between 4.1 and 4.2, since the same deflator is used for both. This is a weakness of the Commerce Department figures on housing. Since owner-occupied dwellings (mostly one-family houses) are different in kind from rental dwellings (mostly apartments), and are also located in different areas (relatively more in suburbs, for instance), it is unlikely that their rental value has evolved in the same manner as that of rented dwellings.

## 4.3 RENTAL VALUE OF FARM HOUSES[11]

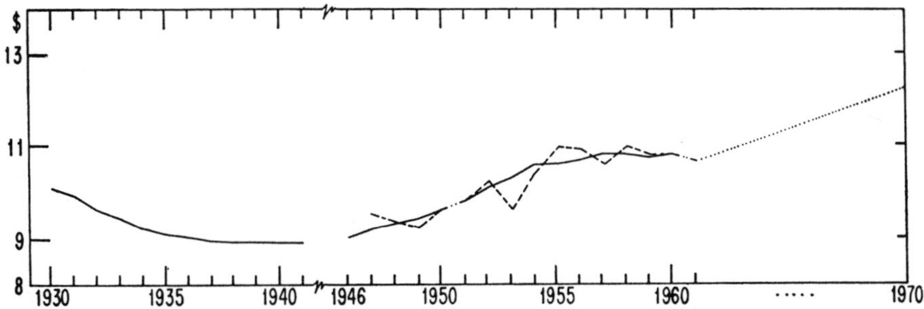


Dynamic model

OLS

$$q_t = \underset{(.0321)}{1.0399}\, q_{t-1} + \underset{(.0076)}{.0138}\, \Delta x_t + \underset{(.0028)}{.0021}\, x_{t-1}$$

$R^2 = .994 \qquad D.W. = 1.98$

$\alpha = 0 \qquad \beta = .2042 \qquad \gamma = .0125 \qquad \gamma' = -.0527$

$\kappa = .1332 \qquad \kappa' = -.0527 \qquad \delta = .1650$

| | 1961 level | 1970 projections | | | |
|---|---|---|---|---|---|
| | | 4% | | 5% | |
| | | I | II | I | II |
| per capita | \$10.73 | \$12.29 | \$12.29 | \$12.34 | \$12.34 |
| aggregate (billions) | | \$2.57 | \$2.57 | \$2.57 | \$2.57 |

The farm population rather than the total population was used as the deflator for this category, and disposable farm income was used as the independent variable. Since the latter was unavailable for the prewar years, the function had to be fitted to 1946–1961 data only. This is the only category for which this has been necessary.

In preparing the projection for 1970, it was assumed that per capita real disposable income for the farm population would grow at a compound rate of $2\frac{1}{2}$ percent per annum for the 4 percent growth rate in GNP, and at $2\frac{3}{4}$ per cent for the 5 percent growth rate.

The negative long-run income elasticity appears to be an anomaly. However, this might be explained by the low level of farm income relative to nonfarm income. The low relative level of farm income may mean that the long-run effect of an increase in income is to increase purchase of household durables, autos, etc., at the expense of housing. But this is highly tentative.

The static model for this item, using total population as the deflator and introducing farm population as a percentage of the total, was very disappointing. The total-expenditure and farm-population coefficients were both negative; the fit was poor; and the residuals had high positive autocorrelation. This model is given below.

$$\ln q_t = \underset{(1.3571)}{5.5710} - \underset{(.1376)}{.2177} \ln x_t - \underset{(.1904)}{.2727} \ln p_t$$
$$- \underset{(.1144)}{.1692} \ln (\text{farm pop. as \% of total})_t + \underset{(.0772)}{.0599}\, d_t$$

$R^2 = .705 \qquad D.W. = .20$

[11] Although the equation for this category was estimated using the farm population as the deflator, the projections have been converted to per capita terms using the total population.

## 4.4 OTHER HOUSING[12]

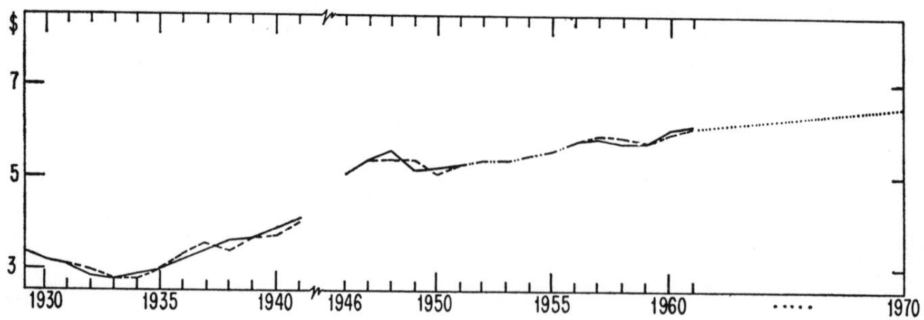


Dynamic model
3PLS/Bergstrom model

$$q_t = \underset{(.1460)}{.3314}\, q_{t-1} + \underset{(.00026)}{.00141}\,(x_t + x_{t-1}) + \underset{(.1124)}{.4380}\, d_t + \underset{(.1051)}{.4338}\, z_t$$

$R^2 = .993 \qquad D.W. = 2.44$

$\xi = 0 \qquad \theta = 1.0044 \qquad \mu = .0042 \qquad \kappa = 1$

| | 1961 level | 1970 projections 4% I | 4% II | 5% I | 5% II |
|---|---|---|---|---|---|
| per capita | \$6.17 | \$6.48 | \$6.43 | \$6.80 | \$6.75 |
| aggregate (billions) | | \$1.35 | \$1.34 | \$1.42 | \$1.41 |

The own-price elasticity was positive when prices were included in the Bergstrom equation. Note that the adjustment of actual to desired consumption is essentially complete within the period for $\theta$ is very close to one. Some preliminary projections were made with the following dynamic model:

$$q_t = \underset{(.2488)}{.6001} + \underset{(.0902)}{.4205}\, q_{t-1} + \underset{(.0004)}{.0026}\, x_t - \underset{(.0026)}{.0121}\, p_t$$

$R^2 = .994 \qquad D.W. = 1.75$

$\alpha = .7040 \qquad \beta = 1.1841 \qquad \gamma = .0018 \qquad \gamma' = .0044 \qquad \kappa = .5062$
$\kappa' = 1.2408 \qquad \lambda = -.0085 \qquad \lambda' = -.0209 \qquad \sigma = -.1874 \qquad \sigma' = -.4594$
$\delta = 2$

Little explanation can be offered for the large values of $\beta$ and $\delta$; however, the close agreement of $\gamma'$ with $\mu$ in the Bergstrom equation should be noted. Note also that prices are important. The projections from this equation differed only slightly from those given above.

The linear static model is also a good equation and is offered as an alternative.

$$q_t = \underset{(.3190)}{.5821} + \underset{(.0003)}{.0037}\, x_t - \underset{(.0033)}{.0100}\, p_t + \underset{(.1602)}{.3683}\, d_t$$

$\kappa = 1.0436 \qquad \sigma = -.2191$

$R^2 = .988 \qquad D.W. = 1.55$

[12] Comprises transient hotels, tourist cabins, clubs, schools, and institutions.

## 5.1 FURNITURE

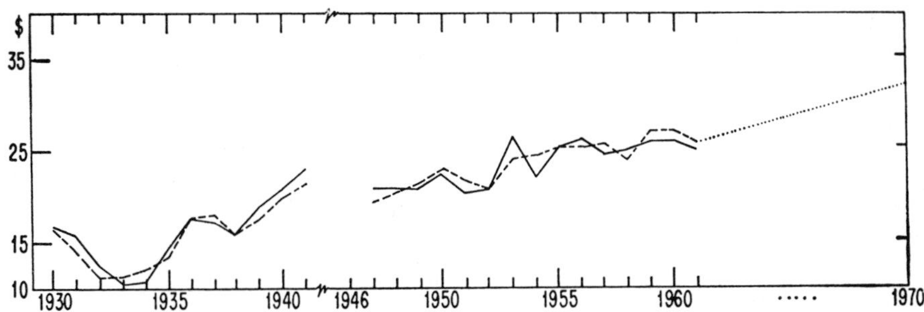


Dynamic model

OLS

$$q_t = .6676\, q_{t-1} + .0406\, \Delta x_t + .0050\, x_{t-1}$$
$$\quad (.1329) \qquad (.0054) \qquad (.0022)$$

$R^2 = .948 \qquad D.W. = 2.06$

$\alpha = 0 \qquad \beta = -.2660 \qquad \gamma = .0456 \qquad \gamma' = .0152$

$\kappa = 2.7964 \qquad \kappa' = .9302 \qquad \delta = .1326$

| | 1961 level | 1970 projections | | | |
|---|---|---|---|---|---|
| | | 4% | | 5% | |
| | | I | II | I | II |
| per capita | \$24.93 | \$32.30 | \$31.89 | \$34.92 | \$34.50 |
| aggregate (billions) | | \$6.75 | \$6.66 | \$7.30 | \$7.21 |

Although one might prefer the $R^2$ to be higher, this equation otherwise is very good. The stock coefficient is negative, as it should be, and the depreciation rate is reasonable. The own-price elasticity was positive when prices were included in the model.

An index of new residential construction per capita was tried in the static model and found to be significant, together with prices and total expenditure. The fit of this model, given below, is slightly better than the model above, but there is some autocorrelation in the residuals.

$$q_t = 160.06 + 30.248 \ln x_t - 7.8374 \ln p_t$$
$$\quad (23.86) \quad (2.857) \qquad (4.2686)$$
$$+ .7676 \ln (\text{index resid. const. per cap.})_t - 4.8923\, d_t$$
$$\quad (.4712). \qquad\qquad\qquad (1.4152)$$

$R^2 = .960 \qquad D.W. = 1.50$

## 5.2 KITCHEN AND OTHER HOUSEHOLD APPLIANCES

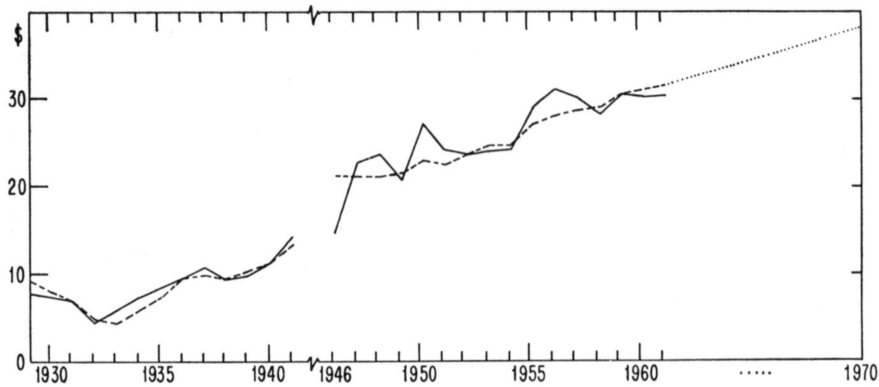


Static model

Linear

$$q_t = .0222\, x_t - .1063\, p_t + 3.5249\, d_t$$
$$\quad (.0020) \qquad (.0161) \qquad (1.3884)$$

$R^2 = .965 \qquad D.W. = 2.00$

$\kappa = 1.5197 \qquad \sigma = -.6253 \qquad s_p = 2.27$

| | 1961 level | 1970 projections 4% | | 5% | |
|---|---|---|---|---|---|
| | | I | II | I | II |
| per capita | \$30.72 | \$38.77 | \$37.72 | \$41.26 | \$40.21 |
| aggregate (billions) | | \$8.10 | \$7.88 | \$8.62 | \$8.40 |

The dynamic model for this category gave a very high negative stock coefficient (−1.76) and a depreciation rate that is clearly too large (1.07). While the assumptions of the dynamic model do not impose any finite bounds on the magnitude of the stock coefficient, practical considerations do. To maintain that kitchen appliances, etc., are goods for which the present purchase of one unit inhibits the future purchase by one and three-fourths units seems untenable. It is unfortunate that for this important item, which is undoubtedly durable, no satisfactory dynamic equation could be found.[13]

The index of residential construction per capita was tried in the static model, but added little to the overall equation. An attempt was also made to incorporate directly into the static model a variable representing the stock of kitchen durable goods. The attempt failed, however, because of a serious inadequacy in our index.

The dynamic equation, with the implausibly large negative stock coefficient, is given below.

$$q_t = -29.111 - .1715\, q_{t-1} + .0411\, \Delta x_t + .0418\, x_{t-1} + .6830\, z_t$$
$$(4.126) \quad (.1504) \qquad (.0059) \qquad (.0057) \qquad (.2208)$$

$R^2 = .988 \qquad D.W. = 1.95$

[13] One reason may be that in this item there was unusually rapid technological change, which our model does not take into account.

## 5.3 CHINA, GLASSWARE, TABLEWARE, AND UTENSILS

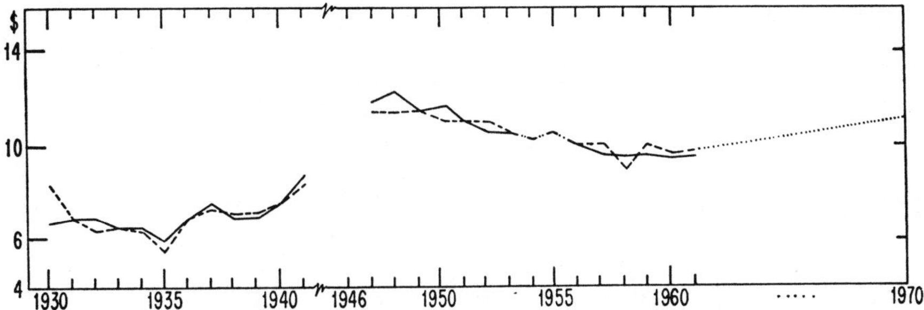


Dynamic model

OLS

$$q_t = 5.3422 + .5836\, q_{t-1} + .0058\, \Delta x_t + .0027\, x_{t-1}$$
$$(3.8824) \quad (.2140) \quad (.0029) \quad (.0017)$$
$$- .1077\, \Delta p_t - .0492\, p_{t-1}$$
$$(.0411) \quad (.0392)$$

$R^2 = .929 \qquad D.W. = 1.57$

$\alpha = 11.3812 \quad \beta = .0669 \quad \gamma = .0057 \quad \gamma' = .0064 \quad \kappa = .7842$

$\kappa' = 8840 \quad \lambda = -.1049 \quad \lambda' = -.1182 \quad \sigma = -1.1635 \quad \sigma' = -1.3115$

$\delta = .5928$

| | 1961 level | 1970 projections 4% | | 5% | |
|---|---|---|---|---|---|
| | | I | II | I | II |
| per capita | \$9.43 | \$11.35 | \$12.01 | \$12.06 | \$12.72 |
| aggregate (billions) | | \$2.37 | \$2.51 | \$2.52 | \$2.66 |

The results indicate that the purchase of this item is subject to slight habit formation. But the habit wears off quite rapidly, for the depreciation rate is substantial. Note also the fairly high own-price elasticity both in the short run and in the long run.

Per capita construction of residential housing was tried in the static model. Unfortunately its coefficient was negative and the model discarded, even though the fit was better than in the dynamic model. This equation is given below.

$$\ln q_t = 2.8649 + 1.0015 \ln x_t - 1.6291 \ln p_t - .0833 \ln (\text{resid. const. per cap.})_t$$
$$(1.0598) \quad (.2176) \quad (.1984) \quad (.0321)$$
$$+ .0823\, d_t$$
$$(.0721)$$

$R^2 = .951 \qquad D.W. = 2.10$

## 5.4 OTHER DURABLE HOUSE FURNISHINGS

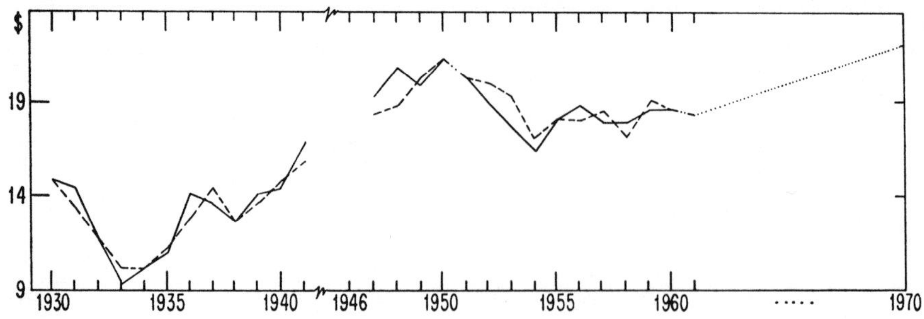


Dynamic model
OLS $\delta = 0$

$$q_t = .9716\, q_{t-1} + .0273\, \Delta x_t$$
$$\quad (.0102) \qquad (.0038)$$

$R^2 = .940 \qquad D.W. = 1.77$

$\alpha =$ indeterminate $\qquad \beta = -.0288 \qquad \gamma = .0277 \qquad \kappa = 2.1101 \qquad \delta = 0$

| | 1961 level | 1970 projections 4% | | 5% | |
|---|---|---|---|---|---|
| | | I | II | I | II |
| per capita | \$18.68 | \$22.11 | \$21.68 | \$24.85 | \$24.41 |
| aggregate (billions) | | \$4.61 | \$4.53 | \$5.19 | \$5.10 |

This equation is another of the special cases of the dynamic model, for it has been estimated under the assumption that δ is equal to zero. The prices were first deleted because of positive coefficients, and then the depreciation rate was found to be very close to zero. Since this rather problematic category is comprised of individual items such as floor coverings, mirrors, picture frames, drafting instruments, etc., which are very durable, the depreciation rate should be quite small. Although it is a rather bald assumption to take δ to be in fact zero, statistically this was indicated to be the case.

Residential construction per capita was found to be important in the static model. The relative price of 5.5 was also tried, but 5.4 and 5.5 were indicated to be substitutes, which seems unreasonable. The own-price elasticity, moreover, was positive in the static model; the fit was poor; and the residuals had positive autocorrelation. In another static model, given below, the amount of residential floor space per capita[14] was tried, but found to have the wrong sign.

$$\ln q_t = 5.0026 + 1.3194 \ln x_t + .1159 \ln p_t$$
$$(8.4156) \quad (.4864) \quad (.7654)$$
$$- 2.2089 \ln (\text{resid. floor space per cap.})_t - .2254\, d_t$$
$$(1.5273) \qquad (.2202)$$

$R^2 = .798 \qquad D.W. = .50$

[14] This series was painstakingly constructed by Alan W. Strout at the Harvard Economic Research Project.

## 5.5 SEMI-DURABLE HOUSE FURNISHINGS

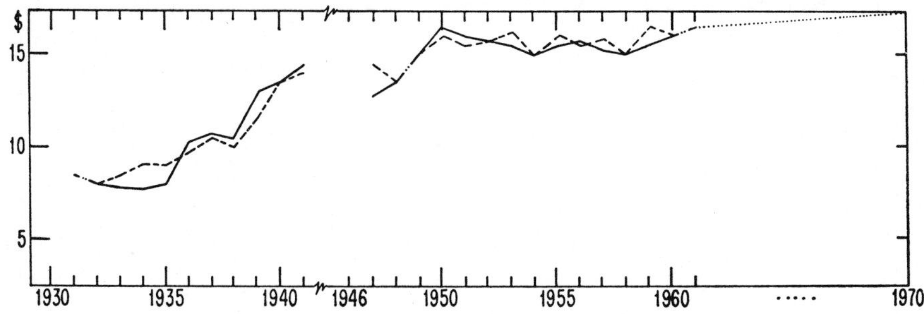


Dynamic model

3PLS

$$q_t = \underset{(.7154)}{1.1247} + \underset{(.2284)}{.3420}\, q_{t-1} + \underset{(.0040)}{.0183}\, \Delta x_t + \underset{(.0017)}{.0038}\, x_{t-1} + \underset{(.3137)}{.6109}\, z_t$$

$R^2 = .948 \qquad D.W. = 1.80$

$\alpha = 71.2759 \qquad \beta = -.7455 \qquad \gamma = .0244 \qquad \gamma' = .0059$

$\kappa = 2.3308 \qquad \kappa' = .5588 \qquad \delta = .2352$

| | 1961 level | 1970 projections 4% | | 5% | |
|---|---|---|---|---|---|
| | | I | II | I | II |
| per capita | \$16.45 | \$17.57 | \$17.43 | \$18.45 | \$18.31 |
| aggregate (billions) | | \$3.67 | \$3.64 | \$3.85 | \$3.83 |

Among the items included in this category are piece goods allocated to house-furnishing use (other than bedding and floor coverings), brushes, brooms, and lampshades; these are durables that are by and large necessities—hence the substantial negative stock coefficient, along with a high short-run but low long-run total-expenditure elasticity, is what we should expect. Moreover, the estimated depreciation rate of .2352 is reasonable.

The relative price of 5.4, per capita new residential construction, total expenditure, and the own relative price were found to be important in the static model. (This equation is given below.) However, the coefficient of the relative price of 5.4 was positive, which seems incorrect.

$$q_t = \underset{(30.80)}{-130.79} + \underset{(3.926)}{14.760} \ln x_t - \underset{(2.7296)}{2.1646} \ln p_t - \underset{(.5353)}{.3249} \ln (\text{price of } 5.4)_t$$
$$+ \underset{(5.514)}{11.565} (\text{resid. const. per cap.})_t - \underset{(1.7122)}{3.2185}\, d_t$$

$R^2 = .903 \qquad D.W. = .89$

## 5.6 CLEANING AND POLISHING PREPARATIONS, AND MISCELLANEOUS HOUSEHOLD SUPPLIES AND PAPER PRODUCTS

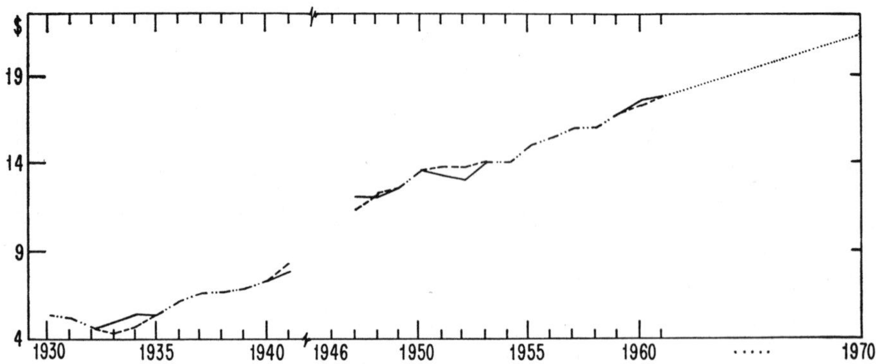


Dynamic model
OLS

$$q_t = -3.7798 + .5455\, q_{t-1} + .0105\, \Delta x_t + .0068\, x_{t-1}$$
$$\quad (.8416) \quad (.0989) \qquad (.0016) \qquad (.0014)$$

$R^2 = .994 \qquad D.W. = 1.76$

$\alpha = -5.0439 \qquad \beta = .3816 \qquad \gamma = .0091 \qquad \gamma' = .0151$

$\kappa = 1.0972 \qquad \kappa' = 1.8092 \qquad \delta = .9698$

| | 1961 level | 1970 projections | | | |
|---|---|---|---|---|---|
| | | 4% | | 5% | |
| | | I | II | I | II |
| per capita | \$17.12 | \$20.86 | \$20.61 | \$22.41 | \$22.17 |
| aggregate (billions) | | \$4.36 | \$4.31 | \$4.68 | \$4.63 |

The own-price elasticity was positive when the relative price was included in the dynamic model. Other than having stronger habit formation than one would expect, this equation does not raise any doubts.

With the various static models tried, the own-price elasticity was always positive, and the residuals invariably had high positive autocorrelation. The double-logarithmic version is given below.

$$\ln q_t = -13.140 + 1.8823 \ln x_t + .4181 \ln p_t + .0528\, d_t$$
$$\quad (2.829) \quad (.1944) \qquad (.3865) \qquad (.0722)$$

$R^2 = .983 \qquad D.W. = .78$

## 5.7 STATIONERY

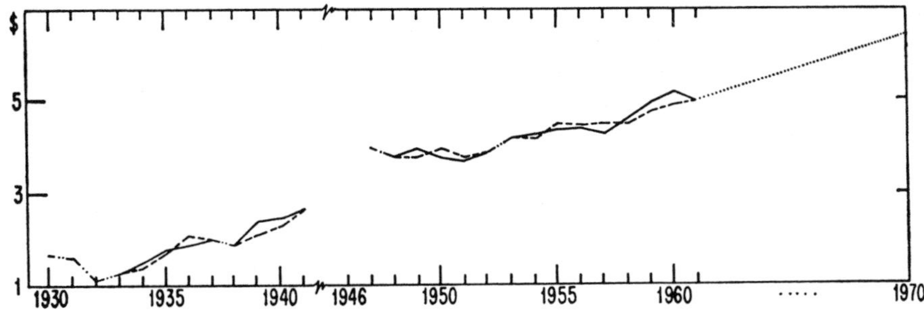


Dynamic model

**OLS**

$$q_t = -.7325 + .2979\, q_{t-1} + .00438\, \Delta x_t + .00331\, x_{t-1}$$
$$\quad (.4865) \quad (.1885) \qquad (.0075) \qquad (.00092)$$
$$- .01565\, \Delta p_t - .01185 d_t$$
$$(.00726) \qquad (.00677)$$

$R^2 = .991 \qquad D.W. = 1.32$

$\alpha = -.9273 \quad \beta = .1353 \quad \gamma = .0042 \quad \gamma' = .0047 \quad \kappa = 1.6372$

$\kappa' = 1.8420 \quad \lambda = -.0150 \quad \lambda' = -.0169 \quad \sigma = -.4750 \quad \sigma' = -.5344$

$\delta = 1.2173$

| | 1961 level | 1970 projections 4% | | 5% | |
|---|---|---|---|---|---|
| | | I | II | I | II |
| per capita | $4.92 | $6.36 | $6.33 | $6.88 | $6.86 |
| aggregate (billions) | | $1.33 | $1.32 | $1.44 | $1.43 |

The results indicate this commodity to be subject to moderate habit formation, but the habit wears off very rapidly. Note also the relatively high total-expenditure elasticities and significant but much smaller own-price elasticities.

The double-logarithmic static model with PCE, prices, and the war dummy is also a good equation. The fit is good, and there is only borderline autocorrelation in the residuals. However, the PCE elasticity of 2.33 may be too high.

$$\ln q_t = -9.5414 + 2.3340 \ln x_t - 1.2875 \ln p_t - .0986\, d_t$$
$$(.8359) \quad (.1313) \qquad (.1771) \qquad (.0579)$$

$R^2 = .989 \qquad D.W. = 1.58$

## 5.8a ELECTRICITY (HOUSEHOLD UTILITY)

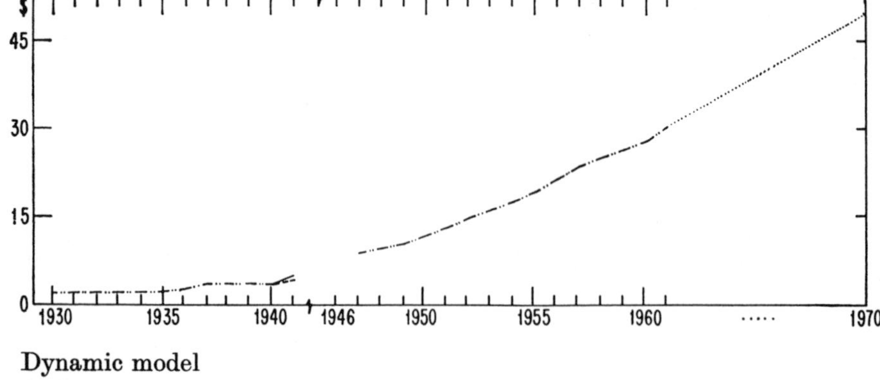


Dynamic model

OLS $\beta = \delta$

$$q_t - q_{t-1} = -\underset{(.6194)}{.9082} + \underset{(.0009)}{.0025}\, \Delta x_t + \underset{(.0003)}{.0018}\, x_{t-1} - \underset{(.0033)}{.0038}\, \Delta p_t - \underset{(.0016)}{.0027}\, p_{t-1}$$

$R^2 = .931$ $D.W. = 1.06$

$\alpha = .9082$ $\beta = \delta = 1.1332$ $\gamma = .0348$ $\kappa = 3.5798$ $\lambda = -.0527$

$\sigma = -.6502$

| | 1961 level | 1970 projections 4% | | 5% | |
|---|---|---|---|---|---|
| | | I | II | I | II |
| per capita | \$30.59 | \$50.63 | \$50.30 | \$51.73 | \$51.39 |
| aggregate (billions) | | \$10.58 | \$10.51 | \$10.81 | \$10.74 |

The price series for this category is a marginal price[15] rather than the implicit deflator ordinarily used. The implicit deflator gave a positive elasticity when it was used. The major drawback to this equation is the positive autocorrelation in the residuals, which arose upon taking the restriction on $\delta$ into account. Unfortunately when $\beta = \delta$ is assumed (as here), 3PLS cannot be used. In view of the dependent variable being a first difference, the fit of the equation is remarkable.

Though the PCE elasticity appears to be high, this is partly because of the very strong trend in the consumption of electricity. When the trend in the dependent variable is stronger than the trend in the independent variable, the elasticity at the means will be overstated. In this case, the elasticity at 1961 levels is 1.8669, a much more plausible figure.

Prices (marginal) were insignificant in the static model. Utilizing a finding of Fisher and Kaysen (1962) on the demand for electricity and our own preliminary cross-section results, we introduced the proportion of the population in the South and West as a predictor in the static model. As can be seen below, it turned out to be highly significant. However, the static models invariably had high positive autocorrelation in the residuals.

$$\ln q_t = \underset{(5.324)}{11.624} + \underset{(.4841)}{.5521} \ln x_t + \underset{(2.293)}{16.126} \ln (\text{prop. of pop. in south and west})_t$$

$R^2 = .958$ $D.W. = .84$

[15] See the Data Sources for a description of this series, and Houthakker (1951) for a justification of the use of the marginal price as an explanatory variable.

## 5.8b GAS (HOUSEHOLD UTILITY)

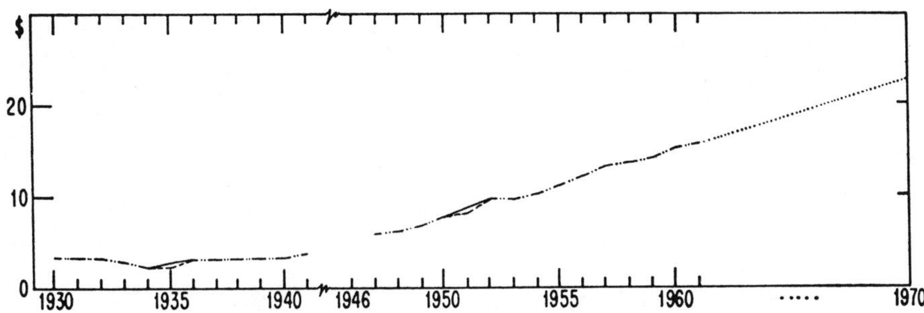


Dynamic model

OLS/Bergstrom model

$$q_t = -1.8230 + .9249\, q_{t-1} + .00111\, (x_t + x_{t-1})$$
$$(.4099) \quad (.0319) \qquad (.00024)$$

$R^2 = .997 \qquad D.W. = 1.98$

$\xi = 1.8941 \qquad \theta = .0780 \qquad \mu = .0295 \qquad \kappa = 4.7628$

| | 1961 level | 1970 projections 4% | | 5% | |
|---|---|---|---|---|---|
| | | I | II | I | II |
| per capita | \$15.98 | \$22.89 | \$22.74 | \$23.82 | \$23.67 |
| aggregate (billions) | | \$4.78 | \$4.75 | \$4.98 | \$4.95 |

The relative price was insignificant in the dynamic model; however, as was the case with 5.8a, a marginal price would be preferred to the implicit deflator, though efforts to construct such a variable were unsuccessful. The adjustment coefficient of .0780 appears to be smaller than one might expect (while the PCE elasticity appears high), but this could result from a supply constraint at some time during the historical period.

Preliminary projections were made from the dynamic model with $\delta = 2$. This equation written out in full is:

$$q_t = -1.7887 + .9301\, q_{t-1} + .0021\, x_t$$
$$(.3915) \quad (.0308) \qquad (.0005)$$

$R^2 = .997 \qquad D.W. = 2.13$

$\alpha = -.9008 \qquad \beta = 1.2757 \qquad \gamma = .0011 \qquad \gamma' = .0030$

$\kappa = .1776 \qquad \kappa' = .4904 \qquad \delta = 2$

The projections from this equation vary little from those given above.

With the static model, the own-price elasticity was positive. The (marginal) price of elasticity was also tried in the static model, but the cross elasticity had the wrong sign for substitutes. The static model with PCE, own price, marginal price of electricity and the war dummy is given below.

$$\ln q_t = -2.5258 + .0028\, x_t + .0062\, p_t - .0026\, (\text{price of 5.8a})_t + .2733\, d_t$$
$$(.7134) \quad (.0003) \qquad (.0018) \qquad (.0011) \qquad\qquad (.2028)$$

$R^2 = .971 \qquad D.W. = 1.03$

## 5.8c WATER

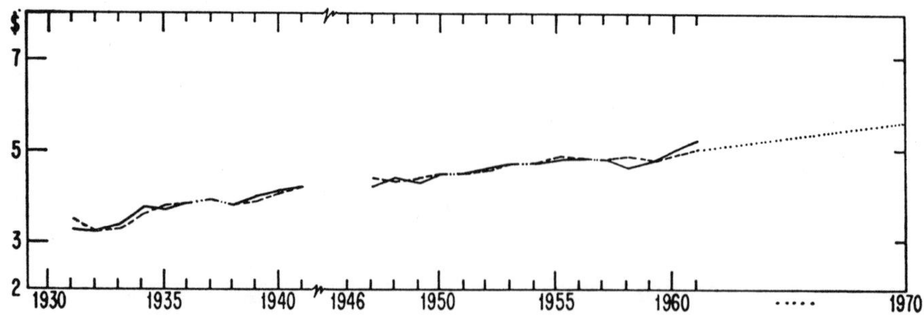


Dynamic model
3PLS

$$q_t = \underset{(.5261)}{1.0240} + \underset{(.2275)}{.5427}\, q_{t-1} + \underset{(.0009)}{.0024}\, \Delta x_t + \underset{(.0005)}{.0009}\, x_{t-1} + \underset{(.2694)}{.1771}\, z_t$$

$R^2 = .951 \quad D.W. = 1.63$

$\alpha = 2.8775 \quad \beta = -.1313 \quad \gamma = .0025 \quad \gamma' = .0018$

$\kappa = .6967 \quad \kappa' = .5426 \quad \delta = .4615$

| | 1961 level | 1970 projections 4% | | 5% | |
|---|---|---|---|---|---|
| | | I | II | I | II |
| per capita | \$5.36 | \$5.68 | \$5.64 | \$5.91 | \$5.87 |
| aggregate (billions) | | \$1.19 | \$1.18 | \$1.23 | \$1.23 |

It is surprising to find a negative stock coefficient for this item; casual observation suggests that lawn watering and car washing (and perhaps even taking a bath) are habit-forming.

The percentages of the population living in the South and West were found to be important with the static model. These variables were introduced after a preliminary cross-section study indicated that the regional distribution of population was important. Unlike the dynamic model, the own-price elasticity was significant in the static. However, total expenditure was insignificant and, moreover, the residuals had positive autocorrelation. This model is given below.

$$q_t = \underset{(11.280)}{-26.263} - \underset{(.4939)}{.6821} \ln p_t + \underset{(3.0010)}{6.2061} \ln (\% \text{ pop. in south})_t$$
$$+ \underset{(.6724)}{5.1595} \ln (\% \text{ pop. in west})_t - \underset{(.3429)}{.8965}\, d_t$$

$R^2 = .953 \quad D.W. = .91$

## 5.8d OTHER FUEL AND ICE

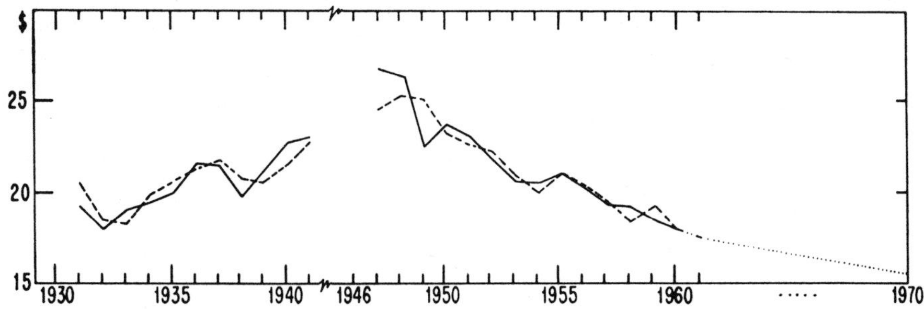


**Dynamic model**
**3PLS**

$$q_t = 3.4777 + .8671\, q_{t-1} + .0142\, \Delta x_t - .0013\, x_{t-1} - .0453\, z_t$$
$$(2.0984) \quad (.0927) \quad (.0052) \quad (.0008) \quad (.1567)$$

$R^2 = .835 \qquad D.W. = 2.19$

$\alpha = 43.660 \qquad \beta = -.2277 \qquad \gamma = .0158 \qquad \gamma' = .0095$

$\kappa = .9538 \qquad \kappa' = -.5717 \qquad \delta = -.0853$

| | 1961 level | 1970 projections 4% | | 5% | |
|---|---|---|---|---|---|
| | | I | II | I | II |
| per capita | \$17.43 | \$15.66 | \$15.57 | \$16.19 | \$16.10 |
| aggregate (billions) | | \$3.27 | \$3.25 | \$3.38 | \$3.36 |

There was great difficulty in finding an acceptable equation for this problematic category. When the relative price was included in the dynamic model, the price coefficients were insignificant and of opposite sign (as are the total-expenditure coefficients above). In order to test for possible substitution effects, the relative prices of 5.8a (electricity) and 5.8b (gas) were tried in both the dynamic and the static models. In each of the trials, the coefficient of the price of the potential substitute was negative.

None of the static models came close to giving reasonable results. The total-expenditure coefficient was always strongly negative, and the fits were very poor. A higher $R^2$ could have been obtained by constraining $\delta$ to be two with the dynamic model (and retaining prices). However, this would have been inconsistent with the value that the models were suggesting the depreciation rate was near. As a result, the above model was chosen largely from the lack of alternatives.

Nonetheless, it is possible to rationalize the dynamic model. This category is comprised largely of coal, ice, and fuel oil. Clearly, the first two have been technologically replaced in recent years by the advent of superior methods of heating and refrigeration. Certainly these are inferior goods in a technical sense, if not possibly in an economic sense also. So it is reasonable to find that the commodity has a negative depreciation rate, for it is a stock whose services are no longer desired. This requires a somewhat broader interpretation of the stock; it must consist, at least in part, of psychological units even when the stock coefficient is negative. The short-run total expenditure can be positive, for the existing furnace or refrigerator is relatively immobile, but the long-run elasticity is negative, for superior substitutes can be put into place. This may well be the dynamics at work in this category.

The linear version of the static model, with total expenditure, own relative price, relative price of 5.8a, and the war dummy, is given below.

$$q_t = \underset{(9.364)}{90.211} - \underset{(.0041)}{.0205}\, x_t - \underset{(.0742)}{.3475}\, p_t - \underset{(.0096)}{.0373}\, (\text{price of 5.8a})_t + \underset{(1.6421)}{.4375}\, d_t$$

$R^2 = .719 \qquad D.W. = 1.55$

## 5.9 TELEPHONE, TELEGRAPH, AND WIRELESS

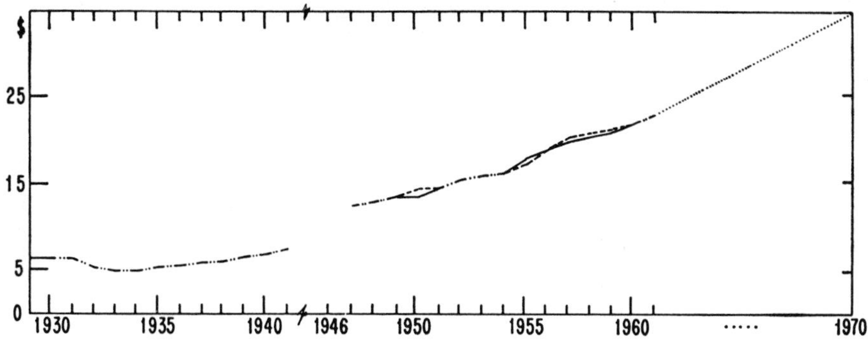


Dynamic model
**OLS** $\beta = \delta$

$$q_t - q_{t-1} = \underset{(.2694)}{-1.2765} + \underset{(.0014)}{.0061}\,\Delta x_t + \underset{(.0021)}{.0013}\,x_{t-1}$$

$R^2 = .733$ $D.W. = 2.02$

$\alpha = -1.2765$ $\beta = \delta = .2453$ $\gamma = .0108$ $\kappa = 1.0896$ $s_p = 1.32$

| | 1961 level | 1970 projections 4% | | 5% | |
|---|---|---|---|---|---|
| | | I | II | I | II |
| per capita | \$23.77 | \$35.55 | \$35.35 | \$36.82 | \$36.62 |
| aggregate (billions) | | \$7.43 | \$7.39 | \$7.69 | \$7.65 |

When prices were included in the dynamic model, $A_1$ was significantly greater than one and the coefficient of $x_{t-1}$ was negative, though the own price elasticities were negative. The drop in the $R^2$ was negligible when the prices were excluded; this equation is given below.

$$q_t = \underset{(.6852)}{-1.8467} + \underset{(.0442)}{.9600}\,q_{t-1} + \underset{(.0014)}{.0061}\,\Delta x_t + \underset{(.0009)}{.0022}\,x_{t-1}$$

$R^2 = .998$ $D.W. = 1.97$

The own-price elasticity was positive in the static model, and there was high positive autocorrelation in the residuals. This equation is given below.

$$\ln q_t = \underset{(2.604)}{-14.194} + \underset{(.2236)}{2.0157}\ln x_t + \underset{(.3092)}{.4340}\ln p_t + \underset{(.1071)}{.2919}\,d_t$$

$R^2 = .968$ $D.W. = .41$

## 5.10 DOMESTIC SERVICES [16]

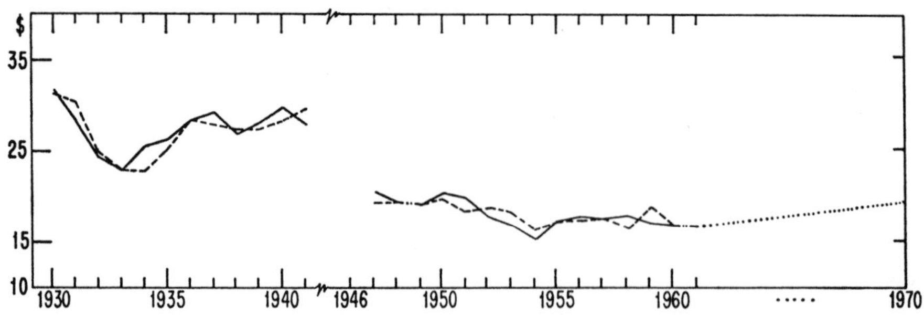


Dynamic model
OLS $\quad \delta = 0$

$$q_t = .9699\, q_{t-1} + .0303\, \Delta x_t + .0186\, \Delta\, (\text{income dist.})_t$$
$$\quad (.0108) \qquad\quad (.0052) \qquad\quad (.0126)$$

$R^2 = .952 \qquad D.W. = 2.17$

$\alpha$ = indeterminate $\qquad \beta = -.0306 \qquad \gamma(\text{upper}) = .0102$

$\gamma$ (lower) $= .0085 \qquad \delta = 0$

| | 1961 level | 1970 projections | | | |
|---|---|---|---|---|---|
| | | 4% | | 5% | |
| | | I | II | I | II |
| per capita | $16.70 | $19.98 | $19.54 | $22.67 | $22.24 |
| aggregate (billions) | | $4.17 | $4.08 | $4.73 | $4.65 |

Much difficulty was encountered in finding an equation for this item. First the dynamic model with PCE and prices appeared promising; however, the moment matrix became negative-definite when the coefficients were constrained. Then prices were excluded, but this gave a negative projection for 1970. Finally, to complete this tale of woe, several static models were tried, but the fits were poor and the residuals invariably had positive autocorrelation. However, the distribution of income was significant in the static model, which led to its trial with the dynamic model. Previous dynamic models had indicated $\delta$ to be near zero, and so the above equation was the final result.

[16] The $\gamma$'s in the dynamic model have been computed as follows:

$$\gamma\ (\text{upper}) = \frac{2}{1.9699}\,\frac{[.0303 + 1.063\,(.0186)]}{5},$$

$$\gamma\ (\text{lower}) = \frac{2}{1.9669}\,[.8\,(.0303) - 1.063\,(.0186)],$$

where 1.063 is the factor for adjusting disposable income to total expenditure while leaving the overall equation unchanged.

One would expect the difference between the marginal propensities to consume of the two income groups to be larger than the above equation indicates. This is probably because of the absence of prices. The distribution of income is no doubt picking up much of the price effect, but this could be merely a statistical illusion. While ordinarily it is not fair to complain about the quality of data, a better wage variable is needed in this instance.

The static model with PCE, income distribution, and prices is given below.

$$q_t = \underset{(4.697)}{19.839} + \underset{(.0062)}{.0256}\, x_t - \underset{(.0768)}{.2999}\, p_t + \underset{(.0107)}{.0499}\, (\text{income dist.})_t$$

$R^2 = .892 \qquad D.W. = .83$

## 5.11 OTHER HOUSEHOLD OPERATION [17]

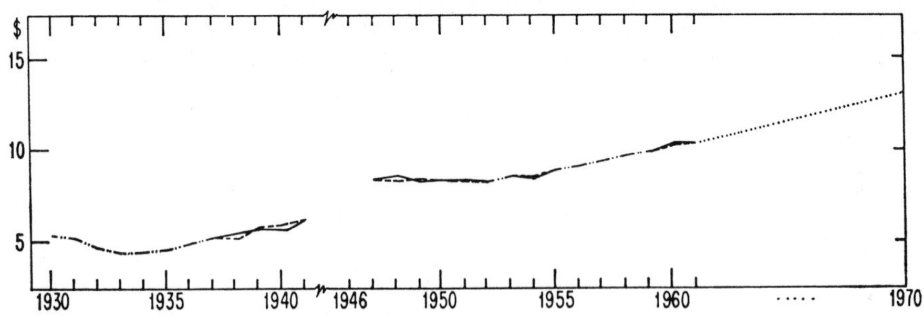


Dynamic model

OLS

$$q_t = -.6478 + .7525\, q_{t-1} + .0046\, \Delta x_t + .0028\, x_{t-1} - .0137\, \Delta p_t$$
$$\quad (.5640) \quad (.1326) \qquad (.0012) \qquad (.0010) \qquad (.0194)$$
$$- .0083\, p_{t-1} - .4275\, d$$
$$(.0077) \qquad (.2433)$$

$R^2 = .996 \qquad D.W. = 1.54$

$\alpha = -.8499 \qquad \beta = .5875 \qquad \gamma = .0037 \qquad \gamma' = .0114$

$\lambda = -.0109 \qquad \lambda' = -.0336 \qquad \sigma = -.1371 \qquad \sigma' = -.4221$

$\kappa = .6219 \qquad \kappa' = 1.9155 \qquad \delta = .8699$

| | 1961 level | 1970 projections 4% | | 1970 projections 5% | |
|---|---|---|---|---|---|
| | | I | II | I | II |
| per capita | \$10.69 | \$13.39 | \$13.39 | \$14.35 | \$14.34 |
| aggregate (billions) | | \$2.80 | \$2.80 | \$3.00 | \$3.00 |

The large positive stock indicates that there is a good deal of inertia and habit formation present in the consumption of the items in this category. But the habit wears off rapidly, for the depreciation rate is quite large. Note that the own-price elasticity only borders on significance; prices could have been left out with little overall effect on the results.

Total expenditure, prices, and the war dummy were important in the double-logarithmic static model, given below; the $R^2$ was high, but the residuals had strong positive autocorrelation.

$$\ln q_t = -4.7585 + 1.0261 \ln x_t - .1446 \ln p_t + .1370\, d_t$$
$$(.6382) \qquad (.0906) \qquad (.1036) \qquad (.0394)$$

$R^2 = .981 \qquad D.W. = .70$

[17] Comprises maintenance services for appliances and house furnishings, moving and warehouse expenses, postage, and express charges, premiums for fire and theft insurance less claims paid, and miscellaneous household-operation services.

## 6.1 DRUG PREPARATIONS AND SUNDRIES

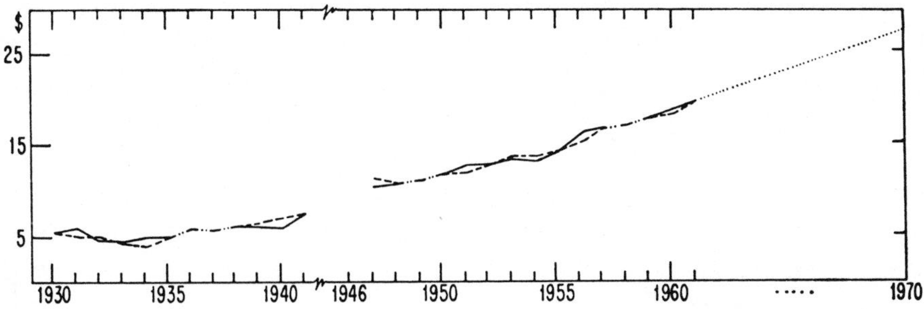


Dynamic model

OLS

$$q_t = -2.9900 + .9004\, q_{t-1} + .0084\, \Delta x_t + .0037\, x_{t-1} - .7255\, d_t$$
$$\quad (1.6491) \quad (.0966) \qquad (.0022) \qquad (.0022) \qquad (.5800)$$

$R^2 = .992 \qquad D.W. = 2.04$

$\alpha = -5.5502 \qquad \beta = .4622 \qquad \gamma = .0069 \qquad \gamma' = .0374$

$\kappa = .8103 \qquad \kappa' = 4.3826 \qquad \delta = .5670$

| | 1961 level | 1970 projections 4% | | 5% | |
|---|---|---|---|---|---|
| | | I | II | I | II |
| per capita | \$19.76 | \$28.05 | \$27.74 | \$30.01 | \$29.70 |
| aggregate (billions) | | \$5.86 | \$5.80 | \$6.27 | \$6.21 |

The price coefficients were both positive when the relative price was included in the dynamic model. The own-price elasticity was also positive in the static model.

The consumption of this item is very highly correlated with total expenditure, since the inverse semi-logarithmic static model, given below, has an $R^2 = .99$ with total expenditure alone.

$$\ln q_t = -.0528 + .00181\, x_t$$
$$\quad (.0460) \quad (.00004)$$

$R^2 = .991 \qquad D.W. = 1.59$

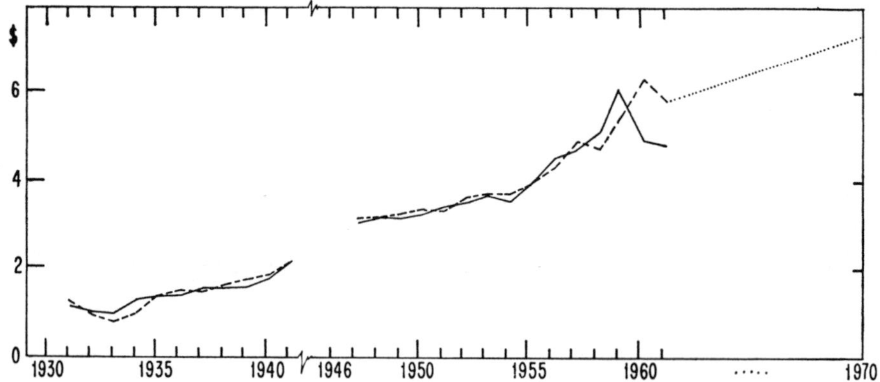


Dynamic model
3PLS

$$q_t = -1.6192 + .6978\, q_{t-1} + .0032\, \Delta x_t + .0021\, x_{t-1} - .3688\, d_t + .3851\, z_t$$
$$\quad (.9039) \quad (.1957) \quad (.0011) \quad (.0011) \quad (.2933) \quad (.3386)$$

$R^2 = .986 \qquad D.W. = 1.97$

$\alpha = -2.0172 \qquad \beta = .5894 \qquad \gamma = .0026 \qquad \gamma' = .0068$

$\kappa = 1.0444 \qquad \kappa' = 2.7743 \qquad \delta = .9454$

| | 1961 level | 1970 projections | | | |
|---|---|---|---|---|---|
| | | 4% | | 5% | |
| | | I | II | I | II |
| per capita | \$5.88 | \$7.44 | \$7.34 | \$8.07 | \$7.97 |
| aggregate (billions) | | \$1.55 | \$1.53 | \$1.69 | \$1.67 |

The positive stock coefficient may appear to be incorrect, for the products included in this category are certainly of a durable nature and would be expected to have a negative stock coefficient. However, these products are not ordinary durable goods; the purchase of eyeglasses, frames, etc., is probably influenced much less in the short run than in the long run by an increase in income. In the short run, glasses, etc., are near necessities, while in the long run an increase in income means that new and better frames, or even contact lenses, can be purchased. This is consistent with a positive stock coefficient.

The price coefficients were both insignificant when the relative price was included in the dynamic model. Prices were also insignificant in the static model. The fit of the static model was good, but, as can be seen below, the own-price elasticity was positive, and the residuals had high positive autocorrelation.

$$\ln q_t = -2.2898 + .0023\, x_t + .0026\, p_t + .0535\, d_t$$
$$\quad (.5666) \quad (.0002) \quad (.0029) \quad (.1328)$$

$R^2 = .98 \qquad D.W. = .99$

## 6.3 PHYSICIANS

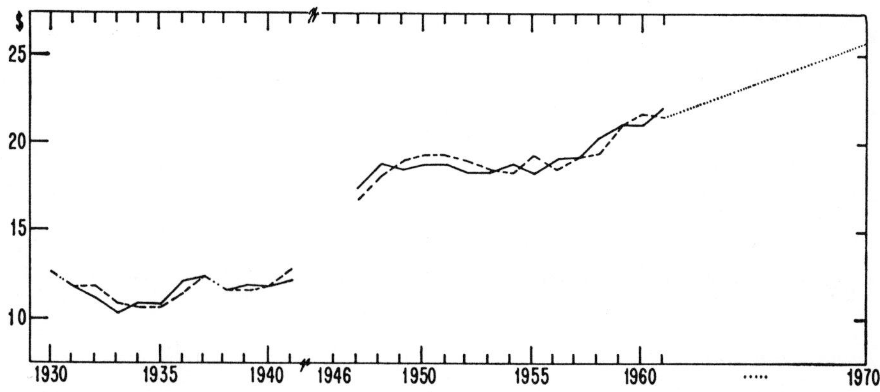


Dynamic model
OLS $\delta = 0$

$$q_t = \underset{(.0144)}{.9946}\, q_{t-1} + \underset{(.0026)}{.0052}\, \Delta x_t - \underset{(.0349)}{.0904}\, \Delta p_t + \underset{(.2996)}{.5037}\, d_t$$

$R^2 = .983 \qquad D.W. = 1.97$

$\alpha =$ indeterminate $\qquad \beta = -.0074 \qquad \gamma = .0552 \qquad \kappa = .4047$

$\lambda = -.0904 \qquad \sigma = -.5753 \qquad \delta = 0$

| | 1961 level | 1970 projections 4% | | 5% | |
|---|---|---|---|---|---|
| | | I | II | I | II |
| per capita | \$22.15 | \$26.03 | \$27.05 | \$26.60 | \$27.62 |
| aggregate (billions) | | \$5.44 | \$5.65 | \$5.56 | \$5.77 |

The bulk of the explanation in this model comes from $q_{t-1}$, for when $\beta = \delta = 0$ was assumed (i.e., the model estimated in first differences, which corresponds to a doubly special case of the dynamic model), the $R^2$ dropped to .33.

The inverse semi-logarithmic static model, with total expenditure and relative price as the explanatory variables, also had a high $R^2$, but the residuals had high positive autocorrelation. This model, along with the dynamic model alluded to above with $\beta = 0$, follow.

$$\ln q_t = \underset{(.1212)}{2.1982} + \underset{(.00003)}{.00088}\, x_t - \underset{(.00113)}{.00554}\, p_t$$

$R^2 = .965 \qquad D.W. = .78$

$$\Delta q_t = \underset{(.0026)}{.0073}\, \Delta x_t - \underset{(.0350)}{.0749}\, \Delta p_t$$

$R^2 = .334 \qquad D.W. = 1.82$

## 6.4 DENTISTS

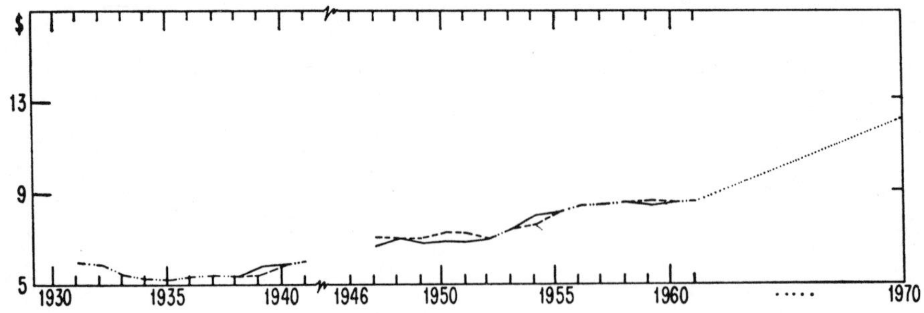


Dynamic model

3PLS

$$q_t = -.2715 + .8535\, q_{t-1} + .0038\, \Delta x_t + .0013\, x_{t-1} - .2810\, z_t$$
$$\qquad (.2482) \quad (.1735) \qquad (.0014) \qquad (.0007) \qquad (.3308)$$

$R^2 = .979 \qquad D.W. = 2.14$

$\alpha = -.6727 \qquad \beta = .2775 \qquad \gamma = .0033 \qquad \gamma' = .0092$

$\kappa = .5757 \qquad \kappa' = 1.5866 \qquad \delta = .4356$

| | 1961 level | 1970 projections 4% | | 5% | |
|---|---|---|---|---|---|
| | | I | II | I | II |
| per capita | $9.71 | $12.03 | $11.92 | $12.69 | $12.59 |
| aggregate (billions) | | $2.51 | $2.49 | $2.65 | $2.63 |

This appears to be a very good equation. The long-run total-expenditure elasticity being three times the short-run elasticity corresponds to expected behavior for the use of dentist's services: the short-run effect of an increase in income is most likely to have interim repairs made (which would probably be made anyway), while gold fillings, new plates, or false teeth are obtained in the long run.

The own-price elasticity was negative but insignificant in the dynamic model, though significant in the static model. The fit of the static model, given below, was poor and the residuals had the usual positive autocorrelation.

$$\ln q_t = 1.4072 + .0011\, x_t - .0078\, p_t - .2199\, d_t$$
$$\qquad (.2748) \quad (.0002) \qquad (.0040) \qquad (.1037)$$

$R^2 = .904 \qquad D.W. = .52$

## 6.5 OTHER PROFESSIONAL SERVICES[18]

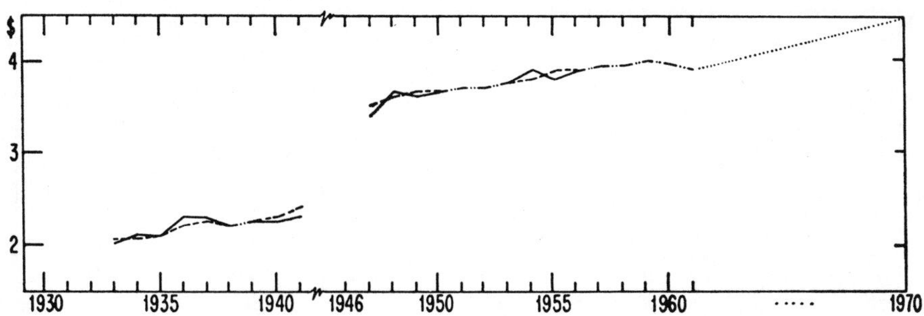


Dynamic model
OLS $\delta = 2$

$$q_t = \underset{(.1625)}{.5792} + \underset{(.1260)}{.2985}\, q_{t-1} + \underset{(.0002)}{.0010}\, x_t + \underset{(.1242)}{.6191}\, d_t$$

$R^2 = .994$ $D.W. = 2.17$

$\alpha = .4466$ $\beta = .9195$ $\gamma = .0008$ $\gamma' = .0014$

$\kappa = .3121$ $\kappa' = .5779$ $\delta = 2$

| | 1961 level | 1970 projections 4% | | 5% | |
|---|---|---|---|---|---|
| | | I | II | I | II |
| per capita | $4.08 | $4.50 | $4.48 | $4.65 | $4.63 |
| aggregate (billions) | | $.94 | $.94 | $.97 | $.97 |

The observations for the first three years of the period (1929–1931)[19] for this item are very much out of line with the rest of the prewar years. They appear simply to be shifted upward. No apparent reason for the higher level for these years could be found, and no subsequent revisions in the data have been made. The exclusion of certain years (except for the war years) is a procedure generally not to be condoned. However, since the first three years are clearly out of line, they have been excluded from the regression analysis.

The results indicate this category to be subject to strong habit formation; however, since $\delta$ was assumed equal to two, the habit wears off very rapidly. The own-relative-price elasticity was positive when prices were included in the dynamic model, as it was also in the static model. The static model is given below.

$$\ln q_t = -\underset{(.6588)}{3.6981} + \underset{(.0759)}{.4965} \ln x_t + \underset{(.1250)}{.2282} \ln p_t - \underset{(.0424)}{.3458}\, d_t$$

$R^2 = .986$ $D.W. = 1.55$

[18] Comprises services of osteopathic physicians, chiropractors, chiropodists and podiatrists, private-duty trained nurses, and miscellaneous curative and healing professions.

[19] The figures are: 1929, $3.57; 1930, $3.31; 1931, $2.86; 1932, $2.33; 1933, $1.99.

## 6.6 PRIVATE HOSPITALS AND SANITARIUMS

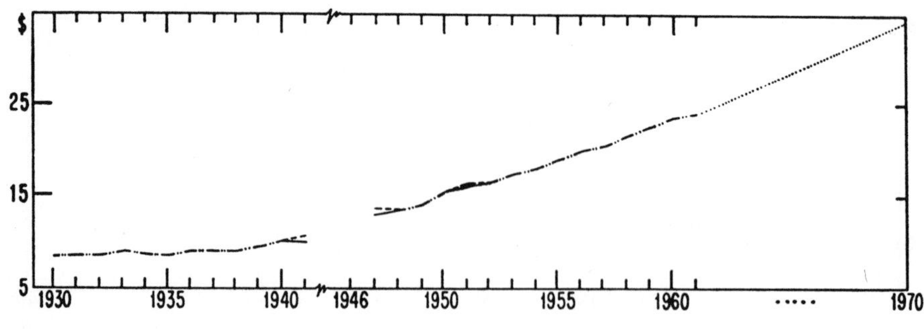


**Dynamic model**
**OLS $\beta = \delta = 2$**

$$\Delta q_t = -.8629 + .0011\, x_t$$
$$\qquad (.2519) \quad (.0002)$$

$R^2 = .552 \qquad D.W. = 2.00$

$\alpha = -.4314 \qquad \gamma = .0005 \qquad \kappa = 1.3599 \qquad \beta = \delta = 2 \qquad s_p = 1.21$

| | 1961 level | 1970 projections 4% | | 5% | |
|---|---|---|---|---|---|
| | | I | II | I | II |
| per capita | \$24.25 | \$34.62 | \$34.53 | \$35.24 | \$35.14 |
| aggregate (billions) | | \$7.23 | \$7.21 | \$7.36 | \$7.34 |

The inverse semi-logarithmic form of the static model with total expenditure and the proportion of total beds in private hospitals per 1000 population, was first used in making projections for this item. (This equation is given below.) The projection was unreasonably high, so the double logarithmic and linear versions were tried, but these also gave projections for 1970 that were more than double the 1961 level. After considerable additional work, the above equation was finally selected.

Since the equation is a very restrictive form of the dynamic model (it is a doubly special case, in which we assume that $\beta = \delta$ and that both are equal to two), it may be instructive if the path followed in arriving at this particular form is traced in full. First, the relative price was excluded because both price coefficients were positive. Then $\delta$ was constrained to be two when the unconstrained value was far greater than this figure. Finally, $\beta$ was assumed equal to $\delta$ when the model estimated with $\delta = 2$ gave $\beta$ a value of 1.994.

The low $R^2$ of .55 should not be viewed with alarm, for the equation was estimated with the dependent variable as a first difference. In terms of levels, the $R^2$ is close to .99.

The static model mentioned above follows.

$$\ln q_t = -1.3536 + .00093\, x_t + .9944\,(\text{prop. of total beds in private hosp.})_t$$
$$\qquad (.6736) \quad (.00013) \qquad (.2946)$$

$R^2 = .971 \qquad D.W. = .48$

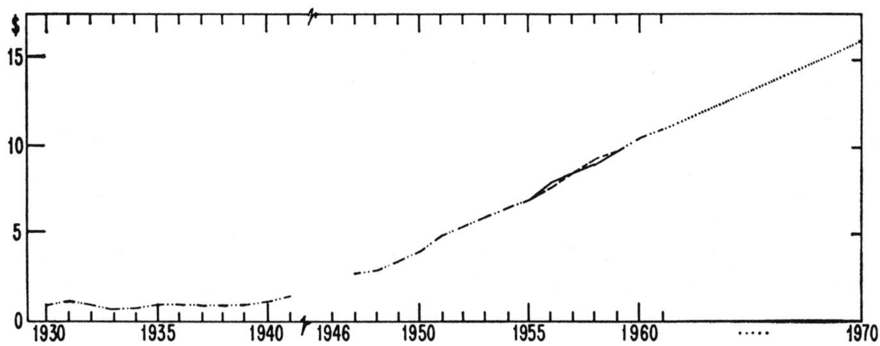


Dynamic model

OLS

$$q_t = .9736\, q_{t-1} + .0021\, \Delta x_t + .00066\, x_{t-1} - .0106\, \Delta p_t - .0033\, p_{t-1}$$
$$\quad (.0299) \qquad (.0007) \qquad (.00020) \qquad (.0024) \qquad (.0011)$$

$R^2 = .999 \qquad D.W. = 2.23$

$\alpha = 0 \qquad \beta = .3459 \qquad \gamma = .0018 \qquad \gamma' = .0248$

$\lambda = -.0090 \qquad \lambda' = -.1257 \qquad \sigma = -.2768 \qquad \sigma' = -3.8569$

$\kappa = .5288 \qquad \kappa' = 7.3666 \qquad \delta = .3727$

| | 1961 level | 1970 projections 4% | | 1970 projections 5% | |
|---|---|---|---|---|---|
| | | I | II | I | II |
| per capita | $11.01 | $16.36 | $16.00 | $16.82 | $16.46 |
| aggregate (billions) | | $3.42 | $3.34 | $3.51 | $3.44 |

The very high long-run total expenditure elasticity is somewhat of an illusion, a result of the strong trend in the dependent variable; if the elasticity is computed at 1961 levels, the value is 1.7162, a much more plausible value.

The inverse semi-logarithmic static model, with total expenditure and own relative price, was a good equation, except for positive autocorrelation in the residuals. This equation is given below.

$$\ln q_t = -1.5204 + .0026\, x_t - .0059\, p_t$$
$$\qquad (.2264) \quad (.0001) \qquad (.0007)$$

$R^2 = .992 \qquad D.W. = .68$

## 6.8 FUNERAL AND BURIAL EXPENSES

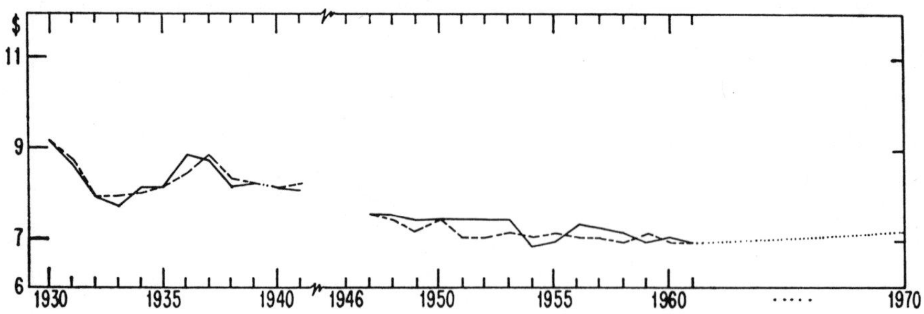


Dynamic model
**OLS** $\delta = 0$

$$q_t = \underset{(.0049)}{.9883}\, q_{t-1} + \underset{(.0007)}{.0047}\, \Delta x_t - \underset{(.0142)}{.0499}\, \Delta p_t$$

$R^2 = .946 \qquad D.W. = 2.28$

$\alpha =$ indeterminate $\qquad \beta = -.0118 \qquad \gamma = .0047 \qquad \lambda = -.0499$

$\kappa = .7623 \qquad \sigma = -.6184 \qquad \delta = 0$

| | 1961 level | 1970 projections 4% | | 5% | |
|---|---|---|---|---|---|
| | | I | II | I | II |
| per capita | \$6.98 | \$7.29 | \$7.61 | \$7.74 | \$8.12 |
| aggregate (billions) | | \$1.51 | \$1.59 | \$1.62 | \$1.70 |

The dynamic model has been used for this category even though the static model, given below, had a higher $R^2$. The variables found to be important in the static model were total expenditure, relative price, the crude death rate per 1000, and the war dummy. The static model was not used because of positive auto-correlation in the residuals.

$$\ln q_t = \underset{(.4902)}{-.7601} + \underset{(.0448)}{.3264} \ln x_t - \underset{(.0818)}{.4071} \ln p_t + \underset{(.1197)}{1.0304} \ln (\text{crude death rate per } 1000)_t - \underset{(.0210)}{.0939}\, d_t$$

$R^2 = .979 \qquad D.W. = 1.30$

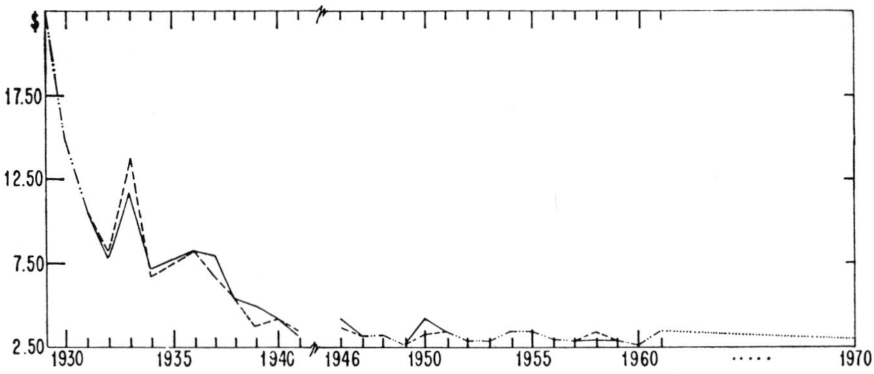


Static model
inverse semi-logarithmic

$$\ln q_t = \underset{(.1114)}{2.5169} - \underset{(.0001)}{.0011}\, x_t - \underset{(.0010)}{.0045}\, p_t + \underset{(.0127)}{.2434}\,(\text{shares traded NYSE per cap})_t$$

$R^2 = .987 \qquad D.W. = 1.91$

$\kappa = -1.4034 \qquad \sigma = -.3786 \qquad s_p = 1.09$

| | 1961 level | 1970 projections 4% | | 5% | |
|---|---|---|---|---|---|
| | | I | II | I | II |
| per capita | \$3.69 | \$3.14 | \$3.45 | \$2.77 | \$3.05 |
| aggregate (billions) | | \$.66 | \$.72 | \$.58 | \$.64 |

It seems strange that the results indicate the services in this category to be an inferior good. Nevertheless, the fact stands that the per capita consumption of this item has decreased nearly sevenfold since 1929; exactly why this is so is not clear. One early idea was that, once the amount of wealth per capita was taken into account, the total-expenditure coefficient would become positive. Accordingly, a wealth variable was constructed and tried in both the static and dynamic models. Partial success was obtained with one of the special cases of the dynamic model ($\delta = 0$). However, though the wealth variable had a positive coefficient, it was insignificant and the $R^2$ of the equation was low. The wealth variable was significant in the static model, but the coefficient of total expenditure remained negative; the own-price elasticity was positive; the $R^2$ was even lower than for the dynamic model; and there was positive autocorrelation in the residuals. These two equations follow.

$$q_t = \underset{(.0407)}{.7995}\, q_{t-1} + \underset{(.0079)}{.0123}\, \Delta x_t + \underset{(.00321)}{.00087}\, \Delta(\text{wealth})_t$$

$R^2 = .819 \qquad D.W. = 2.30$

$$q_t = \underset{(176.63)}{-99.815} - \underset{(8.927)}{18.927} \ln x_t + \underset{(5.2434)}{2.3985} \ln p_t + \underset{(19.293)}{26.800} \ln (\text{wealth})_t - \underset{(3.4057)}{2.5165}\, d_t$$

$R^2 = .640 \qquad D.W. = .77$

## 7.2 BANK SERVICE CHARGES, TRUST SERVICES, AND SAFE-DEPOSIT-BOX RENTAL

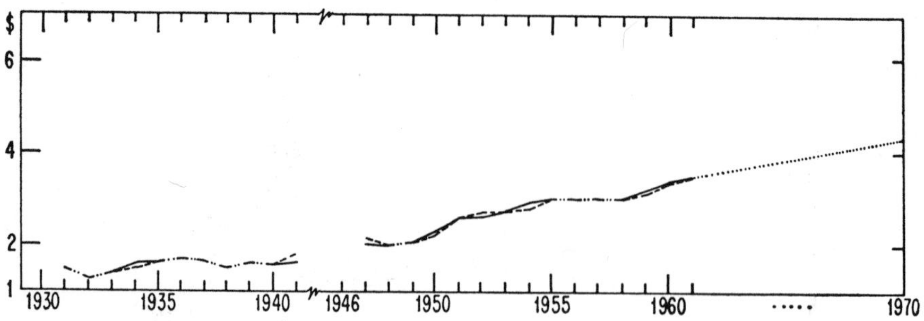


Dynamic model
3PLS $\delta = 0$

$$q_t = \underset{(.0124)}{1.0071}\, q_{t-1} + \underset{(.00029)}{.00035}\, \Delta x_t - \underset{(.0015)}{.0120}\, \Delta p_t + \underset{(.1413)}{.4057}\, z_t$$

$R^2 = .995$  $D.W. = 1.82$

$\alpha =$ indeterminate  $\beta = .0071$  $\gamma = .0003$  $\kappa = .1938$

$\lambda = -.0120$  $\sigma = -.5736$  $\delta = 0$

| | 1961 level | 1970 projections 4% | | 5% | |
|---|---|---|---|---|---|
| | | I | II | I | II |
| per capita | \$3.53 | \$4.32 | \$4.44 | \$4.36 | \$4.49 |
| aggregate (billions) | | \$.90 | \$.93 | \$.91 | \$.94 |

The fit of the above model was .50 when $q_{t-1}$ was taken over to the left-hand side. However, because of severe positive autocorrelation in the residuals, the equation with $\beta = \delta = 0$ could not be used since only least squares can be used with this form of the model.

Total expenditure, prices, and the war dummy were important in all forms of the static model; but the residuals had high positive autocorrelation. The best fit was with the inverse semi-logarithmic version; this equation is given below.

$$\ln q_t = \underset{(.1212)}{-.5955} + \underset{(.0001)}{.0015}\, x_t - \underset{(.0007)}{.0036}\, p_t - \underset{(.0702)}{.2210}\, d_t$$

$R^2 = .965$  $D.W. = .64$

## 7.3 SERVICES FURNISHED WITHOUT PAYMENT BY FINANCIAL INTERMEDIARIES

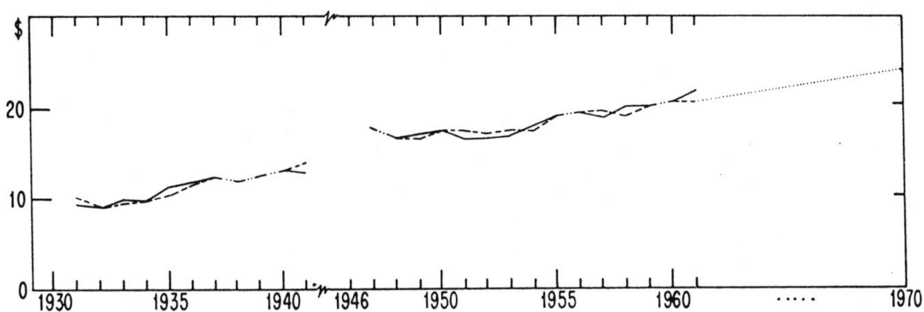


Dynamic model
3PLS $\delta = 2$

$$q_t = -1.0339 + .2774\, q_{t-1} + .0094\, x_t + .3503\, z_t$$
$$(.5441) \quad (.0832) \qquad (.0012) \qquad (.2062)$$

$R^2 = .981$ $D.W. = 1.92$

$\alpha = -.8094$ $\beta = .8686$ $\gamma = .0074$ $\gamma' = .0131$

$\kappa = .6095$ $\kappa' = 10.7744$ $\delta = 2$

| | 1961 level | 1970 projections | | | |
|---|---|---|---|---|---|
| | | 4% | | 5% | |
| | | I | II | I | II |
| per capita | \$21.89 | \$24.36 | \$24.14 | \$25.75 | \$25.53 |
| aggregate (billions) | | \$5.09 | \$5.04 | \$5.38 | \$5.33 |

The relative price added little to the explanation when it was included in the dynamic model. Total expenditure and prices were important in the static model (given below), but the fit was poorer than for the dynamic model.

Because of the artificial nature of this category, already emphasized in Chapter 2, this equation with its implausibly high long-run total-expenditure elasticity should be viewed with caution.

$$\ln q_t = 1.9834 + .00084\, x_t - .0032\, p_t$$
$$(.0894) \quad (.00005) \qquad (.0004)$$

$R^2 = .942$ $D.W. = 1.52$

## 7.4 EXPENSE OF HANDLING LIFE INSURANCE

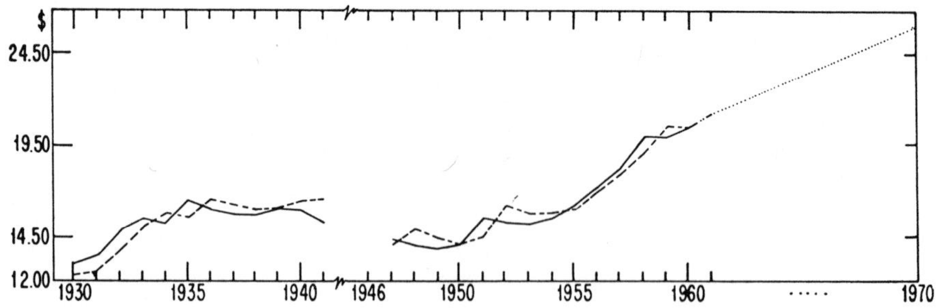


Dynamic model
OLS $\delta = 0$

$$q_t = \underset{(.0128)}{1.0153}\, q_{t-1} - \underset{(.0793)}{.0937}\, \Delta p_t + \underset{(.2941)}{.4222}\, d_t$$

$R^2 = .914 \qquad D.W. = 1.89$

$\alpha = \text{indeterminate} \qquad \beta = .0152 \qquad \lambda = .0930 \qquad \sigma = -.5657 \qquad \delta = 0$

| | 1961 level | 1970 projections 4% I | 4% II | 5% I | 5% II |
|---|---|---|---|---|---|
| per capita | \$21.31 | \$25.88 | \$26.97 | \$25.88 | \$26.97 |
| aggregate (billions) | | \$5.41 | \$5.63 | \$5.41 | \$5.63 |

The equation for this item is not very impressive. Indeed, the indictment can be extended to the category itself, for the item is not a true consumption item in the sense that the expenditure for the service enters independently into the consumer's bundle of consumption goods (see Chapter 2). The equation is essentially an autoregressive scheme on the consumption of the item itself, with a slight assist from the change in the relative price. The dynamic effect is small for $\beta$ is close to zero.

The latter suggests the straightforward use of the static model, but all static models tried were disappointing. Per capita sales of new life insurance was tried in the static model, but the sign was incorrect. The distribution of income was also tried in the static model, but without success. The static equation with total expenditure, prices, income distribution, and the war dummy is given below. As can be seen, the total expenditure and own-relative-price coefficients have wrong signs; the fit is poor; and the residuals have positive autocorrelation.

$$q_t = \underset{(3.705)}{-11.800} - \underset{(.0037)}{.0026}\, x_t + \underset{(.0532)}{.3088}\, p_t - \underset{(.0076)}{.0179}\, (\text{income dist.})_t - \underset{(1.6174)}{2.1237}\, d_t$$

$R^2 = .800 \qquad D.W. = .86$

## 7.5 LEGAL SERVICES

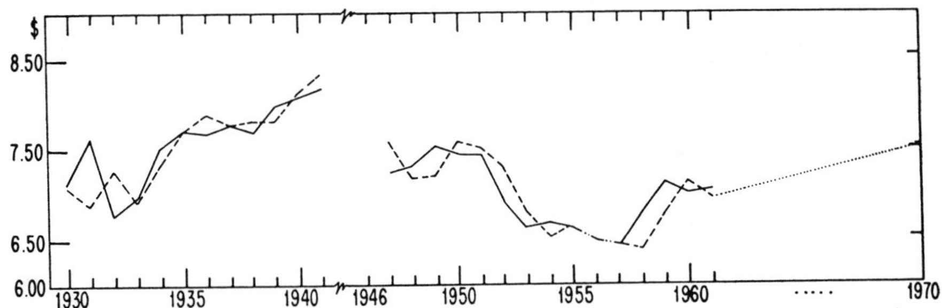


Dynamic model
OLS $\quad \delta = 0$

$$q_t = 1.0085\, q_{t-1} + .0017\, \Delta x_t - .0387\, \Delta p_t$$
$$\quad (.0091) \qquad (.0012) \qquad (.0165)$$

$R^2 = .775 \qquad D.W. = 2.35$

$\alpha =$ indeterminate $\qquad \beta = .0085 \qquad \gamma = .0017 \qquad \kappa = .2980$

$\lambda = -.0385 \qquad \sigma = -.4757 \qquad \delta = 0$

| | 1961 level | 1970 projections | | | |
|---|---|---|---|---|---|
| | | 4% | | 5% | |
| | | I | II | I | II |
| per capita | $7.05 | $7.55 | $8.13 | $7.74 | $8.33 |
| aggregate (billions) | | $1.58 | $1.70 | $1.62 | $1.74 |

Our efforts to find an adequate equation for this category cannot be termed a success. Inspection of a scatter diagram quickly dismissed the distribution of income as being of importance, and attempts to find additional explanatory variables were equally unpromising. It may be worth noting that per capita expenditure on this item varied very little from 1929 to 1961; the high was $8.23 in 1941 and the low $6.45 in 1954 (1954 dollars). Given this small range of variation, the low $R^2$ is perhaps not surprising.

The static model, with total PCE, price, and the war dummy, is given below.

$$\ln q_t = 1.1080 + .3213 \ln x_t - .2954 \ln p_t - .1519\, d_t$$
$$(.6244) \quad (.1035) \qquad (.0629) \qquad (.0419)$$

$R^2 = .672 \qquad D.W. = .80$

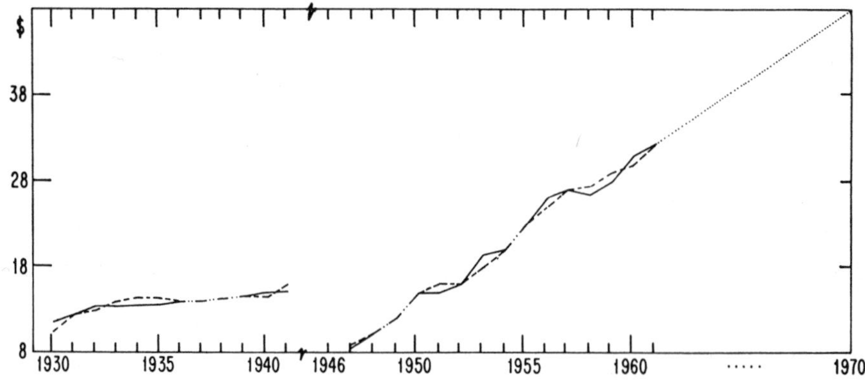


Dynamic model

OLS

$$q_t = .8834\, q_{t-1} + .0176\, \Delta x_t + .0069\, x_{t-1} - .1713\, \Delta p_t - .0674\, p_{t-1}$$
$$\qquad (.0374) \qquad (.0052) \qquad (.0023) \qquad (.0572) \qquad (.0318)$$

$R^2 = .988 \qquad D.W. = 1.55$

$\alpha = 0 \qquad \beta = .3646 \qquad \gamma = .0150 \qquad \gamma' = .0590 \qquad \kappa = 1.0593$

$\kappa' = 4.1516 \qquad \lambda = -.1462 \qquad \lambda' = -.5731 \qquad \sigma = -.6900 \qquad \sigma' = -2.7044$

$\delta = .4895$

| | 1961 level | 1970 projections 4% | | 5% | |
|---|---|---|---|---|---|
| | | I | II | I | II |
| per capita | \$32.59 | \$47.75 | \$47.30 | \$51.39 | \$50.94 |
| aggregate (billions) | | \$9.98 | \$9.88 | \$10.74 | \$10.64 |

*A priori* we might expect that an increase in income in the short run would lead to a decrease in the existing relative level of debt (relative, that is, to total expenditure), while in the long run the relative level would be increased. This is not borne out in the above equation, for the short-run total-expenditure elasticity is greater than one (though not much greater); the long-run elasticity behaves in the expected manner. The cost of debt, while important, exerts a much smaller influence.

With the double-logarithmic static model, PCE had a significant negative elasticity, as did also the relative price. However, the per capita stocks of autos had a highly significant positive influence, which accounts for the negative PCE elasticity. This is because the short-run income elasticity for autos is high, which —because of needed financing—leads to an increase in the relative level of debt; but once this effect is taken into account, an increase in income leads to a decrease in the relative level of debt, consistent with the *a priori* expectation referred to above. This static model is as follows:

$$\ln q_t = 21.579 - 1.1130 \ln x_t - 1.2503 \ln p_t$$
$$\qquad (2.021) \qquad (.3335) \qquad (.2278)$$
$$+ 3.5885 \ln (\text{car stocks per cap.})_t - .3110\, d_t$$
$$\qquad (.1555) \qquad (.0709)$$

$R^2 = .984 \qquad D.W. = 1.17$

## 7.7 OTHER PERSONAL BUSINESS EXPENDITURES[20]

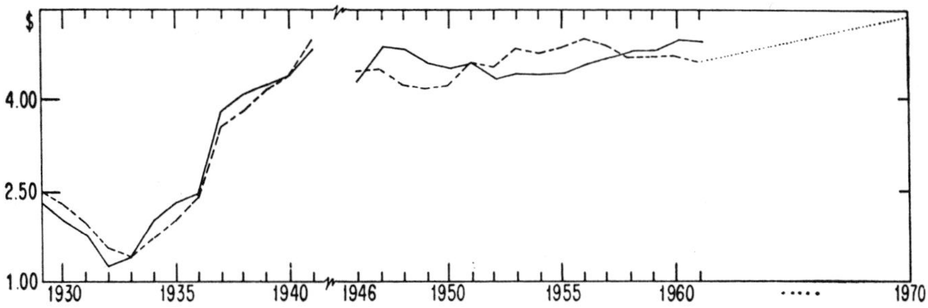


Static model
linear

$$q_t = \underset{(.0006)}{.0022}\, x_t - \underset{(.0053)}{.0129}\, p_t + \underset{(.0481)}{.4728}\, (\%\text{ pop. in union})_t - \underset{(.3215)}{2.3077}\, d_t$$

$R^2 = .948 \qquad D.W. = .51$

$\kappa = .7198 \qquad \sigma = -.3337 \qquad s_p = .95$

| | 1961 level | 1970 projections 4% | | 5% | |
|---|---|---|---|---|---|
| | | I | II | I | II |
| per capita | \$5.01 | \$5.41 | \$5.41 | \$5.66 | \$5.65 |
| aggregate (billions) | | \$1.13 | \$1.13 | \$1.18 | \$1.18 |

This equation, which is one of the poorest in the entire study, was selected after unsuccessful efforts to find a satisfactory dynamic equation. Although the fit of the equation is acceptable and the coefficients are reasonable, the residuals have very high positive autocorrelation. The dynamic model was rejected, although the $R^2$ was higher and autocorrelation in the residuals was absent, because both total-expenditure coefficients were insignificant, a result that makes little sense. The dynamic model is given below.

Since a significant part of this category is comprised of net contributions to labor unions, the percentage of the total population in labor unions is appropriate as an explanatory variable.

$$q_t = \underset{(1.5027)}{1.4840} + \underset{(.1181)}{.8891}\, q_{t-1} + \underset{(.0018)}{.0014}\, \Delta x_t + \underset{(.0008)}{.0008}\, x_{t-1} - \underset{(.0244)}{.0759}\, \Delta p_t$$
$$- \underset{(.0158)}{.0169}\, p_{t-1} - \underset{(.3628)}{.4045}\, d_t$$

$R^2 = .958 \qquad D.W. = 2.04$

[20] Comprises total payments to labor unions minus cash benefits, employment-agency fees, employees' payments to professional associations, miners' expenditures (for explosives, lamps, and smithing), money-order fees, classified advertisements, net purchases from pawnbrokers and miscellaneous secondhand stores, and other personal business services.

## 8.1a NEW CARS AND NET PURCHASES OF USED CARS

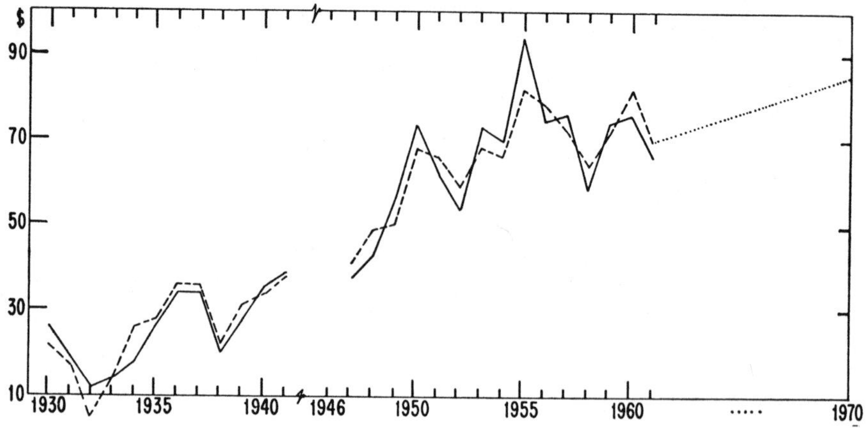


Dynamic model

OLS

$$q_t = .5183\, q_{t-1} + .1544\, \Delta x_t + .0148\, x_{t-1} - .4749\, \Delta p_t$$
$$\quad (.0908) \qquad (.0259) \qquad (.0078) \qquad (.1999)$$
$$- .0457\, p_{t-1} + 14.0725\, d_t$$
$$\quad (.1427) \qquad (3.5786)$$

$R^2 = .958$ $\quad D.W. = 1.95$

$\alpha = 0$ $\quad \beta = -.5335$ $\quad \gamma = .1937$ $\quad \gamma' = .0308$

$\lambda = -.5955$ $\quad \lambda' = -.0948$ $\quad \sigma = -.9578$ $\quad \sigma' = -.1525$

$\kappa = 5.0157$ $\quad \kappa' = .7986$ $\quad \delta = .1010$

| | 1961 level | 1970 projections 4% | | 5% | |
|---|---|---|---|---|---|
| | | I | II | I | II |
| per capita | \$67.03 | \$87.79 | \$88.15 | \$94.42 | \$94.77 |
| aggregate (billions) | | \$18.34 | \$18.42 | \$19.73 | \$19.80 |

The relative price for this item is an average price obtained by dividing PCE in current dollars for the category by the number of domestic new cars sold and deflating by the total PCE implicit deflator. While this price series is not without problems because of the inclusion of net purchases of used cars in the consumption data,[21] it is felt that it reflects more adequately the relative cost of autos than the implicit deflator we usually use. This is particularly true with regard to the shift to compact cars in 1959, which it can be argued led to a decrease in the real cost of automobiles.

Though the $R^2$ could be higher, the above equation is acceptable in its other aspects. The stock coefficient is strongly negative, and the influence of total PCE is much stronger than that of prices. Both of these are expected results. The short-run total PCE elasticity, though large, is consistent with those obtained by Suits

[21] However, Suits (1958) has argued that the full price received by dealers for new automobiles should include the margins on the used cars sold by them.

(1958). The depreciation rate of .10, implying an average lifetime of ten years, agrees well with physical rates of deterioration and depreciation.[22]

Several static models were also tried. In marked contrast to the dynamic model, the stock coefficient was found to be positive when direct estimates of per capita stocks of automobiles were included in the model. This is, of course, counter to most precepts of normal behavior for the purchase of cars. In another static model, the amount of consumer credit outstanding was found to be important. The fits of the static model were not as good as for the dynamic model, and the residuals invariably had high positive autocorrelation.

The importance of consumer credit in the static model, and the success Suits had in his study with a combination price-credit variable,[23] prompted our trying this variable in place of the relative price in the dynamic model. However, this equation was inferior to the one above. We should not conclude from this that credit terms are unimportant; experimentation with a more appropriate credit variable might show the contrary.

The semi-logarithmic static model, with PCE, prices, consumer credit outstanding per capita, and the war dummy, is given below.

$$\begin{aligned} q_t = {} & \underset{(111.56)}{101.52} + \underset{(4.062)}{40.935} \ln x_t - \underset{(19.550)}{46.196} \ln p_t \\ & + \underset{(8.056)}{27.904} (\text{cons. credit outstanding})_t + \underset{(5.4109)}{3.8452} d_t \end{aligned}$$

$R^2 = .963 \qquad D.W. = 1.25$

[22] This compares with values of .16 and .25 for 1952 and 1955 that Houthakker and Haldi (1960) found, using used-car prices. However, these are market depreciation rates, not physical rates.

[23] The definition of this variable can be found in Suits (1958).

## 8.1b TIRES, TUBES, ACCESSORIES, AND PARTS

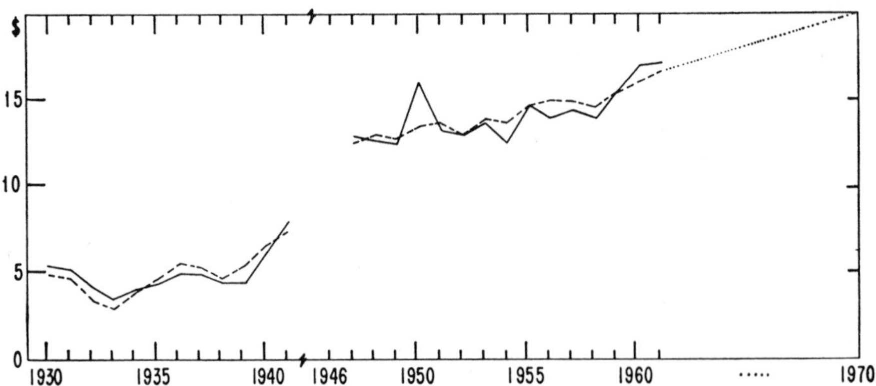


Dynamic model

OLS

$$q_t = .3020\, q_{t-1} + .0140\, \Delta x_t + .0067\, x_{t-1} - .0478\, \Delta p_t - .0228\, p_{t-1} + 2.1092\, d_t$$

Standard errors: (.2368) (.0043) (.0025) (.0467) (.0117) (1.4421)

$R^2 = .977 \qquad D.W. = 1.84$

| | | | |
|---|---|---|---|
| $\alpha = 0$ | $\beta = -.4459$ | $\gamma = .0164$ | $\gamma' = .0096$ |
| $\kappa = 2.0076$ | $\kappa' = 1.1729$ | $\lambda = -.0560$ | $\lambda' = -.0327$ |
| $\sigma = -.6300$ | $\sigma' = -.3681$ | $\delta = .6265$ | |

| | 1961 level | 1970 projections 4% | | 1970 projections 5% | |
|---|---|---|---|---|---|
| | | I | II | I | II |
| per capita | \$17.20 | \$19.83 | \$19.25 | \$20.99 | \$20.41 |
| aggregate (billions) | | \$4.14 | \$4.02 | \$4.39 | \$4.26 |

The static model, with total expenditure, own relative price, per capita stocks of automobiles, and the war dummy, is also a very good equation. The $R^2$ of this equation, given below, is the same as for the dynamic equation, and there is no autocorrelation in the residuals. The coefficient of car stocks may appear to have the wrong sign, but this is consistent with new cars being equipped with new tires.

$$q_t = 10.256 + .0103\, x_t - .0976\, p_t - 12.029\, (\text{car stocks per cap.})_t + 1.6471\, d_t$$

Standard errors: (6.316) (.0032) (.0362) (8.811) (1.0620)

$R^2 = .978 \qquad D.W. = 1.80$

$\kappa = 1.2832 \qquad \sigma = 1.0962$

## 8.1c AUTOMOBILE REPAIR, GREASING, WASHING, PARKING, STORAGE, AND RENTAL

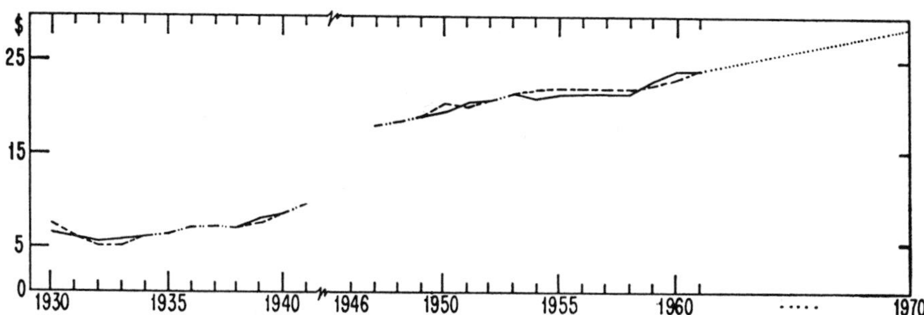


Dynamic model

OLS

$$q_t = .7758\, q_{t-1} + .0114\, \Delta x_t + .0036\, x_{t-1} - .0524\, \Delta p_t$$
$$\quad (.1677) \qquad (.0019) \qquad (.0025) \qquad (.0424)$$
$$- .0164\, p_{t-1} + 1.2201\, d_t$$
$$\quad (.0116) \qquad (1.0848)$$

$R^2 = .998 \qquad D.W. = 1.48$

| | | | |
|---|---|---|---|
| $\alpha = 0$ | $\beta = .1195$ | $\gamma = .0109$ | $\gamma' = .0160$ |
| $\lambda = -.0497$ | $\lambda' = -.0733$ | $\sigma = -.3603$ | $\sigma' = -.5308$ |
| $\kappa = .9152$ | $\kappa' = 1.348$ | $\delta = .3719$ | |

| | 1961 level | 1970 projections 4% I | 4% II | 5% I | 5% II |
|---|---|---|---|---|---|
| per capita | $24.25 | $28.31 | $28.36 | $29.88 | $29.93 |
| aggregate (billions) | | $5.91 | $5.93 | $6.24 | $6.25 |

It is likely that the stock effect in this category is from the stock of automobiles, rather than from the "stock" of auto repairs, etc., for there is nothing inherent in the theory of the dynamic model that does not allow for the stock to be of another commodity. No doubt it would be more appropriate to estimate 8.1a and 8.1c simultaneously, which can be done in principle without difficulty. However, it involves including three additional variables in each equation ($\Delta p_t$, $p_{t-1}$, and $q_{t-1}$, of the other commodity), which is likely to raise problems with multicollinearity when time-series data are being used.

The larger total-expenditure elasticity in the long run can be taken to indicate that more expensive automobiles are purchased in the long run. The low $D.W.$ coefficient in the equation above appeared when the identifying restriction upon $\delta$ was taken into account.

Per capita stocks of automobiles was found to be important in the static model, along with total expenditure, prices, and the war dummy. The fit of this model (the double-logarithmic version is given below) was very good, but the residuals had positive autocorrelation.

$$\ln q_t = -2.0187 + 1.1697 \ln x_t - .7438 \ln p_t$$
$$\quad (3.7608) \qquad (.3437) \qquad (.3336)$$
$$+ .3172\, (\text{car stocks per cap.})_t + .3225\, d_t$$
$$\quad (.2495) \qquad (.1085)$$

$R^2 = .996 \qquad D.W. = 1.13$

## 8.1d GASOLINE AND OIL

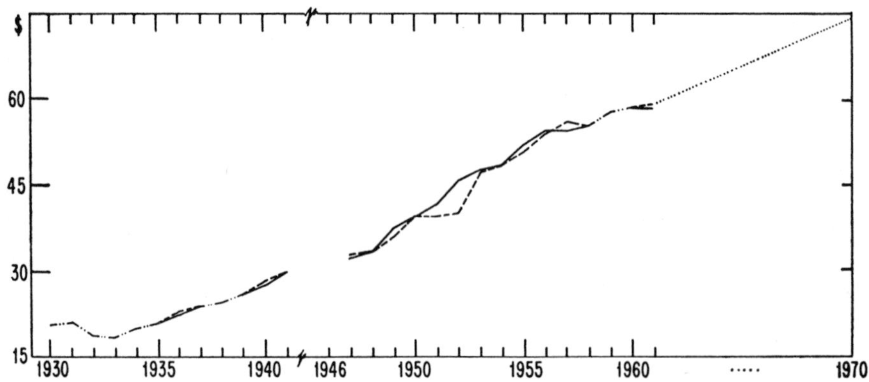


Dynamic model

OLS

$$q_t = .8757\, q_{t-1} + .0189\, \Delta x_t + .0061\, x_{t-1} - .0576\, \Delta p_t - .0187\, p_{t-1}$$
$$\quad (.0310) \qquad (.0037) \qquad (.0013) \qquad (.0308) \qquad (.0053)$$

$R^2 = .998 \qquad D.W. = 1.80$

$\alpha = 0 \qquad \beta = .2554 \qquad \gamma = .0168 \qquad \gamma' = .0493 \qquad \kappa = .5705$

$\kappa' = 1.6694 \qquad \lambda = -.0515 \qquad \lambda' = -.1506 \qquad \sigma = -.1564 \qquad \sigma' = -.4577$

$\delta = .3879$

| | 1961 level | 1970 projections 4% I | 4% II | 5% I | 5% II |
|---|---|---|---|---|---|
| per capita | \$58.37 | \$73.59 | \$72.93 | \$76.98 | \$76.32 |
| aggregate (billions) | | \$15.38 | \$15.24 | \$16.01 | \$15.95 |

The remarks made about the interpretation of the stock effect for 8.1c (auto repairs, etc.) are also appropriate for this category. The higher total-expenditure elasticity in the long run can again be taken to indicate that more costly automobiles are purchased in the long run.

The fit of the static model with total expenditure, own relative price, per capita stocks of autos, and the relative price of 8.2a (local street car, etc.) as a substitute was also very good, but the residuals had high positive autocorrelation. This equation is given below.

$$q_t = -20.879 + .0212\, x_t - .0912\, p_t + .1591\, (\text{price of 8.2a})_t$$
$$\quad (6.977) \quad (.0054) \quad (.0440) \quad (.0383)$$
$$+ 106.04\, (\text{car stocks per cap.})_t$$
$$(24.73)$$

$R^2 = .995 \qquad D.W. = .86$

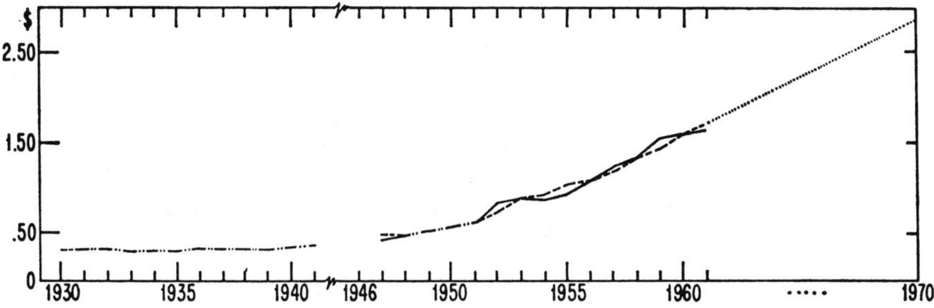


Dynamic model
OLS $\beta = \delta$

$$\Delta q_t = -.1320 + .00019\,\Delta x_t + .00014\,x_{t-1}$$
$$(.0333) \quad (.00017) \quad (.00003)$$

$R^2 = .576 \qquad D.W. = 1.62$

$\alpha = -.1980 \qquad \beta = \delta = .0667 \qquad \gamma = .00015 \qquad \kappa = .2600 \qquad s_p = .16$

| | 1961 level | 1970 projections 4% I | 4% II | 5% I | 5% II |
|---|---|---|---|---|---|
| per capita | $1.67 | $2.84 | $2.83 | $2.92 | $2.91 |
| aggregate (billions) | | $.59 | $.59 | $.61 | $.61 |

The own-price elasticity was negative, but insignificant, when prices were included in the dynamic model. It should be noted that $\beta = \delta$ was assumed in estimating the above equation—hence the $R^2$ of .576 is quite satisfactory; in terms of levels, the $R^2$ is greater than .99.

With the double-logarithmic static model, prices and per capita stocks of autos were significant and their signs were correct. However, the total-expenditure elasticity was negative, a result that is unreasonable. The fit of this equation, given below, was not as good as for the dynamic model, and the residuals had the usual positive autocorrelation.

$$\ln q_t = 14.031 - 1.1200 \ln x_t - .6395 \ln p_t + 2.3829 \ln (\text{car stocks per cap.})_t$$
$$(4.788) \quad (.4921) \quad (.2802) \quad (.3125)$$

$R^2 = .929 \qquad D.W. = .56$

# 8.1f AUTO INSURANCE PREMIUMS, LESS CLAIMS PAID

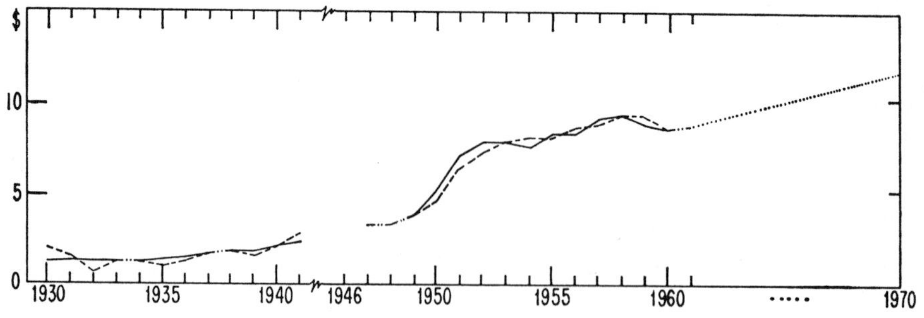


Dynamic model

OLS

$$q_t = .8001\, q_{t-1} + .0043\, \Delta x_t + .0021\, x_{t-1} - .0302\, \Delta p_t - .0147\, p_{t-1}$$
$$\quad (.0693) \qquad (.0021) \qquad (.0006) \qquad (.0065) \qquad (.0053)$$

$R^2 = .987 \qquad D.W. = 1.32$

$\alpha = 0 \qquad \beta = .4196 \qquad \gamma = .0036 \qquad \gamma' = .0104 \qquad \kappa = .9713$

$\kappa' = 2.8065 \quad \lambda = -.0254 \quad \lambda' = -.0734 \quad \sigma = -.5630 \quad \sigma' = -1.6268$

$\delta = .6417$

| | 1961 level | 1970 projections 4% | | 5% | |
|---|---|---|---|---|---|
| | | I | II | I | II |
| per capita | \$8.52 | \$11.63 | \$11.53 | \$12.47 | \$12.38 |
| aggregate (billions) | | \$2.43 | \$2.41 | \$2.61 | \$2.59 |

The high total-expenditure elasticity in the long run for this item may stem from either or both of the following reasons: (1) More expensive automobiles are purchased in the long run, with correspondingly higher insurance rates; (2) there are more accidents as the number of cars increases. Both reasons would be consistent with an interpretation of the "stock" as the stock of autos. This in turn would be consistent with the results of the static model, where per capita stocks of autos were found to be important, together with PCE and prices. The fit of this equation (the double-logarithmic version is given below) was poorer than for the dynamic model, and the residuals had positive autocorrelation. The *D.W.* in the above equation became 1.32 after the identification restriction on $\delta$ was taken into account.

$$\ln q_t = 1.4502 + .8120 \ln x_t - .5892 \ln p_t + 2.2750 \ln (\text{car stocks per cap.})_t$$
$$\quad (3.7223) \quad (.4095) \qquad (.2327) \qquad (.3710)$$

$R^2 = .957 \qquad D.W. = .46$

## 8.2a STREET AND ELECTRIC RAILWAY AND LOCAL BUS

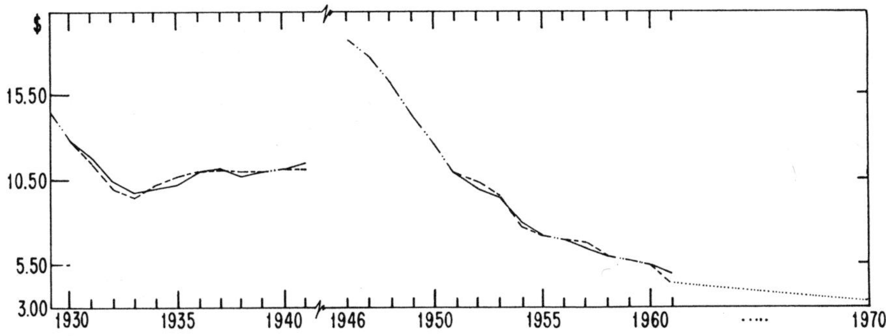


Static model

linear

$$q_t = \underset{(.836)}{22.819} + \underset{(.0013)}{.0159\, x_t} - \underset{(.0073)}{.1156\, p_t} - \underset{(5.438)}{86.106\,(\text{car stocks per cap.})_t} - \underset{(.3052)}{.9841\, d_t}$$

$R^2 = .996 \qquad D.W. = 1.11$

$\kappa = 1.4969 \qquad \sigma = -1.0172 \qquad s_p = 1.33$

| | 1961 level | 1970 projections 4% | | 5% | |
|---|---|---|---|---|---|
| | | I | II | I | II |
| per capita | $5.09 | $3.52 | $4.52 | $5.30 | $6.30 |
| aggregate (billions) | | $.74 | $.94 | $1.11 | $1.32 |

The projections for this category were first made with the following dynamic model:

$$q_t = \underset{(.0149)}{.9973\, q_{t-1}} + \underset{(.0019)}{.0070\, \Delta x_t} - \underset{(.0190)}{.0529\, \Delta p_t} - \underset{(.1357)}{.4934\, d_t} + \underset{(.1849)}{.4282\, z_t}$$

$R^2 = .994 \qquad D.W. = 1.84$

(Note that $\delta = 0$ has been assumed.) However, the initial projection from this equation turned out to be negative, so the equation had to be discarded. The static equation would be more acceptable were it not for the undesirably low *D.W.* coefficient.

## 8.2b TAXICABS

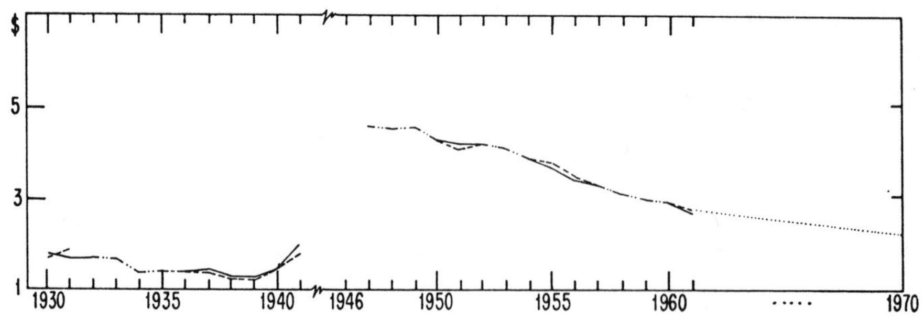


Dynamic model
OLS $\delta = 0$

$$q = .9596\, q_{t-1} + .0016\, \Delta x_t - .0094\, \Delta p_t$$
$$\quad (.0068) \qquad (.0005) \qquad (.0018)$$

$R^2 = .993 \qquad D.W. = 1.86$

$\alpha =$ indeterminate $\quad \beta = -.0412 \quad \gamma = .0016 \quad \kappa = .7206$

$\lambda = -.0095 \quad \sigma = -.4101 \quad \delta = 0$

| | 1961 level | 1970 projections 4% | | 5% | |
|---|---|---|---|---|---|
| | | I | II | I | II |
| per capita | \$2.71 | \$2.28 | \$2.28 | \$2.43 | \$2.43 |
| aggregate (billions) | | \$.48 | \$.48 | \$.51 | \$.51 |

The dynamic model was estimated with the restriction $\delta = 0$ when the coefficients of $x_{t-1}$ and $p_{t-1}$ were found to be very close to zero. The equation indicates that the use of taxicabs is subject to a negative, though small, stock effect, which may appear unusual. However, with $\delta = 0$, the dynamic model is essentially a short-run model, so that judged in this light $\beta < 0$ may not be unreasonable.

Per capita stocks of autos were important in the static model, together with PCE, prices, and the war dummy. The fit of this model, given below, is not as good as for the dynamic model, and the residuals have positive autocorrelation.

$$q_t = 3.3216 + .0029\, x_t - .0061\, p_t - 19.787\, (\text{car stocks per cap.})_t + 2.4978\, d_t$$
$$\quad (.5985) \quad (.0012) \qquad (.0044) \qquad (3.241) \qquad\qquad (.4988)$$

$R^2 = .964 \qquad D.W. = .77$

## 8.2c RAILWAY (COMMUTATION)

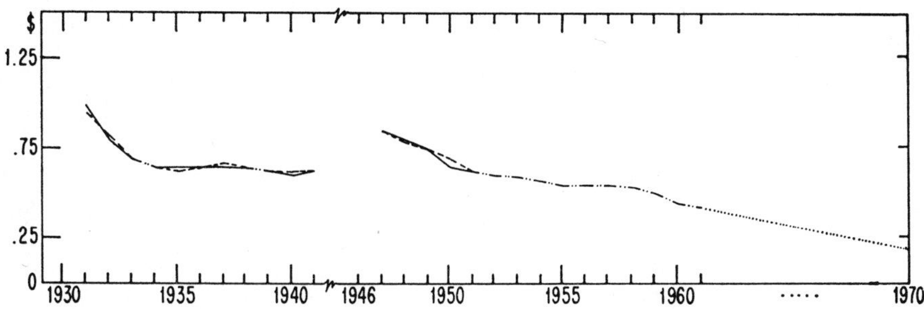


Dynamic model
3PLS

$$q_t = \underset{(.0392)}{.2429} + \underset{(.0357)}{.8198}\, q_{t-1} - \underset{(.0007)}{.0045}\, \Delta p_t - \underset{(.00025)}{.00095}\, p_{t-1} + \underset{(.1357)}{.3753}\, z_t$$

$R^2 = .983$ $\quad D.W. = 2.03$

$\alpha = 1.1162$ $\quad \beta = .0411$ $\quad \lambda = -.0044$ $\quad \lambda' = -.0053$

$\sigma = -.6728$ $\quad \sigma' = -.8121$ $\quad \delta = .2391$

| | 1961 level | 1970 projections 4% | | 5% | |
|---|---|---|---|---|---|
| | | I | II | I | II |
| per capita | \$.44 | \$.18 | \$.48 | \$.18 | \$.48 |
| aggregate (billions) | | \$.04 | \$.10 | \$.04 | \$.10 |

Next to 8.3d (other intercity transportation), this is the smallest category in the study. The elasticity of total expenditure was insignificant, though positive, when total expenditure was included in the model, a not altogether surprising result. Commuting by railway is seen to be subject to habit formation, for $\beta$ is positive, but the effect is small.

All static equations gave very poor results. The own relative price was the only significant variable; the $R^2$'s were very low, and the residuals invariably had high positive autocorrelation. One of these equations is given below.

$$\ln q = \underset{(8.1062)}{6.0729} - \underset{(.8420)}{.4379}\ln x_t - \underset{(.3200)}{.7584}\ln p_t$$
$$- \underset{(.7198)}{.0889}\ln(\text{car stocks per cap.})_t - \underset{(.1536)}{.0066}\, d_t$$

$R^2 = .590$ $\quad D.W. = .21$

## 8.3a INTERCITY RAILWAY

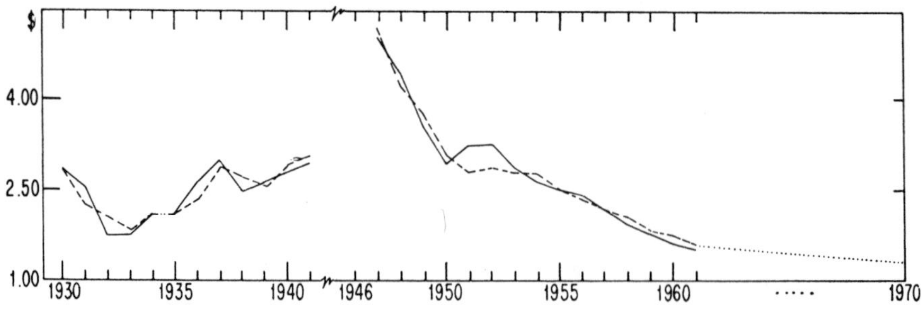


Dynamic model
OLS

$$q_t = \underset{(.4836)}{2.0269} + \underset{(.0440)}{.8029}\, q_{t-1} - \underset{(.0068)}{.0302}\, \Delta p_t - \underset{(.0032)}{.0120}\, p_{t-1} - \underset{(.1444)}{.4688}\, d_t$$

$R^2 = .948 \qquad D.W. = 2.15$

$\alpha = 4.5344 \qquad \beta = .2772 \qquad \lambda = -.0268 \qquad \lambda' = -.0609$

$\sigma = -1.2061 \qquad \sigma' = 2.7353 \qquad \delta = .4959$

| | 1961 level | 1970 projections 4% | | 5% | |
|---|---|---|---|---|---|
| | | I | II | I | II |
| per capita | \$1.53 | \$1.28 | \$1.49 | \$1.28 | \$1.49 |
| aggregate (billions) | | \$.27 | \$.31 | \$.27 | \$.31 |

This item, intercity travel by railway, is seen to be independent of the level of total expenditure, which is in keeping with the results of 8.2c (local commuting travel by railway). However, the own-price elasticities are much larger than for the latter category; indeed the substantial long-run elasticity of −2.74 is somewhat of a surprise.

Per capita stocks of automobiles were found to be highly significant in the static model, along with total expenditure (unlike the dynamic model), own relative price, and the relative price of airline travel. The $R^2$ of this equation, given below, is lower than for the dynamic model, but the amount of positive autocorrelation in the residuals is moderate.

$$q_t = \underset{(1.1903)}{3.1239} + \underset{(.0010)}{.0097}\, x_t - \underset{(.0071)}{.0147}\, p_t + \underset{(.0028)}{.0039}\,(\text{price of 8.3c})_t - \underset{(3.806)}{47.016}\,(\text{car stocks per cap.})_t$$

$R^2 = .905 \qquad D.W. = 1.52$

## 8.3b INTERCITY BUS

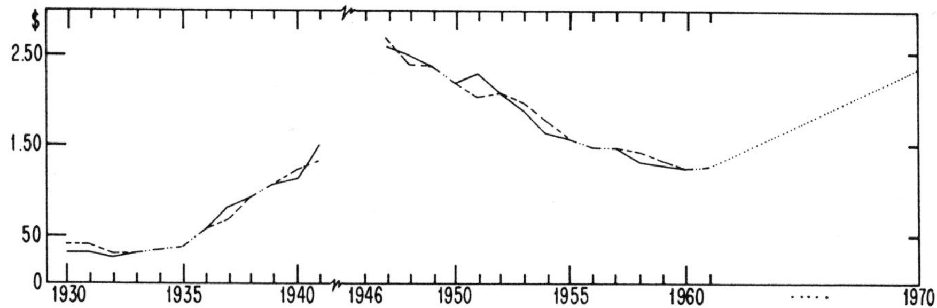


Dynamic model
OLS $\beta = \delta = 2$

$$q_t - q_{t-1} = \underset{(.1716)}{-.5545} + \underset{(.00017)}{.00067\, x_t} \underset{(.0985)}{-.5590\, d_t}$$

$R^2 = .669 \qquad D.W. = 2.16$

$\alpha = -.5545 \qquad \beta = \delta = 2 \qquad \gamma = .0007 \qquad \kappa = .6182 \qquad s_p = .44$

| | 1961 level | 1970 projections | | | |
|---|---|---|---|---|---|
| | | 4% | | 5% | |
| | | I | II | I | II |
| per capita | \$1.32 | \$2.35 | \$2.29 | \$2.72 | \$2.66 |
| aggregate (billions) | | \$.49 | \$.48 | \$.57 | \$.56 |

Prices were insignificant in the dynamic model. The stock of automobiles was also tried at one time in the dynamic model, but the coefficient had the wrong sign.

The relative price of total automotive travel is important in the static model, together with PCE, own price, stocks of autos, and the war dummy. The fit of this equation (given below) is good, and there is only moderate positive autocorrelation in the residuals.

$$q_t = \underset{(1.4289)}{1.3874} + \underset{(.00095)}{.00216\, x_t} - \underset{(.0015)}{.0104\, p_t} + \underset{(.0080)}{.0156}\text{ (price total auto. travel)}_t$$
$$- \underset{(2.359)}{14.759}\text{ (car stocks per cap.)}_t + \underset{(.2025)}{1.0381\, d_t}$$

$R^2 = .964 \qquad D.W. = 1.37$

## 8.3c AIRLINE TRAVEL

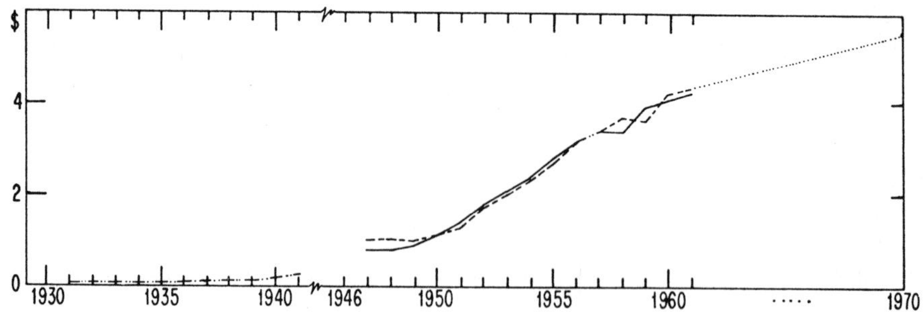


Dynamic model
3PLS $\delta = 2$

$$q_t = .9519\, q_{t-1} + .00025\, x_t - .0012\, p_t + .2742\, z_t$$
$$(.0617) \quad (.00009) \quad (.0005) \quad (.2526)$$

$R^2 = .994 \qquad D.W. = 2.22$

$\alpha = 0 \qquad \beta = 1.9507 \qquad \gamma = .00012 \qquad \gamma' = .0051 \qquad \kappa = .1115$

$\kappa' = 4.5267 \qquad \lambda = -.0006 \qquad \lambda' = -.0239 \qquad \sigma = -.0582 \qquad \sigma' = -2.3603$

$\delta = 2$

| | 1961 level | 1970 projections 4% I | 4% II | 5% I | 5% II |
|---|---|---|---|---|---|
| per capita | \$4.32 | \$5.63 | \$5.62 | \$5.75 | \$5.74 |
| aggregate (billions) | | \$1.18 | \$1.17 | \$1.20 | \$1.20 |

The implausibly high stock coefficient for this item can be attributed to the very strong trend in the dependent variable. Similarly, if the total-expenditure elasticity is computed at the 1961 levels rather than at the means, the value is 1.96, a much more plausible figure.

The distribution of income was tried in the static model and the results indicated that, as one would expect, the marginal propensity to consume of the upper-income group is higher than for the lower-income groups. In another static model, the price of intercity rail travel (8.3a) was found to be important, along with total expenditure and own relative price. Per capita stocks of automobiles were insignificant, although the coefficient was negative. The double-logarithmic form of this equation is given below. To vary an old theme, note that this is one of the rare instances where the residuals have high negative autocorrelation.[24]

$$\ln q_t = -39.824 + 5.9561 \ln x_t - 3.4498 \ln p_t + 2.7728 \ln (\text{price of 8.3a})_t$$
$$(34.433) \quad (3.8745) \quad (1.7301) \quad (2.3754)$$
$$- .3304\, (\text{car stocks per cap.})_t - .1673\, d_t$$
$$(2.4942) \quad (1.0444)$$

$R^2 = .971 \qquad D.W. = 2.96$

[24] This was also true for the inverse semi-logarithmic form of the equation. Interestingly enough, the other two forms had high positive autocorrelation. This suggests that the *D.W.*'s are highly sensitive to the choice of functional forms.

## 8.3d OTHER INTERCITY TRANSPORTATION[25]

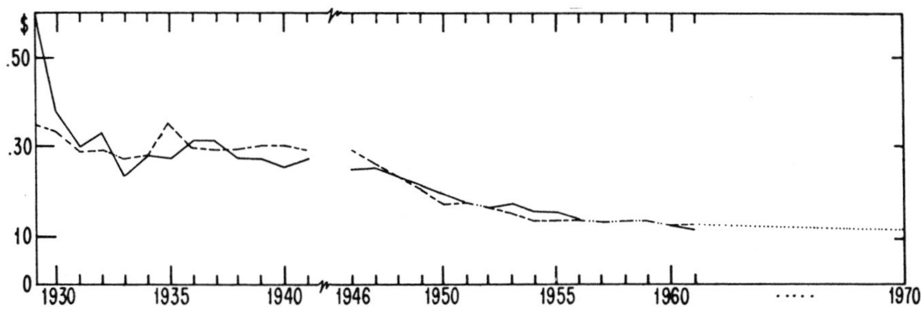


Static model
inverse semi-logarithmic

$$\ln q_t = \underset{(.4928)}{-.5222} + \underset{(.0006)}{.0015}\, x_t - \underset{(.0017)}{.0024}\, p_t - \underset{(1.6677)}{9.1129}\,(\text{car stocks per cap.})_t - \underset{(.1895)}{.6333}\, d_t$$

$R^2 = .735$ $D.W. = .97$

$\kappa = 1.9207$ $\sigma' = -.3235$ $s_p = .20$

| | 1961 level | 1970 projections 4% | | 1970 projections 5% | |
|---|---|---|---|---|---|
| | | I | II | I | II |
| per capita | $.12 | $.13 | $.12 | $.15 | $.15 |
| aggregate (billions) | | $.03 | $.03 | $.03 | $.03 |

Since this is the smallest item of all the consumption categories, this equation and the dynamic equation given below were the only ones estimated.

$$q_t = \underset{(.1535)}{.1793} + \underset{(.1961)}{.5840}\, q_{t-1} + \underset{(.0002)}{.0001}\, \Delta x_t - \underset{(.0001)}{.0001}\, x_{t-1} + \underset{(.0003)}{.0003}\, \Delta p_t + \underset{(.0005)}{.0001}\, p_{t-1} + \underset{(.0344)}{.0122}\, d_t - \underset{(.2609)}{.3222}\, z_t$$

$R^2 = .911$ $D.W. = 2.11$

[25] Comprises baggage charges, and coastal, inland-waterway, and ferry foot-passenger fares.

## 9.1 BOOKS AND MAPS

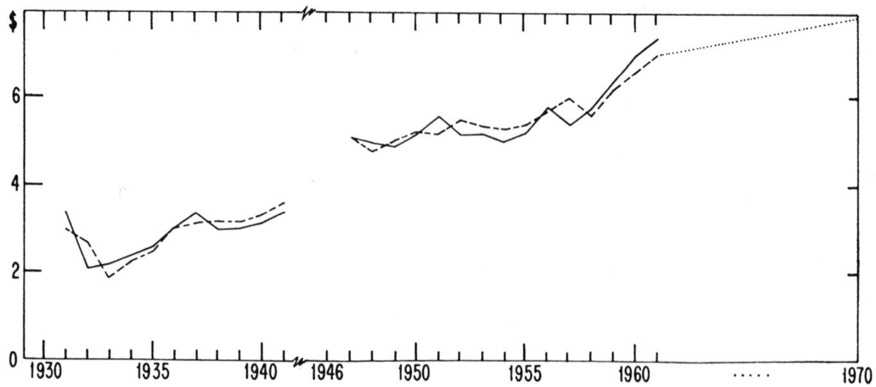


Dynamic model
3PLS

$$q_t = -1.7994 + .2649\, q_{t-1} + .0041\, \Delta x_t + .0038\, x_{t-1} - .4836\, z_t$$
$$\quad (.4331) \quad (.1629) \quad (.0018) \quad (.0008) \quad (.2462)$$

$R^2 = .957$ $\quad D.W. = 1.99$

$\alpha = 1.6312$ $\quad \beta = .5820$ $\quad \gamma = .0035$ $\quad \gamma' = .0052$

$\kappa = .9759$ $\quad \kappa' = 1.4648$ $\quad \delta = 1.7442$

| | 1961 level | 1970 projections | | | |
|---|---|---|---|---|---|
| | | 4% | | 5% | |
| | | I | II | I | II |
| per capita | \$7.49 | \$7.87 | \$7.78 | \$8.42 | \$8.33 |
| aggregate (billions) | | \$1.64 | \$1.63 | \$1.76 | \$1.74 |

The results indicate that this category is subject to considerable habit formation. However, the habit wears off rapidly, for $\delta$ is very large.

The distribution of income was important in the static model, along with total expenditure and the war dummy. The marginal propensity to consume for the upper-income group was considerably higher than for the lower-income groups; indeed, it was even negative for the latter (but probably not significantly different from zero). This is in keeping with a preliminary cross-section study which indicated that the education of the head of the household and race were important factors determining expenditures for books and maps. Although income distribution as we have defined it is not an ideal proxy for these demographic factors, it represents them to a considerable extent.

The static equation, with total expenditure, own relative price, income distribution, and the war dummy, is given below.

$$q_t = -2.2216 + .0062\, x_t - .0093\, p_t + .0068\, (\text{income dist.})_t + .8749\, d_t$$
$$\quad (1.5334) \quad (.0011) \quad (.0137) \quad (.0030) \quad (.6601)$$

MPC (upper) = .0269 $\quad$ MPC (lower) = −.000079

$R^2 = .923$ $\quad D.W. = 1.42$

## 9.2 NEWSPAPERS AND MAGAZINES

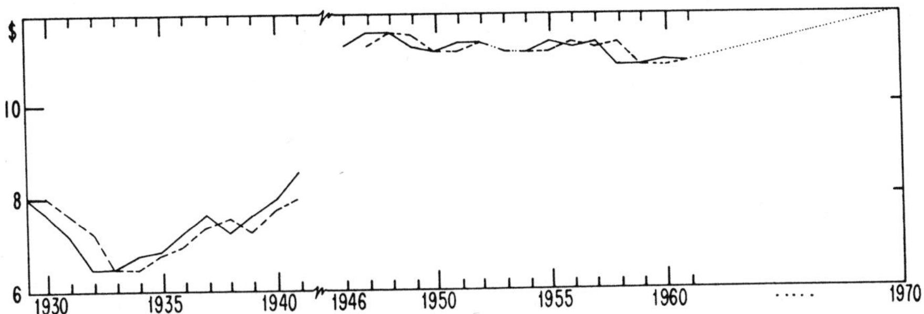


Dynamic model
OLS $\beta = \delta = 0$

$$q_t - q_{t-1} = \underset{(.00010)}{.00037}\, \Delta x_t - \underset{(.0007)}{.0015}\, \Delta p_t$$

$R^2 = .564 \qquad D.W. = 1.95$

$\alpha =$ indeterminate $\qquad \beta = \delta = 0 \qquad \gamma = .0004 \qquad \kappa = .5246$

$\lambda = -.0015 \qquad \sigma = -.1067$

| | 1961 level | 1970 projections 4% | | 5% | |
|---|---|---|---|---|---|
| | | I | II | I | II |
| per capita | \$11.02 | \$12.16 | \$12.12 | \$12.58 | \$12.54 |
| aggregate (billions) | | \$2.54 | \$2.53 | \$2.63 | \$2.62 |

Ordinarily we would expect to find habit formation present for newspapers and magazines. However, when the coefficients were unrestricted, the depreciation rate was negative and the coefficient of $q_{t-1}$ was greater than one.

With the static model, the stock of television sets per capita was highly significant, along with PCE, prices, and the war dummy. The fit was also very good, though there was positive autocorrelation in the residuals. This equation is given below.

$$q_t = \underset{(.9759)}{5.1269} + \underset{(.0006)}{.0050}\, x_t - \underset{(.0069)}{.0244}\, p_t - \underset{(.9576)}{4.7474}\, (\text{TV sets per cap.})_t + \underset{(.2420)}{1.8987}\, d_t$$

$R^2 = .991 \qquad D.W. = 1.45$

## 9.3 NONDURABLE TOYS

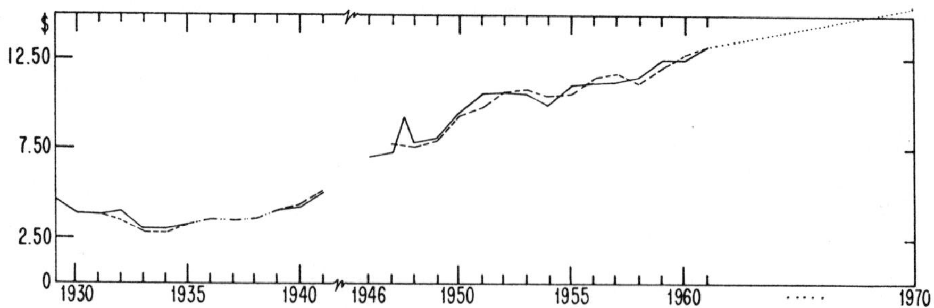


Dynamic model
3PLS $\delta = 2$

$$q_t = \underset{(2.8505)}{4.0270} + \underset{(.1127)}{.5160}\, q_{t-1} + \underset{(.0010)}{.0048}\, x_t - \underset{(.0247)}{.0648}\, p_t + \underset{(.2530)}{.4996}\, z_t$$

$R^2 = .993$ $D.W. = 2.06$

$\alpha = 2.6563$ $\beta = 1.3193$ $\gamma = .0032$ $\gamma' = .0093$ $\kappa = .5257$

$\kappa' = 1.5497$ $\lambda = -.0427$ $\lambda' = -.1255$ $\sigma = -.5841$ $\sigma' = -1.7161$

$\delta = 2$

| | 1961 level | 1970 projections 4% | | 5% | |
|---|---|---|---|---|---|
| | | I | II | I | II |
| per capita | \$13.39 | \$14.76 | \$14.50 | \$15.68 | \$15.42 |
| aggregate (billions) | | \$3.40 | \$3.23 | \$3.60 | \$3.44 |

This equation leaves some doubts, for though the fit is good and the price and PCE elasticities are reasonable, the stock coefficient is implausibly large; little explanation can be offered for this. Some preliminary projections were made from the following static model:

$$\ln q_t = \underset{(2.2081)}{-4.7345} + \underset{(.1994)}{1.1812} \ln x_t - \underset{(.3304)}{.9487} \ln p_t + \underset{(.3054)}{1.0143} \ln (\%\ \text{pop.} < 14)_t - \underset{(.2560)}{.5297}\, d_t$$

$R^2 = .982$ $D.W. = 1.08$

This would be an acceptable equation were it not for the low $D.W.$

## 9.4 WHEEL GOODS, DURABLE TOYS, SPORTS EQUIPMENT, BOATS, AND PLEASURE AIRCRAFT

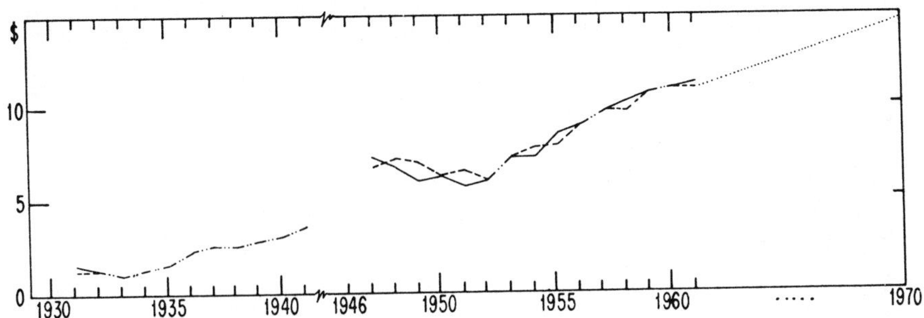


Dynamic model

3PLS

$$q_t = .8419\, q_{t-1} + .0056\, \Delta x_t + .0018\, x_{t-1} - .0317\, \Delta p_t - .0100\, p_{t-1}$$
$$\quad (.1056) \qquad (.0025) \qquad (.0010) \qquad (.0216) \qquad (.0054)$$
$$+ .4268\, z_t$$
$$(.2248)$$

$R^2 = .990 \qquad D.W. = 1.95$

$\alpha = 0 \qquad \beta = .2028 \qquad \gamma = .0052 \qquad \gamma' = .0112 \qquad \kappa = 1.1463$

$\kappa' = 2.5007 \qquad \lambda = -.0290 \qquad \lambda' = -.0633 \qquad \sigma = -.5975 \qquad \sigma' = -1.3036$

$\delta = .3744$

| | 1961 level | 1970 projections 4% I | 4% II | 5% I | 5% II |
|---|---|---|---|---|---|
| per capita | \$11.31 | \$14.76 | \$14.50 | \$15.68 | \$15.42 |
| aggregate (billions) | | \$3.08 | \$3.03 | \$3.28 | \$3.22 |

It might seem at first that the stock coefficient should be negative, since the items in this category are durables. However, sports equipment, pleasure boats, aircraft, etc., in many respects are luxuries in the short run and are complementary to leisure in the long run. Also these goods are subject to substantial demonstration effects in the long run. Hence the long run total-expenditure elasticity should be larger than in the short run.

The percentage of the population under age fourteen was tried in the static model, but its coefficient was insignificant. The own-price elasticity was always positive, and there was the usual positive autocorrelation. A static equation, with total expenditure and the percentage of the population under fourteen, is given below.

$$\ln q_t = -21.325 + 3.1895 \ln x_t + .0287 \ln (\%\ \text{pop.} < 14)_t$$
$$\qquad (1.432) \qquad (.2440) \qquad (.1137)$$

$R^2 = .979 \qquad D.W. = .53$

## 9.5 RADIO AND TELEVISION RECEIVERS, RECORDS, AND MUSICAL INSTRUMENTS

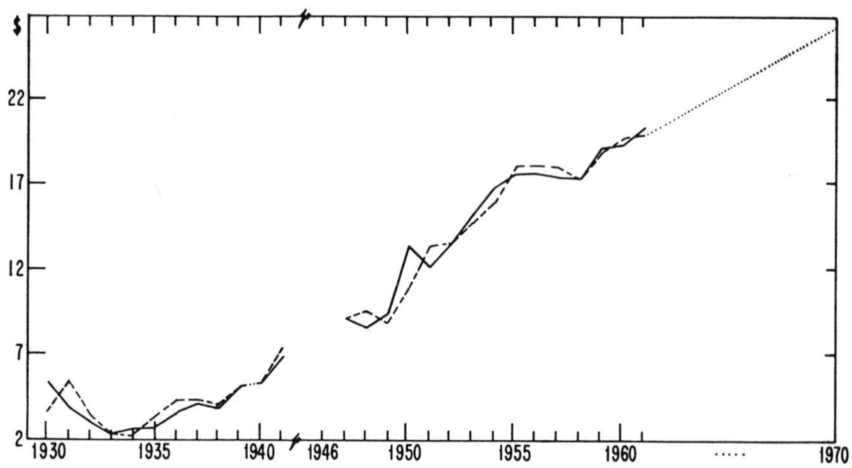


Dynamic model

OLS

$$q_t = .6599\, q_{t-1} + .0167\, \Delta x_t + .0060\, x_{t-1} - .0946\, \Delta p_t - .0340\, p_{t-1}$$
$$\quad (.2093) \qquad (.0050) \qquad (.0035) \qquad (.0499) \qquad (.0197)$$

$R^2 = .983 \qquad D.W. = 2.26$

$\alpha = 0 \qquad \beta = .0282 \qquad \gamma = .0165 \qquad \gamma' = .0176 \qquad \kappa = 1.9834$

$\kappa' = 2.1201 \qquad \lambda = -.0935 \qquad \lambda' = -.0999 \qquad \sigma = -1.1904 \qquad \sigma' = -1.2725$

$\delta = .4380$

| | 1961 level | 1970 projections 4% | | 5% | |
|---|---|---|---|---|---|
| | | I | II | I | II |
| per capita | \$20.60 | \$25.90 | \$25.33 | \$27.85 | \$27.28 |
| aggregate (billions) | | \$5.41 | \$5.29 | \$5.82 | \$5.70 |

The positive stock coefficient (although it is probably not statistically different from zero) is disturbing. However, it possibly reflects the fact that, once television became available, the stocks of television sets were below the equilibrium level (relative to total expenditure) until recent years.[26]

A preliminary cross-section study indicated that several demographic variables may have an important influence on consumption in this category. These include age of head of household, tenure, class of residence, and size of family. However, none of these has been incorporated into the regression analyses because none shows enough year-to-year variation.

[26] The remark about technological change made in connection with item 5.2 (household appliances) is also relevant here.

The static model, with total expenditure and per capita stocks of television sets, was also a very good equation. The $R^2$ of this equation, given below, is actually higher than for the dynamic model, and there was only marginal positive autocorrelation in the residuals.

$$q_t = \underset{(.9135)}{-8.4321} + \underset{(.0008)}{.0130}\, x_t + \underset{(2.188)}{26.340}\, (\text{TV sets per cap.})_t$$

$R^2 = .990 \qquad D.W. = 1.62$

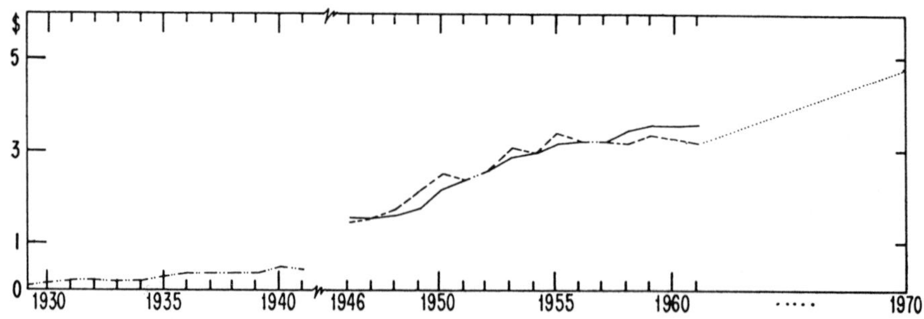


Static model
double-logarithmic

$$\ln q_t = -10.752 + 2.0940 \ln x_t - 1.0149 \ln p + .1610 \ln (\text{TV sets per cap.})_t$$
$$\quad (1.797) \quad (.2623) \quad (0.0904) \quad (.0157)$$
$$+ 1.4907\, d_t$$
$$(.1415)$$

$R^2 = .982 \qquad D.W. = 1.07$

$\kappa = 2.0940 \qquad \sigma = -1.0149 \qquad s_p = 1.14$

| | 1961 level | 1970 projections 4% | | 5% | |
|---|---|---|---|---|---|
| | | I | II | I | II |
| per capita | \$3.94 | \$4.79 | \$5.29 | \$5.38 | \$5.94 |
| aggregate (billions) | | \$1.00 | \$1.10 | \$1.12 | \$1.24 |

The dynamic equation for this category, given below, was unacceptable because of the implausibly large coefficient of $q_{t-1}$. As a result, the above static model has been used in spite of the presence of positive autocorrelation in the residuals. Apart from this defect, the equation is all right.

$$q_t = 1.8927 + 1.4247\, q_{t-1} + .0017\, \Delta x_t - .0007\, x_{t-1} - .0332\, \Delta p_t - .0146\, p_{t-1}$$
$$\quad (1.2166) \quad (.2132) \quad (.0015) \quad (.0009) \quad (.0162) \quad (.0081)$$
$$- .4617\, d_t$$
$$(.3857)$$

$R^2 = .977 \qquad D.W. = 1.95$

## 9.7 FLOWERS, SEEDS, AND POTTED PLANTS

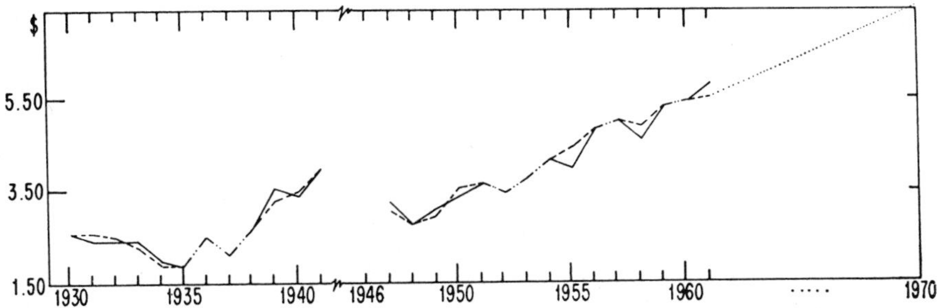


Dynamic model
OLS $\delta = 2$

$$q_t = \underset{(.4622)}{-1.2281} + \underset{(.0891)}{.0932}\, q_{t-1} + \underset{(.0006)}{.0057}\, x_t - \underset{(.0026)}{.0203}\, p_t - \underset{(.2199)}{1.3343}\, d_t$$

$R^2 = .982 \qquad D.W. = 2.13$

$\alpha = -1.1234 \quad \beta = .3412 \quad \gamma = .0052 \quad \gamma' = .0063 \quad \kappa = 1.8617$

$\kappa' = 2.2446 \quad \lambda = -.0186 \quad \lambda' = -.0224 \quad \sigma = -.5165 \quad \sigma' = -.6228$

$\delta = 2$

| | 1961 level | 1970 projections 4% | | 5% | |
|---|---|---|---|---|---|
| | | I | II | I | II |
| per capita | \$5.91 | \$7.74 | \$7.46 | \$8.43 | \$8.15 |
| aggregate (billions) | | \$1.62 | \$1.56 | \$1.76 | \$1.70 |

The results indicate purchase of flowers, etc., to be subject to habit formation. Note that both of the PCE elasticities are substantial, while the price effect though significant is considerably smaller.

The static model, with PCE, prices, and the war dummy, is also a good equation; indeed it differs very little from the equation given above.

$$q_t = \underset{(.4850)}{-1.1251} + \underset{(.0004)}{.0059}\, x_t - \underset{(.0024)}{.0215}\, p_t - \underset{(.2088)}{1.2907}\, d_t$$

$R^2 = .976 \qquad D.W. = 1.67$

## 9.8a MOTION PICTURES

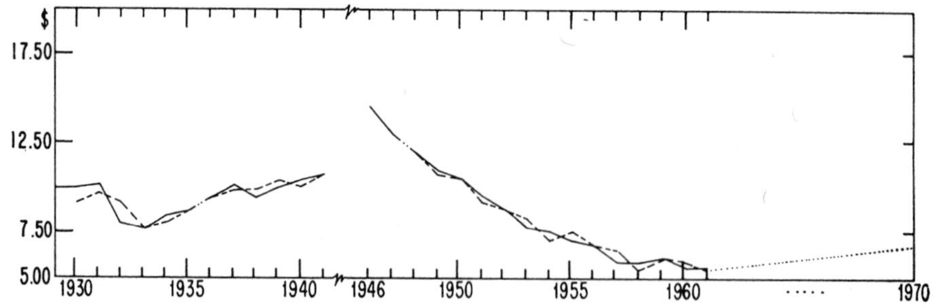


Dynamic model

OLS

$$q_t = .8920\, q_{t-1} + .0080\, x_t + .00105\, x_{t-1} - 1.3885\, d_t$$
$$\quad (.0325) \qquad (.0021) \qquad (.00033) \qquad (.2849)$$

$R^2 = .954 \qquad D.W. = 2.42$

$\alpha = 0 \qquad \beta = .0269 \qquad \gamma = .0079 \qquad \gamma' = .0098$

$\kappa = 1.1460 \qquad \kappa' = 1.4157 \qquad \delta = .1411$

| | 1961 level | 1970 projections | | | |
|---|---|---|---|---|---|
| | | 4% | | 5% | |
| | | I | II | I | II |
| per capita | \$5.52 | \$6.73 | \$6.58 | \$7.68 | \$7.53 |
| aggregate (billions) | | \$1.41 | \$1.37 | \$1.60 | \$1.57 |

The price elasticities were both positive when prices were included in the dynamic model. There was no indication of differing MPC's between upper- and lower-income groups when the distribution of income was included in the static model. The percentage of population under age eighteen was also unsuccessful in the static model. A scatter diagram of the proportion of the population between fourteen and eighteen and the dependent variable indicated a slight relationship, but opposite to what would be expected.

The static model, with PCE, prices, TV stocks, and the war dummy, is given below.

$$q_t = 8.0140 \ln x_t - 9.8166 \ln p_t - 1.4690 \ln (\text{TV sets per cap.})_t - 8.4644\, d_t$$
$$\quad (1.2614) \qquad (1.8657) \qquad (.0888) \qquad (.7080)$$

$R^2 = .918 \qquad D.W. = .77$

## 9.8b LEGITIMATE THEATER AND OPERA

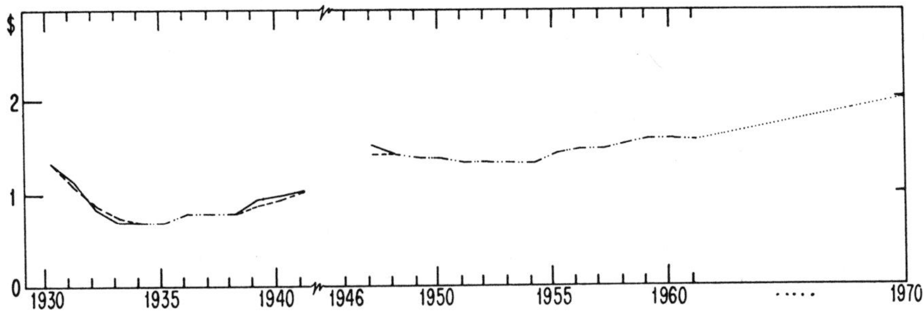


Dynamic model

OLS

$$q_t = -.1736 + .6071\, q_{t-1} + .00093\, \Delta x_t + .00050\, x_{t-1}$$
$$\qquad (.0394) \quad (.0555) \qquad (.00026) \qquad (.00006)$$

$R^2 = .984 \qquad D.W. = 1.84$

$\alpha = -.2905 \qquad \beta = .2533 \qquad \gamma = .0008 \qquad \gamma' = .0013$

$\kappa = .8668 \qquad \kappa' = 1.3146 \qquad \delta = .7423$

| | 1961 level | 1970 projections 4% | | 1970 projections 5% | |
|---|---|---|---|---|---|
| | | I | II | I | II |
| per capita | \$1.67 | \$2.04 | \$2.02 | \$2.17 | \$2.15 |
| aggregate (billions) | | \$.43 | \$.42 | \$.45 | \$.45 |

The own-price elasticities were negative but insignificant when the relative price was included in the dynamic model. The distribution of income, which was important in the static model, was tried in place of prices in the dynamic model, but when the coefficients were constrained in taking account of the identifying restriction on $\delta$, the moment matrix became negative-definite.

The results show theater and opera to be subject to habit formation, for $\beta$ is positive; but the large value of $\delta$ indicates the habit wears off quickly.

With the static model, TV stocks per capita together with PCE and income distribution were important as predictors. However, the price elasticity was positive; the $R^2$ was low; and the residuals had high positive autocorrelation. Moreover, the MPC for the lower-income groups was negative.

$$q_t = -.5079 + .00090\, x_t + .0049\, p_t + .00204\, (\text{income dist.})_t - 1.4775\, (\text{TV sets per cap.})_t$$
$$\qquad (.7885) \quad (.00035) \qquad (.0069) \qquad (.00109) \qquad\qquad (.7604)$$

MPC (upper) = .00061 $\qquad$ MPC (lower) = −.00102

$R^2 = .739 \qquad D.W. = .38$

## 9.8c SPECTATOR SPORTS

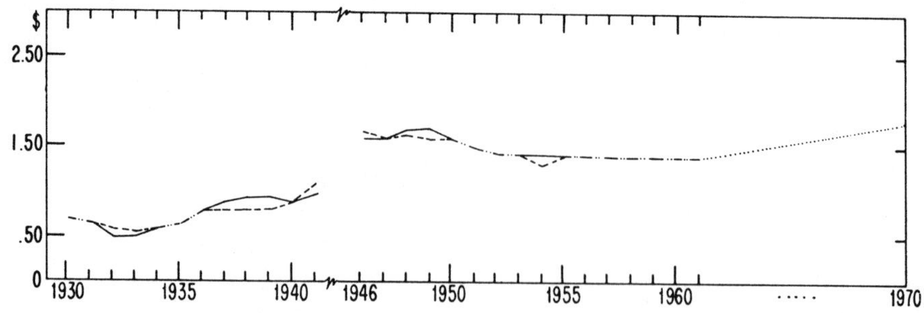


Static model
linear

$$q_t = -.4212 + .0012\, x_t - .0010\,(\text{income dist.})_t - 2.5185\,(\text{TV sets per cap.})_t + .2317\, d_t$$
$$\quad (.1969) \quad (.0002) \quad (.0004) \quad (.2318) \quad (.0832)$$

$R^2 = .978 \qquad D.W. = 1.15$

MPC (upper) = .000027 MPC (lower) = .001810 $s_p = .09$

| | 1961 level | 1970 projections 4% I | 4% II | 5% I | 5% II |
|---|---|---|---|---|---|
| per capita | $1.39 | $1.79 | $1.77 | $1.92 | $1.90 |
| aggregate (billions) | | $.37 | $.37 | $.40 | $.40 |

Both total-expenditure coefficients were insignificant in the dynamic model and, since this seemed an unreasonable result, further work with the dynamic model was not attempted. With the static model, on the other hand, the own-price elasticity turned up positive, so prices were excluded. However, other than the low $D.W.$ coefficient, the static model given above is reasonable. The marginal propensity to consume of the upper-income group is indicated to be close to zero, while it is much larger for the lower-income groups. The dynamic model is given below.

$$q_t = -.1760 + .8594\, q_{t-1} + .00002\, \Delta x_t + .00008\, x_{t-1} - .0060\, \Delta p_t + .0015\, p_{t-1} + .0874\, d_t$$
$$\quad (.4682) \quad (.0825) \quad (.00037) \quad (.00015) \quad (.0029) \quad (.0022) \quad (.1127)$$

$R^2 = .984 \qquad D.W. = 2.12$

## 9.9 CLUBS AND FRATERNAL ORGANIZATIONS EXCEPT INSURANCE

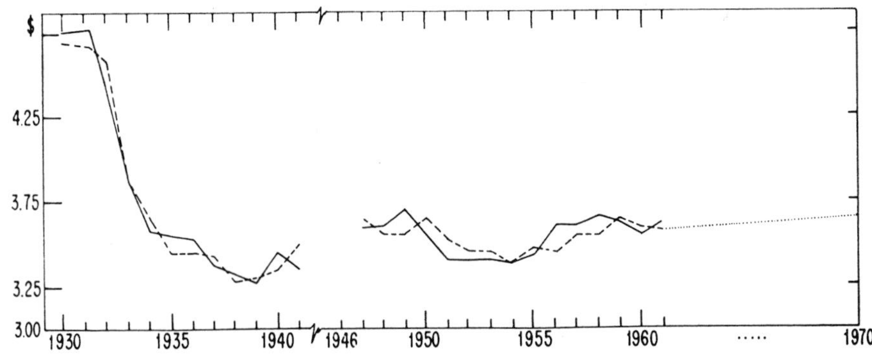


Dynamic model

OLS

$$q_t = \underset{(.4830)}{1.3018} + \underset{(.1064)}{.6299}\, q_{t-1} + \underset{(.00085)}{.00094}\, \Delta x_t + \underset{(.00015)}{.00033}\, x_{t-1} - \underset{(.0102)}{.0139}\, \Delta p_t - \underset{(.0066)}{.0048}\, p_{t-1} + \underset{(.1299)}{.5502}\, (\text{prohib. dummy})_t$$

$R^2 = .954 \quad D.W. = 2.09$

$\alpha = 3.7864 \quad \beta = -.0322 \quad \gamma = .0009 \quad \gamma' = .0008 \quad \kappa = .3257$

$\kappa' = .3026 \quad \lambda = -.0141 \quad \lambda' = -.0131 \quad \sigma = -.3683 \quad \sigma' = -.3422$

$\delta = .4219$

| | 1961 level | 1970 projections 4% | | 5% | |
|---|---|---|---|---|---|
| | | I | II | I | II |
| per capita | $3.65 | $3.66 | $3.72 | $3.75 | $3.82 |
| aggregate (billions) | | $.76 | $.78 | $.78 | $.80 |

The observations for the first four years of the period (1929–1932) are markedly above the pattern for the rest of the early part of the period. A probable explanation is that this reflects one of the "legitimate" substitute forms of entertainment during Prohibition. Accordingly, a dummy variable has been incorporated into the model; it takes the value 1 for 1929–1932, and 0 thereafter.

The negative stock coefficient suggests that people tire of going to clubs, a result that appears somewhat unusual, but the coefficient is probably not significant. When the distribution of income was included in the static model, the marginal propensity to consume of the upper-income group was decidedly higher than for the lower-income groups. Indeed, the latter was negative. This could account for the negative stock coefficient if the expenditure of the lower-income groups were a large enough part of the total, or if the income distribution were becoming more equal.

The static model, with total expenditure, own relative price, income distribution, and the prohibition dummy, is given below. As can be seen, the intercept and the prohibition dummy are the most significant variables (the others only border on significance), and the $R^2$ is much lower than for the dynamic model.

$$q_t = \underset{(.6073)}{3.2718} + \underset{(.00048)}{.00053}\, x_t - \underset{(.0013)}{.0031}\, p_t + \underset{(.0011)}{.0011}\, (\text{income dist.})_t + \underset{(.1295)}{1.1049}\, (\text{prohib. dummy})_t$$

MPC (upper) = .000335 MPC (lower) = −.000453

$R^2 = .882$ $D.W. = 1.62$

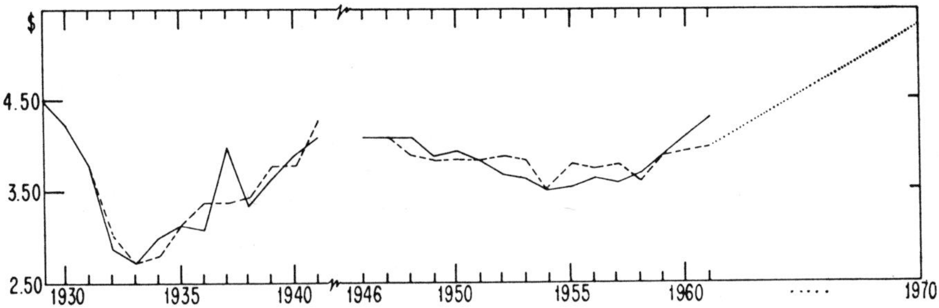


Dynamic model
3PLS

$$q_t = .7171\, q_{t-1} + .0040\, \Delta x_t + .0019\, x_{t-1} - .0224\, \Delta p_t - .0110\, p_{t-1}$$
$$(.1564) \quad (.0014) \quad (.0013) \quad (.0198) \quad (.0012)$$
$$- .6234\, d_t - .5774\, z_t$$
$$(.4138) \quad (.2579)$$

$R^2 = .817 \qquad D.W. = 2.40$

$\alpha = 0 \qquad \beta = .3208 \qquad \gamma = .0035 \qquad \gamma' = .0069 \qquad \kappa = 1.1938$

$\kappa' = 2.3563 \lambda \quad = -.0197 \qquad \lambda' = -.0388 \qquad \sigma = -.4689 \qquad \sigma' = -.9254$

$\delta = .6503$

| | 1961 level | 1970 projections 4% | | 5% | |
|---|---|---|---|---|---|
| | | I | II | I | II |
| per capita | $4.31 | $5.32 | $5.83 | $5.96 | $6.48 |
| aggregate (billions) | | $1.11 | $1.22 | $1.25 | $1.35 |

There is substantial, though plausible, habit formation present for this item. Moreover, the PCE elasticities are considerably higher than the price elasticities, not a surprising result. The major drawback to this equation is the low $R^2$.

Some preliminary projections were made from the following static equation:

$$q_t = .0055\, x_t + .0052\, \mathrm{ID}_t - .0266\, p_t - 1.9780\, (\text{TV sets per cap.})_t - .3759\, d_t$$
$$(.0004) \quad (.0012) \quad (.0056) \quad (.6809) \quad (.2521)$$

MPC (upper) = .002183 MPC (lower) = .000064

$R^2 = .835 \qquad D.W. = 1.95$

In view of the low $R^2$ for both the dynamic and the static models, we consider this equation an acceptable alternative to the dynamic model given above.

## 9.11 PARI-MUTUEL RECEIPTS

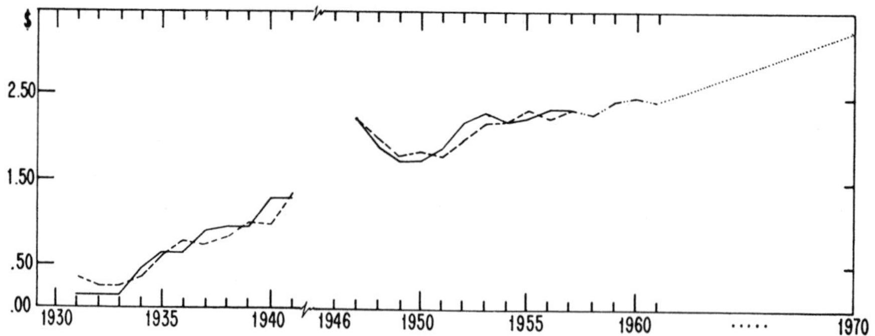


Dynamic model
3PLS

$$q_t = -.9697 + .4628\, q_{t-1} + .0021\, \Delta x_t + .0014\, x_{t-1} + .2935\, z_t$$
$$\quad (.2285) \quad (.0887) \quad (.0007) \quad (.0003) \quad (.2273)$$

$R^2 = .980 \qquad D.W. = 2.07$

$\alpha = -1.2861 \qquad \beta = .2964 \qquad \gamma = .0019 \qquad \gamma' = .0026$

$\kappa = 1.5248 \qquad \kappa' = 2.1398 \qquad \delta = 1.0309$

| | 1961 level | 1970 projections 4% | | 5% | |
|---|---|---|---|---|---|
| | | I | II | I | II |
| per capita | $2.42 | $3.29 | $3.25 | $3.57 | $3.53 |
| aggregate (billions) | | $.69 | $.68 | $.75 | $.74 |

Both of the price coefficients were insignificant (and positive) when prices were included in the dynamic model. The results show the total-expenditure elasticity to be substantial in both short run and long run, and indicate that "going to the races" is subject to habit formation. But the habit wears off quickly.

The own-price elasticity was negative in the static model. There was also evidence from the static model that distribution of income is of some importance. The derived marginal propensity to consume was much higher for the lower-income groups than for the higher-income group. However, the fit of this model, given below, is poorer than of the dynamic model, and there is positive autocorrelation in the residuals.

$$q_t = 1.0220 + .00063\, x_t - .0130\, p_t - .0077\, (\text{income dist.})_t + .0354\, d_t$$
$$\quad (.6823) \quad (.00056) \quad (.0071) \quad (.0017) \quad (.3087)$$

MPC (upper) $= -.001452$ MPC (lower) $= .006852$

$R^2 = .940 \qquad D.W. = .93$

## 9.12 OTHER RECREATION[27]

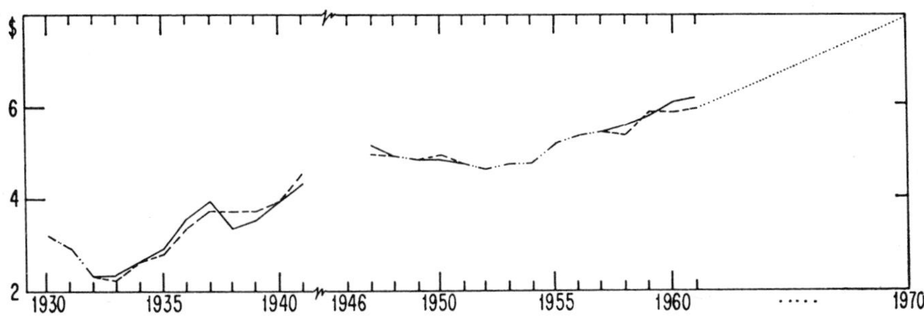


Dynamic model

OLS

$$q_t = .7807\, q_{t-1} + .0050\, \Delta x_t + .0016\, x_{t-1} - .0223\, \Delta p_t$$
$$\quad (.1134) \qquad (.0009) \qquad (.0006) \qquad (.0096)$$
$$- .0071\, p_{t-1} - .5236\, d_t$$
$$\quad (.0036) \qquad (.2402)$$

$R^2 = .986$ $\quad D.W. = 1.89$

$\alpha = 0$ $\quad \beta = .1319$ $\quad \gamma = .0047$ $\quad \gamma' = .0073$ $\quad \kappa = 1.3428$

$\kappa' = 2.0618$ $\quad \lambda = -.0210$ $\quad \lambda' = -.0323$ $\quad \sigma = -.4901$ $\quad \sigma' = -.7526$

$\delta = .3781$

| | 1961 level | 1970 projections 4% | | 1970 projections 5% | |
|---|---|---|---|---|---|
| | | I | II | I | II |
| per capita | \$6.23 | \$7.87 | \$8.02 | \$8.57 | \$8.72 |
| aggregate (billions) | | \$1.64 | \$1.68 | \$1.79 | \$1.82 |

Most of the items included in this category can be considered complementary with leisure; hence the positive stock coefficient and the substantial total-expenditure elasticities are appropriate.

Total expenditure, the distribution of income, per capita stocks of television sets, and the war dummy were important in the static model. However, the own-price elasticity was positive with this model (given below), and the marginal propensity to consume for the lower-income groups was higher than for the upper-income group. It is difficult to accept the latter result.

$$q_t = -5.7490 + .0070\, x_t + .0202\, p_t + .0018\, (\text{income dist.})_t$$
$$\quad (1.2120) \quad (.0006) \qquad (.0079) \qquad (.0014)$$
$$- 4.8939\, (\text{TV sets per cap.})_t - .4368\, d_t$$
$$\quad (.8562) \qquad\qquad (.3095)$$

MPC (upper) = .001789 $\quad$ MPC (lower) = .004124

$R^2 = .976$ $\quad D.W. = 1.36$

[27] Comprises photo developing and printing, photographic studios, collectors' net acquisitions of stamps and coins, hunting-dog purchase and training, sports guide service, veterinary service, purchase of pets, camp fees, nonvending coin-machine receipts minus payoff, and other commercial amusements.

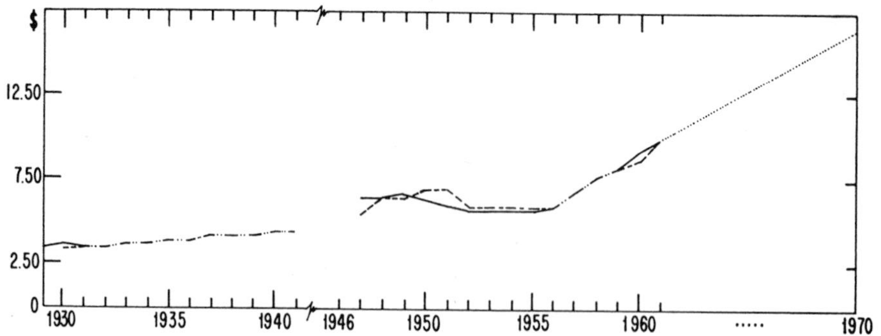


Dynamic model
OLS $\beta = \delta = -2$

$$q_t - q_{t-1} = \underset{(.5999)}{-1.2322} + \underset{(.0006)}{.0014}\, x_{t-1} - \underset{(.3385)}{.4918}\, d_t$$

$R^2 = .260 \qquad D.W. = 1.67$

$\alpha = -1.2322 \qquad \beta = \delta = -2 \qquad \gamma = .0014 \qquad s_p = 1.96$

| | 1961 level | 1970 projections 4% | | 1970 projections 5% | |
|---|---|---|---|---|---|
| | | I | II | I | II |
| per capita | \$9.99 | \$16.95 | \$16.85 | \$17.56 | \$17.46 |
| aggregate (billions) | | \$3.54 | \$3.52 | \$3.67 | \$3.65 |

This equation should be viewed as the best of a large number of poor equations from which to choose. It presents a number of anomalies, particularly the large negative stock coefficient and negative depreciation rate. However, the $R^2$ of .26 should not be viewed with alarm; in terms of levels, the $R^2$ is well over .9. Prior to assuming $\beta = \delta$, the short-run PCE elasticity was negative, while the long-run elasticity was positive. This is plausible for expenditure for higher education.

A static model with the percentage of the population of college age (18–24) as a predictor, together with PCE, prices, income distribution, and the war dummy, is given below.

$$q_t = \underset{(2.0888)}{-6.6084} + \underset{(.0016)}{.0044}\, x_t + \underset{(.0172)}{.0572}\, p_t + \underset{(.0665)}{.0696}\, (\%\text{ pop. } 18\text{–}24)_t$$
$$+ \underset{(.0041)}{.0037}\, (\text{income dist.})_t + \underset{(.8203)}{1.5533}\, d_t$$

$R^2 = .914 \qquad D.W. = .574$

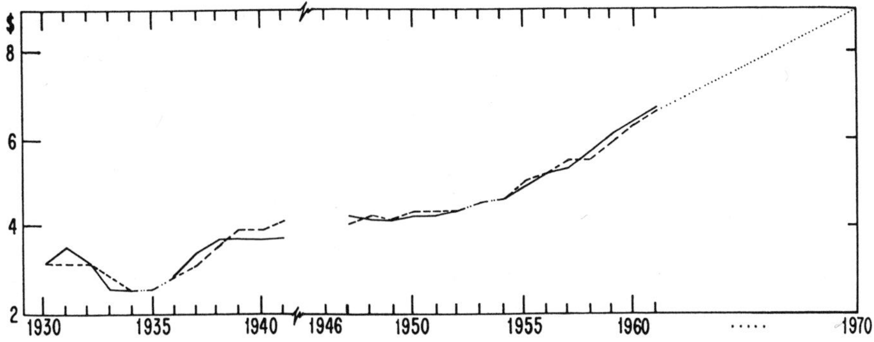


Dynamic model
OLS $\delta = 2$

$$q_t = -1.5100 + .7546\, q_{t-1} + .0024\, x_t - .7524\, d_t$$
$$\quad (.4020) \quad (.0941) \qquad (.0006) \qquad (.2319)$$

$R^2 = .974 \qquad D.W. = 1.67$

$\alpha = -.8605 \qquad \beta = 1.7203 \qquad \gamma = .0014 \qquad \gamma' = .0099$

$\kappa = .4090 \qquad \kappa' = 2.9243 \qquad \delta = 2$

| | 1961 level | 1970 projections 4% | | 1970 projections 5% | |
|---|---|---|---|---|---|
| | | I | II | I | II |
| per capita | \$6.81 | \$9.09 | \$8.97 | \$9.84 | \$9.72 |
| aggregate (billions) | | \$1.90 | \$1.87 | \$2.06 | \$2.03 |

When prices were included in the dynamic model, both price coefficients were positive; the price elasticity was also positive in the static model. While the PCE elasticities appear to be plausible, little justification can be given for the large values for $\beta$ and $\delta$.

Inclusion of the distribution of income in the static model added nothing. The $R^2$ of this model (given below) is lower than for the dynamic model, and the residuals have positive autocorrelation.

$$q_t = -2.6436 + .0060\, x_t - .0001\, (\text{income dist.})_t - 1.3380\, d_t$$
$$\quad (.7267) \quad (.0008) \qquad (.0028) \qquad\qquad (.5174)$$

$R^2 = .89 \qquad D.W. = .71$

## 10.3 OTHER EDUCATIONAL EXPENDITURES[28]

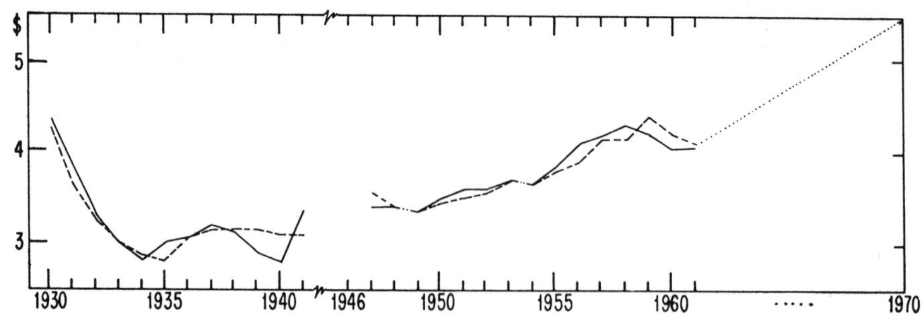


Dynamic model

OLS

$$q_t = .8139\, q_{t-1} + .0023\, \Delta x_t + .0012\, x_{t-1} - .0143\, \Delta p_t$$
$$\quad (.1099) \quad (.0010) \quad (.0004) \quad (.0118)$$
$$- .0075\, p_{t-1} - .3154\, d_t$$
$$\quad (.0048) \quad (.1632)$$

$R^2 = .932$  $D.W. = 2.04$

$\alpha = 0$  $\beta = .5068$  $\gamma = .0018$  $\gamma' = .0064$  $\kappa = .6501$

$\kappa' = 2.2558$  $\lambda = -.0116$  $\lambda' = -.0403$  $\sigma = -.3035$  $\sigma' = -1.0531$

$\delta = .7120$

| | 1961 level | 1970 projections | | | |
|---|---|---|---|---|---|
| | | 4% | | 5% | |
| | | I | II | I | II |
| per capita | \$4.07 | \$5.51 | \$5.76 | \$6.00 | \$6.24 |
| aggregate (billions) | | \$1.15 | \$1.20 | \$1.25 | \$1.30 |

The static models tried for this category were very disappointing. A variable representing the importance of foundation grants would no doubt be significant in the static model; however, we were unable to construct such a variable. Given the heterogeneous collection of items included in this category (some of them purely conventional), the above dynamic equation appears plausible.

The static model, with PCE, prices, and war dummy, is given below.

$$q_t = 1.2790 + .0020\, x_t + .00099\, p_t - .6131\, d_t$$
$$\quad (1.0608) \quad (.0010) \quad (.01378) \quad (.4612)$$

$R^2 = .354$  $D.W. = .25$

[28] Comprises fees paid to commercial, trade, and correspondence schools; fees for musical, dancing, and other instruction except athletics; and current expenditures (including depreciation) of foundations for education and research.

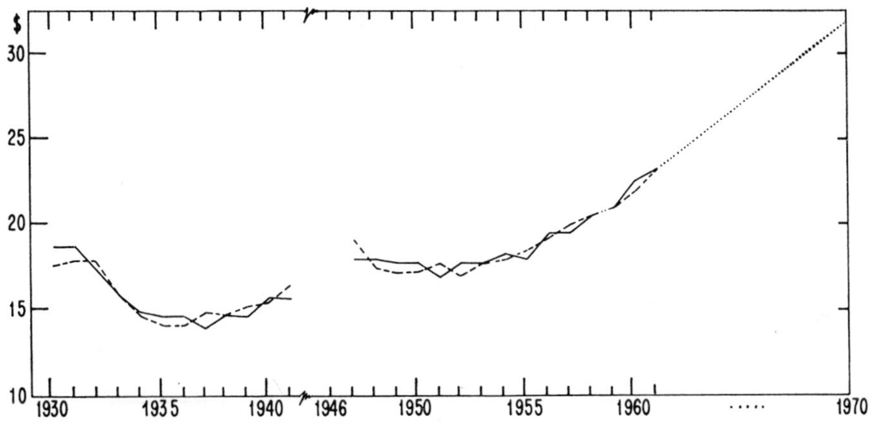


Dynamic model
OLS $\delta = -2$

$$q_t = \underset{(1.4771)}{-3.7950} + \underset{(.0813)}{.8003}\, q_{t-1} + \underset{(.0014)}{.0071}\, x_{t-1} \underset{(.6991)}{-2.7156}\, d_t$$

$R^2 = .942 \qquad D.W. = 2.17$

$\alpha = 2.1080 \qquad \beta = -2.2219 \qquad \gamma = -.0039 \qquad \gamma' = .0355$

$\kappa = -.2808 \qquad \kappa' = 2.5312 \qquad \delta = -2$

| | 1961 level | 1970 projections | | | |
|---|---|---|---|---|---|
| | | 4% | | 5% | |
| | | I | II | I | II |
| per capita | \$23.23 | \$31.64 | \$31.31 | \$33.70 | \$33.37 |
| aggregate (billions) | | \$6.61 | \$6.54 | \$7.04 | \$6.97 |

Prices were insignificant when they were included in the dynamic model. While the negative short-run but positive long-run PCE elasticities are plausible for such an item, the large negative values for $\beta$ and $\delta$ are difficult to interpret. However, if we recast the model in a context of a classical distributed lag, as was suggested in Chapter 1 for the case of $\delta = -2$, then the equation is plausible.

None of the static models tried was of any assistance. A static equation, with PCE, prices, income distribution, and the war dummy, is given below.

$$q_t = \underset{(6.8018)}{1.8606} + \underset{(.0033)}{.0155}\, x_t - \underset{(.0777)}{.0208}\, p_t + \underset{(.0090)}{.0361}\, (\text{income dist.})_t + \underset{(1.8797)}{3.4942}\, d_t$$

MPC (upper) = .0175 MPC (lower) = .0183

$R^2 = .746 \qquad D.W. = 1.06$

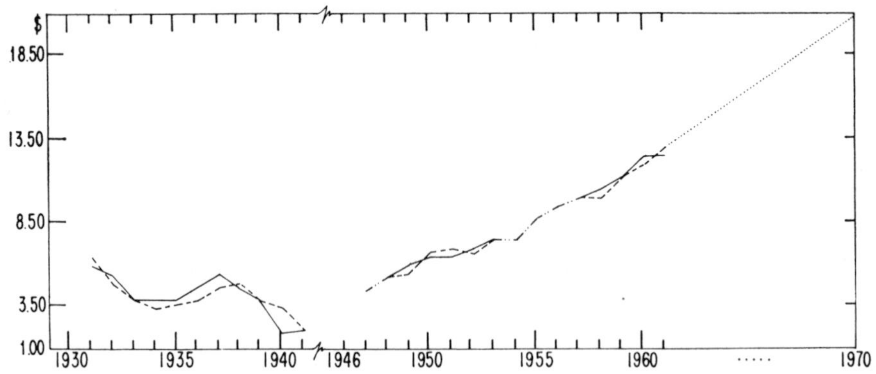


Dynamic model
3PLS

$$q_t = .9415\, q_{t-1} + .0059\, \Delta x_t + .0018\, x_{t-1} - .0468\, \Delta p_t - .0147\, p_{t-1} + .2640\, z_t$$
$$(.0750) \quad (.0031) \quad (.0006) \quad (.0237) \quad (.0037) \quad (.1857)$$

$R^2 = .972 \qquad D.W. = 1.67$

$\alpha = 0 \qquad \beta = .3109 \qquad \gamma = .0051 \qquad \gamma' = .0316 \qquad \kappa = .9646$

$\kappa' = 5.9432 \qquad \lambda = -.0407 \qquad \lambda' = -.2508 \qquad \sigma = -.6590 \qquad \sigma' = -4.0607$

$\delta = .3711$

| | 1961 level | 1970 projections | | | |
|---|---|---|---|---|---|
| | | 4% | | 5% | |
| | | I | II | I | II |
| per capita | $12.48 | $20.65 | $19.90 | $21.89 | $21.13 |
| aggregate (billions) | | $4.31 | $4.16 | $4.57 | $4.41 |

It is interesting to note the high negative long-run own-price elasticity. That the long-run total-expenditure elasticity is high is not surprising, though it should probably be not as high as nearly six. This may be due to the linear form of the dynamic model.

A linear static model (given below), using total expenditure, own relative price, departures of U.S. citizens for abroad per capita, income distribution, and the war dummy, gave a slightly higher $R^2$. In view of the positive autocorrelation in the residuals, the dynamic model was deemed superior.

$$q_t = 4.0452 + .0050\, x_t - .0520\, p_t + .4196\, (\text{departures of citizens abroad})_t + .0192\, (\text{income dist.})_t + 1.3029\, d_t$$
$$(2.5084) \quad (.0031) \quad (.0285) \quad (.0756) \quad (.0502) \quad (.10611)$$

MPC (upper) = .00507 MPC (lower) = $-.00123$

$R^2 = .964 \qquad D.W. = 1.13$

## 12.2 EXPENDITURES ABROAD BY U.S. GOVERNMENT PERSONNEL (MILITARY AND CIVILIAN)

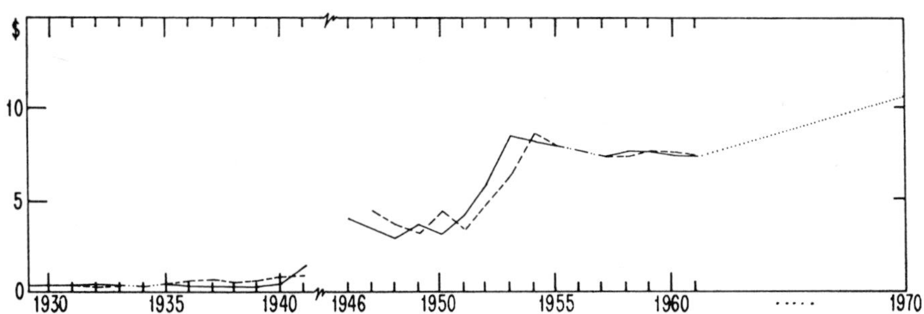


Dynamic model
3PLS $\delta = 2$

$$q_t = -2.7286 + .7353\, q_{t-1} + .0031\, x_t + .3930\, z_t$$
$$(1.3802) \quad (.1234) \qquad (.0014) \qquad (.2242)$$

$R^2 = .965$ $D.W. = 2.04$

$\alpha = -1.5724$ $\beta = 1.6949$ $\gamma = .0018$ $\gamma' = .0117$

$\kappa = .5925$ $\kappa' = 3.8840$ $\delta = 2$

| | 1961 level | 1970 projections 4% | | 5% | |
|---|---|---|---|---|---|
| | | I | II | I | II |
| per capita | $7.45 | $10.73 | $10.59 | $11.67 | $11.52 |
| aggregate (billions) | | $2.24 | $2.21 | $2.44 | $2.41 |

Ideally, expenditure for this item should be deflated by U.S. government personnel abroad, with total expenditure correspondingly being the total expenditure of these individuals. Unfortunately, these data are not available for each year of the period; however, the number abroad can be introduced as a proportion. This was done in the static model. Moreover, the category itself is ill-defined, for included within the category is a mixture of services, durable goods, and nondurable goods, which are classified by type of product in the domestic accounts. Accordingly, the above equation should be viewed with caution.

The inverse semi-logarithmic static model, with total expenditure, prices, percentage of the total United States population in the armed forces abroad, and the war dummy, is given below. This equation was used to make the projections at first, but the initial projection was unquestionably too high (about $22).

$$\ln q_t = -2.4853 + .0025\, x_t - .0114\, p_t$$
$$(.8019) \quad (.0005) \qquad (.0081)$$
$$+ .9694\,(\%\text{ total pop. in armed forces abroad})_t + 1.1278)\, d_t$$
$$(.3402) \qquad\qquad\qquad (.3764)$$

$R^2 = .941$ $D.W. = 1.72$

## 12.3 NET PERSONAL CASH REMITTANCES TO FOREIGN COUNTRIES

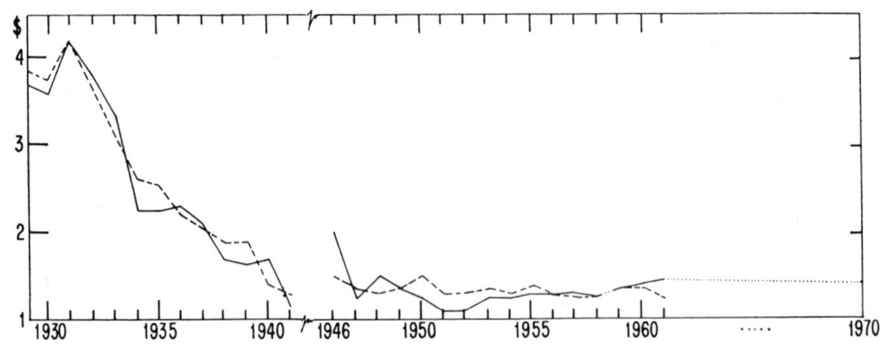


Static model
inverse semi-logarithmic

$$\ln q_t = -1.5448 + .0012\, x_t - .0181\, p_t + .3007\, (\%\text{ pop. foreign born})_t$$
$$\qquad (.6966) \quad (.0003) \qquad (.0028) \qquad (.0358)$$

$R^2 = .964 \qquad D.W. = 2.16$

$\kappa = 1.4917 \qquad \sigma = -1.8266 \qquad s_p = .34$

| | 1961 level | 1970 projections 4% | | 5% | |
|---|---|---|---|---|---|
| | | I | II | I | II |
| per capita | $1.43 | $1.44 | $1.35 | $1.65 | $1.54 |
| aggregate (billions) | | $.30 | $.28 | $.34 | $.32 |

The fit of the dynamic model (given below) was poorer than the above equation, and both total-expenditure coefficients were insignificant. Although less obvious, there is a deflation problem with this category, somewhat similar to the one encountered in 12.2.

$$q_t = 2.1045 + .6772\, q_{t-1} + .0003\, \Delta x_t + .0002\, x_{t-1} - .0476\, \Delta p_t$$
$$\qquad (1.9386) \quad (.1815) \qquad (.0019) \qquad (.0007) \qquad (.0121)$$
$$- .0159\, p_{t-1} - .3335\, d_t$$
$$\qquad (.0119) \qquad (.3107)$$

$R^2 = .925 \qquad D.W. = 2.24$

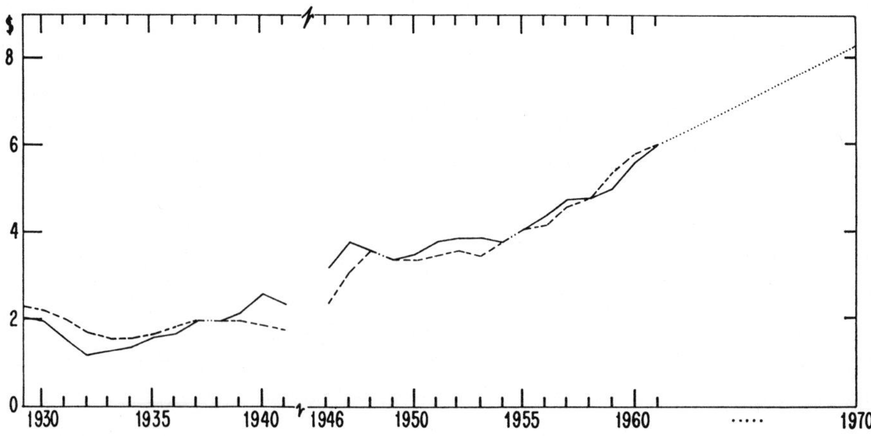


Static model
linear

$$q_t = \underset{(.0001)}{.0011}\, x_t + \underset{(38.12)}{478.99}\,(\text{nonimmigrant aliens admitted per cap.})_t + \underset{(.1157)}{.7185}\, d_t$$

$R^2 = .983 \qquad D.W. = 1.42$

$\kappa = .4569$

| | 1961 level | 1970 projections 4% | | 5% | |
|---|---|---|---|---|---|
| | | I | II | I | II |
| per capita | − $6.01 | − $8.50 | − $8.48 | − $8.62 | − $8.60 |
| aggregate (billions) | | − $1.78 | − $1.77 | − $1.80 | − $1.80 |

There is little that can be said for this category, since it is a balancing item for the rest of the consumption accounts. It is rather surprising that United States consumer expenditure is so important in the explanation of this item; it is perhaps a measure of general world prosperity.

The dynamic model is given below.

$$q_t = \underset{(1.0437)}{.4710} \quad \underset{(.2013)}{1.4164}\, q_{t-1} + \underset{(.0012)}{.0012}\, \Delta x_t - \underset{(.0015)}{.0039}\, x_{t-1} - \underset{(.0130)}{.0402}\, \Delta p_t + \underset{(.0106)}{.0236}\, p_{t-1}$$
$$+ \underset{(.4359)}{1.3166}\, d_t - \underset{(.2755)}{.3097}\, z_t$$

$R^2 = .985 \qquad D.W. = 2.25$

# 5

# *Discussion of the Demand Equations*

This chapter discusses our empirical results and the projections to 1970 from a broader perspective. Of particular interest are the overall success (or lack of it) of the dynamic model, the overall influence of habit formation on consumption, and the general influence of prices. These empirical questions, together with several related issues, are discussed in section I. Section II analyzes in some detail the projections to 1970. Among other things, the budget shares for the projections are computed, and the distribution of these shares is compared to the distribution that prevailed in 1961. In making this comparison we also aggregate the 84 commodity categories into two larger classifications: the twelve-group aggregates (food, clothing, and so on) and the traditional aggregates of durables, nondurables, and services. Section III presents a test of the performance of our equations in forecasting consumption in 1962 and 1963, and section IV contains a comparison with recently published demand studies for six European countries.

## *I. An Overview of the Empirical Results*

One of the most striking results of the investigation is the large number of categories in which the dynamic model gave the best equation. Of the 83 equations, 72 are dynamic. Although this is the expected result, it nevertheless takes on added significance in view of the fact that the nature of the projection exercise precluded complete commitment to the dynamic model.

Another successful aspect of the dynamic model is that the harmful effects of autocorrelation in the error term have for the most part been sidestepped. This is attributable in large part to the superior specification of the dynamic equation, for only 21 of the 72 dynamic equations required 3PLS in estimation. To see that our early fear of facing a major problem of autocorrelation with the static model had substance, we need only note the very low *D.W.*'s for a large majority of the static equations presented in Chapter 4. For the static equations that remain, autocorrelation is still a problem.

In general, the $R^2$'s of the equations are satisfactory, for they are typically very high. Fifty-five of the 83 have $R^2 \geqslant .950$ and 70 have $R^2 \geqslant .900$ (see Table 5.1). For the equations with $q_t$ as the dependent variable, the lowest $R^2$ with the dynamic equation is for item 7.5 ($R^2 = .775$), while the lowest $R^2$ with the static equation is with item 8.3d ($R^2 = .735$). Of the equations with $q_t$ as the dependent variable, these two are the only equations with $R^2 < .800$.

Table 5.1. Summary of the 84 PCE Categories

| Item | Form* | 3PLS† | Stock coefficient | PCE† | Prices† | $R^2$ | $D.W.$ |
|---|---|---|---|---|---|---|---|
| 1.0 | D | | 1.0869 | x | | 0.916 | 1.85 |
| 1.1 | D | | 0.1182 | x | | 0.988 | 1.85 |
| 1.2 | D | | −0.1618 | x | x | 0.974 | 2.30 |
| 1.3 | D | x | −0.2718 | x | | 0.892 | 1.81 |
| 1.4 | DL | | | x | x | 0.965 | 1.50 |
| 1.5 | D | x | 0.1743 | x | | 0.989 | 1.99 |
| 2.1 | L | | | x | x | 0.857 | 1.86 |
| 2.2 | D | x | 0.1923 | x | x | 0.981 | 1.96 |
| 2.3 | D | | −0.2065 | x | | 0.904 | 2.03 |
| 2.4 | | | no equation estimated | | | | |
| 2.5 | D | | 0.0185 | x | x | 0.997 | 2.13 |
| 2.6 | D | | 0.3380 | x | x | 0.916 | 2.33 |
| 2.7 | D | | 0.3888 | x | x | 0.991 | 2.50 |
| 2.8 | D | | −0.0706 | x | | 0.944 | 1.94 |
| 3.1 | D | | 0.5384 | | x | 0.990 | 2.13 |
| 3.2 | D | x | 0.2819 | x | | 0.892 | 1.99 |
| 4.1 | B | x | | x | | 0.999 | 1.46 |
| 4.2 | D | x | 1.6396 | x | | 0.985 | 1.71 |
| 4.3 | D | | 0.2042 | x | | 0.994 | 1.98 |
| 4.4 | B | x | | x | | 0.993 | 2.44 |
| 5.1 | D | | −0.2660 | x | | 0.948 | 2.06 |
| 5.2 | L | | | x | x | 0.965 | 2.00 |
| 5.3 | D | | 0.0669 | x | x | 0.929 | 1.57 |
| 5.4 | D | | −0.0288 | x | | 0.940 | 1.77 |
| 5.5 | D | x | −0.7455 | x | | 0.948 | 1.80 |
| 5.6 | D | | 0.3816 | x | | 0.994 | 1.76 |
| 5.7 | D | | 0.1353 | x | x | 0.991 | 1.32 |
| 5.8a | D | | 1.1332 | x | x | 0.931 | 1.06 |
| 5.8b | B | | | x | | 0.997 | 1.97 |
| 5.8c | D | x | −0.1313 | x | | 0.951 | 1.63 |
| 5.8d | D | x | −0.2277 | x | | 0.835 | 2.19 |
| 5.9 | D | | 0.2453 | x | | 0.733 | 2.02 |
| 5.10 | D | | −0.0306 | x | | 0.952 | 2.17 |
| 5.11 | D | | 0.5875 | x | x | 0.996 | 1.54 |
| 6.1 | D | | 0.4622 | x | | 0.992 | 2.04 |
| 6.2 | D | x | 0.5894 | x | | 0.986 | 1.97 |
| 6.3 | D | | −0.0074 | x | x | 0.983 | 1.97 |
| 6.4 | D | x | 0.2775 | x | | 0.979 | 2.14 |
| 6.5 | D | | 0.9195 | x | | 0.994 | 2.17 |
| 6.6 | D | | 2 | x | | 0.552 | 2.00 |
| 6.7 | D | | 0.3459 | x | x | 0.998 | 2.23 |
| 6.8 | D | | −0.0118 | x | x | 0.946 | 2.28 |
| 7.1 | IL | | | x | x | 0.987 | 1.91 |
| 7.2 | D | x | 0.0071 | x | x | 0.995 | 1.82 |
| 7.3 | D | x | 0.8686 | x | | 0.981 | 1.92 |
| 7.4 | D | | 0.0152 | x | x | 0.914 | 1.89 |
| 7.5 | D | | 0.0085 | x | x | 0.775 | 2.35 |
| 7.6 | D | | 0.3646 | x | x | 0.988 | 1.55 |
| 7.7 | L | | | x | x | 0.948 | 0.51 |

Table 5.1.—*continued*

| Item | Form* | 3PLS† | Stock coefficient | PCE† | Prices† | $R^2$ | *D.W.* |
|---|---|---|---|---|---|---|---|
| 8.1a | D | | −0.5335 | x | x | 0.958 | 1.95 |
| 8.1b | D | | −0.4459 | x | x | 0.977 | 1.84 |
| 8.1c | D | | 0.1195 | x | x | 0.998 | 1.48 |
| 8.1d | D | | 0.2554 | x | x | 0.998 | 1.80 |
| 8.1e | D | | 0.0667 | x | | 0.576 | 1.62 |
| 8.1f | D | | 0.4196 | x | x | 0.987 | 1.32 |
| 8.2a | L | | | x | x | 0.996 | 1.11 |
| 8.2b | D | | −0.0412 | x | x | 0.993 | 1.86 |
| 8.2c | D | x | 0.0411 | | x | 0.983 | 2.03 |
| 8.3a | D | | 0.2772 | | x | 0.948 | 2.15 |
| 8.3b | D | | 2 | x | | 0.669 | 2.16 |
| 8.3c | D | x | 1.9507 | x | x | 0.994 | 2.22 |
| 8.3d | IL | | | x | x | 0.735 | 0.97 |
| 9.1 | D | x | 0.3909 | x | | 0.957 | 1.98 |
| 9.2 | D | | 0 | x | x | 0.564 | 1.95 |
| 9.3 | D | x | 1.3193 | x | x | 0.993 | 2.06 |
| 9.4 | D | x | 0.2028 | x | x | 0.990 | 1.95 |
| 9.5 | D | | 0.0282 | x | x | 0.983 | 2.26 |
| 9.6 | DL | | | x | x | 0.982 | 1.07 |
| 9.7 | D | | 0.3412 | x | x | 0.982 | 2.13 |
| 9.8a | D | | 0.0269 | x | | 0.954 | 2.42 |
| 9.8b | D | | 0.2533 | x | | 0.984 | 1.84 |
| 9.8c | L | | | x | | 0.978 | 1.15 |
| 9.9 | D | | −0.0322 | x | x | 0.954 | 2.09 |
| 9.10 | D | x | 0.3208 | x | x | 0.817 | 2.40 |
| 9.11 | D | | 0.2964 | x | | 0.980 | 2.07 |
| 9.12 | D | | 0.1319 | x | x | 0.986 | 1.89 |
| 10.1 | D | | −2 | x | | 0.260 | 1.67 |
| 10.2 | D | | 1.7203 | x | | 0.974 | 1.67 |
| 10.3 | D | | 0.5068 | x | x | 0.932 | 2.04 |
| 11.0 | D | | −2.2219 | x | | 0.942 | 2.17 |
| 12.1 | D | x | 0.3109 | x | x | 0.972 | 1.67 |
| 12.2 | D | x | 1.6949 | x | | 0.965 | 2.04 |
| 12.3 | IL | | | x | x | 0.964 | 2.16 |
| 12.4 | L | | | x | | 0.983 | 1.42 |

* Definitions of the symbols are:

| | |
|---|---|
| D | dynamic model |
| B | Bergstrom model |
| L | linear static model |
| DL | double-logarithmic static model |
| IL | inverse semi-logarithmic static model |

† An "x" indicates that the equation has the characteristic.

However, high $R^2$'s with time-series data are commonplace, so that this in itself is little reason for self-congratulation. More important in many respects is the statistical significance of the regression coefficients. On this score the overall results must also be termed a success, for in most equations the coefficients of $q_{t-1}$ and $\Delta x_t$ are several times their standard errors, while the coefficient of $\Delta p_t$ is typically $1\frac{1}{2}$ to $2\frac{1}{2}$ times its standard error.

As has been noted, one of the strong features of the dynamic model is that it enables the effect of habit formation to be clearly separated from the effect of inventory adjustment: $\beta > 0$ indicates presence of habit formation, while $\beta < 0$ indicates inventory adjustment. Hence it becomes an interesting exercise to analyze the stock coefficients of the dynamic equations in order to see whether habit formation or inventory adjustment predominates in United States consumption.

A count of signs of the stock coefficient in Table 5.1 shows that 50 are positive, 18 are negative, and 1 is zero.[1] The 50 categories subject to habit formation (by this criterion) accounted for 58.4 percent of total expenditure in 1961 (1954 dollars), while the commodities subject to inventory adjustment accounted for 28.2 percent of total expenditure in 1961. Hence, even after allowing for the 14 categories for which stock coefficients are missing, habit formation quite clearly predominates in United States consumption.

It is difficult to say whether or not this is an expected result. Perhaps the general strength of habit formation is the only surprising result, and not the predominance of habit formation as such. Quite clearly, if income levels are high enough, it is possible for all commodities to become subject to habit formation. Our results indicate that the United States may be well along toward this end.

Clearly the most important factor explaining the pattern of consumption in the United States is total expenditure. PCE is excluded from only three of the 83 categories, namely: 3.1 (toilet articles and preparations), 8.2c (commuting by railway), and 8.3a (intercity railway travel). Of these, only the independence of expenditure on toilet articles and preparations from total expenditure is surprising. Moreover, there are only two categories with negative long-run total-expenditure coefficients. These are 5.8d (other fuel and ice) and 7.1 (brokerage charges and interest, and investment counseling); of these, only 7.1 is the surprise. However, this anomaly may be because banks and mutual investor funds have taken over many of the services previously performed by brokerage houses.

Prices, on the other hand, are much less important than PCE in explaining United States consumption. Of the 83 equations, prices appear in only 45, and they only border on significance in many of these. Moreover, as was noted in Chapter 1, the price coefficients may be biased in a negative direction because of the manner in which the price series are derived. In light of this possible bias, it is interesting to note that, of the 45 categories with prices, 29 are classified as services by the Department of Commerce.

The lack of a strong overall influence of prices is consistent with the predominance of habit formation. Prices should be expected to exert less of an influence on consumption at high levels of income, because income becomes

[1] This makes a total of 69; the other three dynamic equations are the Bergstrom model and thus do not have stock coefficients.

less of a constraining factor and because more commodities become subject to habit formation. It should be an interesting exercise to test the implications of this hypothesis with data for countries with incomes lower than in the United States.[2]

With regard to the influence of other factors on consumption, the stock of automobiles, the stock of television sets, the distribution of income, and several population variables are the most important. As expected, the stock of automobiles typically was found to be important (using the static model) in the categories of the transportation group (Group VIII) and the stock of television sets in the categories of the recreation group (Group IX). The distribution of income was found to exert some influence on owner-occupied and rental housing, domestic services, and several of the categories in recreation. Finally, the influence of population in one form or another was found to be important in the use of tobacco, in the utilities, in purchases of toys, and in expenditures on education.

Before moving on to the projections, we should point out that, while we are satisfied in general with the set of equations, there are several equations that leave much to be desired. The equations for 3.1, 5.4, 5.10, 7.4, 7.5, 10.1, and 11.0 clearly fall into this category. Many reasons for the poor quality of these equations can be advanced, but in the end we must acknowledge the fact that our dynamic theory itself is only a modest step forward.

## *II. An Overview of the Projections for 1970*

Since the object of the investigation was to provide several sets of projections for 1970, it is appropriate that we devote this section to an analysis of our projections. The analysis so far has been entirely in real terms (1954 dollars); but in many respects the projections in current dollars are of more interest. By multiplying the projections by their respective relative prices in 1970, we can put the projections into 1970 dollars deflated by the aggregate deflator for 1970 (with 1954 = 100). The budget shares will then be in terms of current 1970 dollars. It is not necessary to do this for the second set of relative prices, because they are identical with the 1961 relative prices.

The four sets of projections in 1970 in both per capita and aggregate terms, together with the projections in current relative prices for the first set of prices and the 4 percent and 5 percent growth rates, are tabulated in Table 5.2.

We mentioned at the end of Chapter 1 that a good deal of emphasis was given to the projections in selecting the equations. Hence, on the whole, we are satisfied with the projections. We might note, however, that the projections of $88 and $94 per capita (in 1954 dollars) for 8.1a (new cars and net

[2] Taylor (1964) has found in a similar study of 64 categories of consumption in Sweden, 1931–1958, that prices are much more important and that inventory adjustment predominates.

purchases of used cars) may be too low in view of the fact that in 1955—the best automobile year prior to 1961—there were expenditures of over $93 per capita. If the economy is to be in full employment in 1970 (as is the assumption), expenditures on cars may have to be greater than the 1955 level. Similarly, in light of recent innovations in air travel, the projections for 8.3c also appear too low, though in this instance (unlike cars) there is a less compelling reason for believing them to be higher.

Table 5.2. Personal Consumption Expenditure Projections in 1970

| | Per capita in 1954 dollars | | | | | Per capita in current relative prices* | | | Total in billions of 1954 dollars | | | |
|---|---|---|---|---|---|---|---|---|---|---|---|---|
| | | 4% Growth | | 5% Growth | | | 4% Growth | 5% Growth | 4% Growth | | 5% Growth | |
| Item | 1961 | Price set I† | Price set II | Price set I | Price set II | 1961 | Price set I | Price set I | Price set I | Price set II | Price set I | Price set II |
| 1.0 | 53.24 | 57.69 | 57.90 | 59.84 | 60.06 | 50.58 | 50.58 | 52.54 | 12.05 | 12.10 | 12.50 | 12.55 |
| 1.1 | 286.05 | 334.87 | 332.62 | 349.20 | 346.93 | 271.75 | 308.42 | 321.61 | 69.96 | 69.49 | 72.96 | 72.48 |
| 1.2 | 59.77 | 66.55 | 73.71 | 71.55 | 78.70 | 61.74 | 74.74 | 80.35 | 13.90 | 15.40 | 14.95 | 16.44 |
| 1.3 | 7.71 | 10.31 | 10.23 | 10.85 | 10.76 | 6.36 | 8.09 | 8.52 | 2.15 | 2.14 | 2.27 | 2.25 |
| 1.4 | 6.10 | 4.01 | 3.76 | 4.10 | 3.85 | 5.43 | 3.06 | 3.13 | 0.84 | 0.79 | 0.86 | 0.80 |
| 1.5 | 35.89 | 44.47 | 44.12 | 46.64 | 46.29 | 37.29 | 48.16 | 50.51 | 9.29 | 9.22 | 9.74 | 9.67 |
| 2.1 | 19.99 | 23.98 | 23.91 | 27.32 | 27.25 | 21.71 | 27.24 | 31.04 | 5.01 | 5.00 | 5.71 | 5.67 |
| 2.2 | 1.13 | 1.11 | 1.30 | 1.20 | 1.40 | 1.30 | 1.38 | 1.49 | 0.23 | 0.27 | 0.25 | 0.29 |
| 2.3 | 123.98 | 140.46 | 139.49 | 146.62 | 145.64 | 118.03 | 123.60 | 129.03 | 29.35 | 29.14 | 30.63 | 30.43 |
| 2.4 | 0.28 | 0.24 | 0.24 | 0.24 | 0.24 | 0.26 | 0.21 | 0.21 | 0.05 | 0.05 | 0.05 | 0.05 |
| 2.5 | 9.54 | 9.66 | 9.63 | 10.25 | 10.21 | 9.89 | 10.22 | 10.84 | 2.01 | 2.01 | 2.14 | 2.13 |
| 2.6 | 3.84 | 2.92 | 4.06 | 3.93 | 5.07 | 4.28 | 3.56 | 4.79 | 0.61 | 0.85 | 0.82 | 1.06 |
| 2.7 | 13.24 | 17.22 | 16.29 | 18.32 | 17.40 | 10.67 | 11.19 | 11.91 | 3.59 | 3.40 | 3.83 | 3.64 |
| 2.8 | 2.83 | 3.49 | 3.46 | 3.71 | 3.68 | 2.86 | 3.48 | 3.70 | 0.73 | 0.72 | 0.78 | 0.77 |
| 3.1 | 15.31 | 28.93 | 28.83 | 28.93 | 28.83 | 15.37 | 28.93 | 28.93 | 6.04 | 6.02 | 6.04 | 6.02 |
| 3.2 | 11.53 | 14.66 | 14.49 | 15.75 | 15.58 | 12.99 | 17.93 | 19.26 | 3.06 | 3.03 | 3.29 | 3.26 |
| 4.1 | 137.84 | 178.42 | 177.56 | 183.89 | 183.02 | 138.67 | 176.81 | 182.23 | 37.28 | 37.10 | 38.42 | 38.24 |
| 4.2 | 58.57 | 65.76 | 65.48 | 67.51 | 67.23 | 58.92 | 65.17 | 66.90 | 13.74 | 13.68 | 14.10 | 14.05 |
| 4.3 | 10.73 | 12.29 | 12.29 | 12.34 | 12.34 | 9.83 | 10.68 | 10.72 | 2.57 | 2.57 | 2.57 | 2.57 |
| 4.4 | 6.17 | 6.48 | 6.43 | 6.80 | 6.75 | 6.80 | 7.45 | 7.82 | 1.35 | 1.34 | 1.42 | 1.41 |
| 5.1 | 24.93 | 32.30 | 31.89 | 34.92 | 34.50 | 23.33 | 28.75 | 31.08 | 6.75 | 6.66 | 7.30 | 7.21 |
| 5.2 | 30.72 | 38.77 | 37.72 | 41.26 | 40.21 | 26.48 | 31.02 | 33.01 | 8.10 | 7.88 | 8.62 | 8.40 |
| 5.3 | 9.43 | 11.35 | 12.01 | 12.06 | 12.72 | 10.72 | 13.67 | 14.52 | 2.37 | 2.51 | 2.52 | 2.66 |
| 5.4 | 18.68 | 22.11 | 21.68 | 24.85 | 24.41 | 18.33 | 21.45 | 24.10 | 4.61 | 4.53 | 5.19 | 5.10 |
| 5.5 | 16.45 | 17.57 | 17.43 | 18.45 | 18.31 | 15.36 | 15.00 | 15.76 | 3.67 | 3.64 | 3.85 | 3.83 |
| 5.6 | 17.12 | 20.86 | 20.61 | 22.41 | 22.17 | 16.95 | 20.90 | 22.45 | 4.36 | 4.31 | 4.68 | 4.63 |
| 5.7 | 4.92 | 6.36 | 6.33 | 6.88 | 6.86 | 5.32 | 7.09 | 7.66 | 1.33 | 1.32 | 1.44 | 1.43 |
| 5.8a | 30.59 | 50.64 | 50.30 | 51.73 | 51.39 | 24.99 | 35.45 | 36.21 | 10.58 | 10.51 | 10.81 | 10.74 |
| 5.8b | 15.98 | 22.89 | 22.74 | 23.82 | 23.67 | 16.46 | 24.13 | 25.11 | 4.78 | 4.75 | 4.98 | 4.95 |
| 5.8c | 5.36 | 5.68 | 5.64 | 5.91 | 5.87 | 6.41 | 7.75 | 8.07 | 1.19 | 1.18 | 1.23 | 1.23 |
| 5.8d | 17.43 | 15.66 | 15.57 | 16.19 | 16.10 | 17.50 | 15.50 | 16.03 | 3.27 | 3.25 | 3.38 | 3.36 |
| 5.9 | 23.77 | 35.55 | 35.35 | 36.82 | 36.62 | 22.39 | 34.84 | 36.08 | 7.43 | 7.39 | 7.69 | 7.65 |
| 5.10 | 16.70 | 19.98 | 19.54 | 22.67 | 22.24 | 18.44 | 24.64 | 27.95 | 4.17 | 4.08 | 4.73 | 4.65 |
| 5.11 | 10.69 | 13.39 | 13.39 | 14.35 | 14.34 | 11.30 | 14.92 | 15.99 | 2.80 | 2.80 | 3.00 | 3.00 |
| 6.1 | 19.76 | 28.05 | 27.74 | 30.01 | 29.70 | 19.66 | 28.47 | 30.46 | 5.86 | 5.80 | 6.27 | 6.21 |
| 6.2 | 5.88 | 7.44 | 7.34 | 8.07 | 7.97 | 6.12 | 7.63 | 8.27 | 1.55 | 1.53 | 1.69 | 1.67 |
| 6.3 | 22.15 | 26.03 | 27.05 | 26.60 | 27.62 | 25.45 | 33.16 | 33.89 | 5.44 | 5.65 | 5.56 | 5.77 |
| 6.4 | 9.71 | 12.03 | 11.92 | 12.69 | 12.59 | 10.20 | 13.25 | 13.97 | 2.51 | 2.49 | 2.65 | 2.63 |
| 6.5 | 4.08 | 4.50 | 4.48 | 4.65 | 4.63 | 4.59 | 5.40 | 5.58 | 0.94 | 0.94 | 0.97 | 0.97 |
| 6.6 | 24.25 | 34.62 | 34.53 | 35.24 | 35.14 | 27.69 | 44.35 | 45.14 | 7.23 | 7.21 | 7.36 | 7.34 |
| 6.7 | 11.01 | 16.36 | 16.00 | 16.82 | 16.46 | 8.04 | 9.82 | 10.09 | 3.42 | 3.34 | 3.51 | 3.44 |
| 6.8 | 6.98 | 7.24 | 7.61 | 7.74 | 8.12 | 8.21 | 9.20 | 9.84 | 1.51 | 1.59 | 1.62 | 1.70 |
| 7.1 | 3.69 | 3.14 | 3.45 | 2.77 | 3.05 | 5.89 | 5.53 | 4.88 | 0.66 | 0.72 | 0.58 | 0.64 |

Table 5.2—*continued*

| | Per capita in 1954 dollars | | | | | Per capita in current relative prices* | | | Total in billions of 1954 dollars | | | |
|---|---|---|---|---|---|---|---|---|---|---|---|---|
| | | 4% Growth | | 5% Growth | | | 4% Growth | 5% Growth | 4% Growth | | 5% Growth | |
| Item | 1961 | Price set I† | Price set II | Price set I | Price set II | 1961 | Price set I | Price set I | Price set I | Price set II | Price set I | Price set II |
| 7.2 | 3.53 | 4.32 | 4.44 | 4.36 | 4.49 | 4.35 | 5.78 | 5.83 | 0.90 | 0.93 | 0.91 | 0.94 |
| 7.3 | 21.89 | 24.36 | 24.14 | 25.75 | 25.53 | 25.50 | 34.49 | 36.46 | 5.09 | 5.04 | 5.38 | 5.33 |
| 7.4 | 21.31 | 25.88 | 26.97 | 25.88 | 26.97 | 23.80 | 31.73 | 31.73 | 5.41 | 5.63 | 5.41 | 5.63 |
| 7.5 | 7.05 | 7.55 | 8.13 | 7.74 | 8.33 | 8.98 | 7.54 | 7.73 | 1.58 | 1.70 | 1.62 | 1.74 |
| 7.6 | 32.29 | 47.75 | 47.30 | 51.39 | 50.94 | 32.13 | 51.47 | 55.40 | 9.98 | 9.88 | 10.74 | 10.64 |
| 7.7 | 5.01 | 5.41 | 5.41 | 5.66 | 5.65 | 5.28 | 5.89 | 6.16 | 1.13 | 1.13 | 1.18 | 1.18 |
| 8.1a | 67.03 | 87.79 | 88.15 | 94.42 | 94.77 | 67.83 | 63.82 | 68.64 | 18.34 | 18.42 | 19.73 | 19.80 |
| 8.1b | 17.20 | 19.83 | 19.25 | 20.99 | 20.41 | 14.45 | 14.42 | 15.26 | 4.14 | 4.02 | 4.39 | 4.26 |
| 8.1c | 24.25 | 28.31 | 28.36 | 29.88 | 29.93 | 26.07 | 31.74 | 33.50 | 5.91 | 5.93 | 6.24 | 6.25 |
| 8.1d | 58.37 | 73.59 | 72.93 | 76.98 | 76.32 | 58.19 | 72.41 | 75.75 | 15.38 | 15.24 | 16.01 | 15.95 |
| 8.1e | 1.67 | 2.84 | 2.83 | 2.92 | 2.91 | 1.50 | 2.21 | 2.27 | 0.59 | 0.59 | 0.61 | 0.61 |
| 8.1f | 8.58 | 11.63 | 11.53 | 12.47 | 12.38 | 9.33 | 12.72 | 13.64 | 2.43 | 2.41 | 2.61 | 2.59 |
| 8.2a | 5.09 | 3.52 | 4.52 | 5.30 | 6.30 | 6.05 | 4.58 | 6.89 | 0.74 | 0.94 | 1.11 | 1.32 |
| 8.2b | 2.71 | 2.28 | 2.28 | 2.43 | 2.43 | 2.95 | 2.55 | 2.72 | 0.48 | 0.48 | 0.51 | 0.51 |
| 8.2c | 0.44 | 0.18 | 0.48 | 0.18 | 0.48 | 0.48 | 0.31 | 0.31 | 0.04 | 0.10 | 0.04 | 0.10 |
| 8.3a | 1.53 | 1.28 | 1.49 | 1.28 | 1.49 | 1.61 | 1.41 | 1.41 | 0.27 | 0.31 | 0.27 | 0.31 |
| 8.3b | 1.32 | 2.35 | 2.29 | 2.72 | 2.66 | 1.57 | 3.14 | 3.63 | 0.49 | 0.48 | 0.57 | 0.56 |
| 8.3c | 4.32 | 5.63 | 5.62 | 5.75 | 5.74 | 4.44 | 5.91 | 6.04 | 1.18 | 1.17 | 1.20 | 1.20 |
| 8.3d | 0.12 | 0.13 | 0.12 | 0.15 | 0.15 | 0.11 | 0.11 | 0.13 | 0.03 | 0.03 | 0.03 | 0.03 |
| 9.1 | 7.49 | 7.87 | 7.78 | 8.42 | 8.33 | 8.44 | 10.09 | 10.79 | 1.64 | 1.63 | 1.76 | 1.74 |
| 9.2 | 11.02 | 12.16 | 12.12 | 12.58 | 12.54 | 12.42 | 15.58 | 16.11 | 2.54 | 2.53 | 2.63 | 2.62 |
| 9.3 | 13.39 | 16.25 | 15.48 | 17.22 | 16.46 | 12.84 | 14.74 | 15.62 | 3.40 | 3.23 | 3.60 | 3.44 |
| 9.4 | 11.31 | 14.76 | 14.50 | 15.68 | 15.42 | 10.63 | 13.49 | 14.33 | 3.08 | 3.03 | 3.28 | 3.22 |
| 9.5 | 20.60 | 25.90 | 25.33 | 27.85 | 27.28 | 18.70 | 22.82 | 24.54 | 5.41 | 5.29 | 5.82 | 5.70 |
| 9.6 | 3.66 | 4.79 | 5.29 | 5.38 | 5.94 | 4.14 | 6.08 | 6.83 | 1.00 | 1.10 | 1.12 | 1.24 |
| 9.7 | 5.91 | 7.74 | 7.46 | 8.43 | 8.15 | 5.18 | 6.19 | 6.74 | 1.62 | 1.56 | 1.76 | 1.70 |
| 9.8a | 5.52 | 6.73 | 6.58 | 7.68 | 7.53 | 6.71 | 9.32 | 10.64 | 1.41 | 1.37 | 1.60 | 1.57 |
| 9.8b | 1.67 | 2.04 | 2.02 | 2.17 | 2.15 | 1.97 | 2.65 | 2.82 | 0.43 | 0.42 | 0.45 | 0.45 |
| 9.8c | 1.39 | 1.79 | 1.77 | 1.92 | 1.90 | 1.37 | 1.71 | 1.83 | 0.37 | 0.37 | 0.40 | 0.40 |
| 9.9 | 3.65 | 3.66 | 3.72 | 3.75 | 3.82 | 3.92 | 4.15 | 4.25 | 0.76 | 0.78 | 0.78 | 0.80 |
| 9.10 | 4.31 | 5.32 | 5.83 | 5.96 | 6.48 | 5.11 | 7.30 | 8.18 | 1.11 | 1.22 | 1.25 | 1.35 |
| 9.11 | 2.42 | 3.29 | 3.25 | 3.57 | 3.53 | 2.56 | 3.68 | 4.00 | 0.69 | 0.68 | 0.75 | 0.74 |
| 9.12 | 6.23 | 7.87 | 8.02 | 8.57 | 8.72 | 6.85 | 9.37 | 10.21 | 1.69 | 1.68 | 1.79 | 1.82 |
| 10.1 | 9.99 | 16.95 | 16.85 | 17.56 | 17.46 | 11.81 | 22.93 | 23.76 | 3.54 | 3.52 | 3.67 | 3.65 |
| 10.2 | 6.81 | 9.09 | 8.97 | 9.84 | 9.72 | 8.71 | 14.37 | 15.56 | 1.90 | 1.87 | 2.06 | 2.03 |
| 10.3 | 4.07 | 5.51 | 5.76 | 6.00 | 6.24 | 4.51 | 6.76 | 7.36 | 1.15 | 1.20 | 1.25 | 1.30 |
| 11.0 | 23.23 | 31.64 | 31.31 | 33.70 | 33.37 | 24.35 | 34.36 | 36.60 | 6.61 | 6.54 | 7.04 | 6.97 |
| 12.1 | 12.48 | 20.65 | 19.90 | 21.89 | 21.13 | 11.42 | 17.59 | 18.65 | 4.31 | 4.16 | 4.57 | 4.41 |
| 12.2 | 7.45 | 10.73 | 10.59 | 11.67 | 11.52 | 6.88 | 9.12 | 9.92 | 2.24 | 2.21 | 2.44 | 2.41 |
| 12.3 | 1.43 | 1.44 | 1.35 | 1.65 | 1.54 | 1.40 | 1.37 | 1.57 | 0.30 | 0.28 | 0.34 | 0.32 |
| 12.4 | −6.01 | −8.50 | −8.48 | −8.62 | −8.60 | −5.31 | −7.48 | −7.59 | −1.78 | −1.77 | −1.80 | −1.80 |

* The projections in current relative prices are obtained by multiplying the projections in 1954 dollars by their respective projected relative price in 1970.

† The roman numerals refer to the two sets of relative prices projected in 1970. These prices are tabulated in Table 4.1 (Chapter 4).

On the other hand, the projections for 5.8a (electricity) of about $50 per capita (in 1954 dollars) may seem too large an increase from $30.59 per capita in 1961. However, as can be seen in the graph for that item, there has been a very strong trend in electricity consumption since 1929, and the projections do not appear to be out of line with this trend. Also, it should be noted that the projected increase in current dollars is much smaller.

Though there are a few exceptions, the projections generally are insensitive to prices. The most noteworthy exceptions are 1.2 (purchased meals), 1.4 (food produced and consumed on farms), 2.6 (laundering in establishments), 8.2a (street and electric railway and local bus), and 8.2c (commuting by railway). Of these, the largest dollar change (in 1954 dollars) is with 1.2 ($1.5 billion for both growth rates), while the largest percentage change is with 8.2c (150 percent for both growth rates).

Another interesting exercise is to compare the distribution of budget shares in 1961 with its projection in 1970. This has been done for the projections for the first set of prices and the 4 percent growth rate. The results, in both constant and current dollars, are tabulated in Table 5.3.

Table 5.3. Distribution of Total Personal Consumption Expenditures (Budget Shares)*

| | 1954 dollars | | Current dollars | |
|---|---|---|---|---|
| Item | 1961 | 1970 | 1961 | 1970 |
| 1.0 | .0283 | .0322 | .0252 | .0306 |
| 1.1 | .1643 | .1728 | .1533 | .1643 |
| 1.2 | .0326 | .0361 | .0372 | .0373 |
| 1.3 | .0051 | .0047 | .0040 | .0038 |
| 1.4 | .0020 | .0037 | .0015 | .0033 |
| 1.5 | .0218 | .0218 | .0239 | .0225 |
| 2.1 | .0118 | .0121 | .0135 | .0131 |
| 2.2 | .0005 | .0007 | .0007 | .0008 |
| 2.3 | .0689 | .0749 | .0615 | .0714 |
| 2.4 | .0001 | .0002 | .0001 | .0002 |
| 2.5 | .0047 | .0058 | .0051 | .0060 |
| 2.6 | .0014 | .0023 | .0018 | .0026 |
| 2.7 | .0084 | .0080 | .0056 | .0065 |
| 2.8 | .0017 | .0017 | .0017 | .0017 |
| 3.1 | .0142 | .0092 | .0144 | .0093 |
| 3.2 | .0072 | .0070 | .0089 | .0079 |
| 4.1 | .0875 | .0832 | .0879 | .0838 |
| 4.2 | .0323 | .0354 | .0324 | .0356 |
| 4.3 | .0060 | .0065 | .0053 | .0059 |
| 4.4 | .0032 | .0037 | .0037 | .0041 |
| 5.1 | .0158 | .0151 | .0143 | .0141 |
| 5.2 | .0190 | .0186 | .0154 | .0160 |
| 5.3 | .0056 | .0056 | .0068 | .0065 |
| 5.4 | .0108 | .0113 | .0107 | .0111 |
| 5.5 | .0086 | .0099 | .0075 | .0093 |
| 5.6 | .0102 | .0103 | .0104 | .0102 |
| 5.7 | .0031 | .0030 | .0035 | .0032 |

* The 1970 budget shares are based on the projections from the first set of prices and the 4 percent growth rate.

Table 5.3—*continued*

| Item | 1954 dollars | | Current dollars | |
|---|---|---|---|---|
| | 1961 | 1970 | 1961 | 1970 |
| 5.8a | .0248 | .0185 | .0176 | .0151 |
| 5.8b | .0112 | .0097 | .0120 | .0100 |
| 5.8c | .0028 | .0032 | .0039 | .0039 |
| 5.8d | .0077 | .0105 | .0077 | .0106 |
| 5.9 | .0174 | .0144 | .0173 | .0135 |
| 5.10 | .0098 | .0101 | .0123 | .0112 |
| 5.11 | .0066 | .0065 | .0074 | .0068 |
| 6.1 | .0138 | .0119 | .0142 | .0119 |
| 6.2 | .0037 | .0036 | .0038 | .0037 |
| 6.3 | .0128 | .0134 | .0165 | .0154 |
| 6.4 | .0059 | .0059 | .0066 | .0062 |
| 6.5 | .0022 | .0025 | .0027 | .0028 |
| 6.6 | .0170 | .0146 | .0221 | .0167 |
| 6.7 | .0080 | .0066 | .0049 | .0049 |
| 6.8 | .0036 | .0042 | .0046 | .0050 |
| 7.1 | .0015 | .0022 | .0027 | .0036 |
| 7.2 | .0021 | .0021 | .0029 | .0026 |
| 7.3 | .0120 | .0132 | .0171 | .0154 |
| 7.4 | .0127 | .0129 | .0158 | .0144 |
| 7.5 | .0037 | .0043 | .0037 | .0054 |
| 7.6 | .0234 | .0195 | .0256 | .0194 |
| 7.7 | .0027 | .0030 | .0029 | .0032 |
| 8.1a | .0431 | .0405 | .0317 | .0410 |
| 8.1b | .0097 | .0104 | .0072 | .0087 |
| 8.1c | .0139 | .0146 | .0158 | .0158 |
| 8.1d | .0361 | .0353 | .0360 | .0352 |
| 8.1e | .0014 | .0010 | .0011 | .0009 |
| 8.1f | .0057 | .0052 | .0063 | .0056 |
| 8.2a | .0017 | .0031 | .0023 | .0037 |
| 8.2b | .0011 | .0016 | .0013 | .0018 |
| 8.2c | .0001 | .0003 | .0002 | .0003 |
| 8.3a | .0006 | .0009 | .0007 | .0010 |
| 8.3b | .0012 | .0008 | .0016 | .0009 |
| 8.3c | .0028 | .0026 | .0029 | .0027 |
| 8.3d | .0001 | .0001 | .0001 | .0001 |
| 9.1 | .0039 | .0045 | .0050 | .0051 |
| 9.2 | .0060 | .0067 | .0077 | .0075 |
| 9.3 | .0080 | .0081 | .0073 | .0078 |
| 9.4 | .0072 | .0068 | .0067 | .0064 |
| 9.5 | .0127 | .0124 | .0113 | .0113 |
| 9.6 | .0023 | .0022 | .0030 | .0025 |
| 9.7 | .0038 | .0036 | .0031 | .0031 |
| 9.8a | .0033 | .0033 | .0046 | .0041 |
| 9.8b | .0010 | .0010 | .0013 | .0012 |
| 9.8c | .0009 | .0008 | .0009 | .0008 |
| 9.9 | .0018 | .0022 | .0021 | .0024 |
| 9.10 | .0026 | .0026 | .0036 | .0031 |
| 9.11 | .0016 | .0015 | .0018 | .0015 |

Table 5.3—*continued*

| Item | 1954 dollars | | Current dollars | |
|---|---|---|---|---|
| | 1961 | 1970 | 1961 | 1970 |
| 9.12 | .0039 | .0038 | .0047 | .0041 |
| 10.1 | .0083 | .0060 | .0114 | .0071 |
| 10.2 | .0045 | .0041 | .0071 | .0053 |
| 10.3 | .0027 | .0025 | .0034 | .0027 |
| 11.0 | .0155 | .0140 | .0171 | .0147 |
| 12.1 | .0101 | .0075 | .0087 | .0069 |
| 12.2 | .0053 | .0045 | .0045 | .0042 |
| 12.3 | .0007 | .0009 | .0007 | .0008 |
| 12.4 | −.0042 | −.0036 | −.0037 | −.0032 |

The distribution of budget shares for the projections in 1970 does not appear to reveal any inconsistencies that have so far escaped attention. For the most part, the projected distribution in 1970 is not greatly different from what it was in 1961 in both constant and current dollars. In keeping with Engel's law, the shares for the major food items (1.1 and 1.2) decrease, as do the shares for clothing (2.3). The most significant increases are for 3.1 (toilet articles and preparations), the utilities (5.8a [electricity], 5.8b [gas], and 5.9 [telephone and telegraph]), and 7.6 (interest on personal debt). However, the increase in the share for 5.8a is smaller in current than in constant dollars. It is also interesting to note that, while the share for 4.1 (space rental value of owner-occupied housing) increases, this increase is largely offset by a decrease in the share for 4.2 (space rental value of tenant-occupied housing). Together these two housing items will continue to account for about 12 percent of total expenditure in 1970 (in both constant and current dollars).

The next part of our analysis involves aggregating the projections into the twelve large categories of consumption defined by the Department of Commerce: (I) food and tobacco; (II) clothing, accessories, and jewelry; (III) personal care; (IV) housing; (V) household operation; (VI) medical care and death expenses; (VII) personal business; (VIII) transportation; (IX) recreation; (X) private education and research; (XI) religious and welfare activities; (XII) foreign travel and remittances—net. The projected budget shares for these twelve groups for the first set of prices and both growth rates, together with the budget shares in 1961, are given in Table 5.4.

In keeping with our previous finding for the major food items, we see that the most significant change in budget shares is the share for food and tobacco (Group I). It is projected at about $25\frac{1}{2}$ percent of total expenditure (in 1954 dollars), down from 27.1 percent in 1961. The share for clothing, accessories, and jewelry (Group II) is the only other group to show a noticeable decline in 1970, while the shares for personal care (Group III), housing operation (Group V), medical and death expenses (Group VI), private education and

Table 5.4. Distribution of Total Personal Consumption Expenditures (Budget Shares)*

| | 1954 dollars | | | Current dollars | | |
|---|---|---|---|---|---|---|
| | 1961 | 1970 | | 1961 | 1970 | |
| Group | | 4% | 5% | | 4% | 5% |
| I | .2710 | .2541 | .2563 | .2619 | .2452 | .2440 |
| II | .1056 | .0977 | .0974 | .1022 | .0899 | .0911 |
| III | .0162 | .0214 | .0213 | .0171 | .0233 | .0234 |
| IV | .1288 | .1290 | .1285 | .1295 | .1293 | .1264 |
| V | .1466 | .1536 | .1522 | .1415 | .1467 | .1483 |
| VI | .0627 | .0669 | .0671 | .0665 | .0752 | .0742 |
| VII | .0572 | .0581 | .0588 | .0641 | .0708 | .0700 |
| VIII | .1163 | .1174 | .1177 | .1177 | .1071 | .1087 |
| IX | .0595 | .0590 | .0585 | .0610 | .0632 | .0646 |
| X | .0126 | .0155 | .0155 | .0151 | .0219 | .0220 |
| XI | .0140 | .0155 | .0154 | .0147 | .0171 | .0173 |
| XII | .0093 | .0119 | .0115 | .0087 | .0102 | .0106 |

* The 1970 budget shares are based on the projections from the first set of prices.

research (Group X), religious and welfare activities (Group XI), and the foreign sector (Group XII) show moderate increases. The projected shares of the remaining groups, housing (Group IV), personal business (Group VII), and transportation (Group VIII), are about the same as they were in 1961.

In current dollars, the picture is generally the same as for constant dollars. However, transportation (Group VIII) shows a decline of about 1 percent from its 1961 budget share, while the share for personal business (Group VII) is projected to increase about .5 percent.

A salient feature of Table 5.4 is the finding that the projected budget shares are generally insensitive to the growth rate in GNP. The projected shares in constant dollars are virtually the same for the 4 percent and 5 percent growth rates, while the projected shares in current dollars differ only slightly. But it would have been more meaningful in this context to have used more disparate growth rates, say 3 percent and 6 percent.

The final step in the analysis of this section is to aggregate the projections into the traditional categories of durables, nondurables, and services (according to the definitions of the Department of Commerce), and then to compute the budget shares. These results are tabulated in Table 5.5. A glance at the table shows that since 1954 the budget share (in 1954 dollars) of durables has been roughly constant at about 13.6 percent, while the shares for services has been increasing at the expense of nondurables. The projections for 1970 are in keeping with this historical experience, though the increase in the relative share for services is slowed down somewhat.

Table 5.5. Distribution of Total Personal Consumption Expenditures (Budget Shares)*

| | 1954 dollars | | | | | | | Current dollars | | |
|---|---|---|---|---|---|---|---|---|---|---|
| | | | | | | 1970 | | | 1970 | |
| Category | 1954 | 1956 | 1958 | 1960 | 1961 | 4% | 5% | 1961 | 4% | 5% |
| Durables | .136 | .144 | .130 | .142 | .137 | .140 | .138 | .130 | .119 | .121 |
| Nondurables | .501 | .493 | .488 | .474 | .471 | .452 | .452 | .459 | .437 | .436 |
| Services | .363 | .363 | .382 | .384 | .392 | .408 | .410 | .411 | .445 | .443 |

* The 1970 budget shares are based on the projections from the first set of prices.

## *III. Personal Consumption Expenditures for 1962 and 1963*

Just before press time, data for 1962 and 1963 became available for the 84 PCE categories. Since the only true test of an econometric model is to confront it with new data, it is a useful exercise to compare the projections for 1962 and 1963 with the actual values for those years.

The procedure is plagued from the outset by an annoying problem, however, because the data for 1960 and 1961 that are consistent with the data for 1962 and 1963 are not the same data used in estimating the regression equations.[3] The correct procedure would be to re-estimate the equations with the revised data. But this seems ill advised in view of the fact that the PCE data from 1954 on are being revised again to 1958 Census of Manufactures benchmarks. Accordingly, we have used the revised data with the original equations. This amounts to assuming that the revisions in the 1960 and 1961 data do not affect the slope coefficients.

Current dollar data for PCE for 1960, 1961, 1962, and 1963 are available in the July 1964 *Survey of Current Business*; constant dollar data were made available to us on worksheets by the Office of Business Economics. The relative prices were obtained by dividing the current dollar by the constant dollar data, dividing by the overall PCE deflator, and then multiplying by 100. Data for the other independent variables are available in the sources listed in the Data Sources.

Table 5.6 tabulates the predicted and actual values for 1962 and 1963. We have made the predictions for 1963 in two ways. The first way is to predict 1963 using the predicted values for 1962. This would be the procedure if total PCE for 1962 and 1963 were known at the time of prediction but not

[3] Data revisions, of course, are not a problem peculiar to our study. Much econometric work can never be adequately tested because of subsequent data revisions. Anyone who, in the 1970s, wanted to test our projections for 1970 (assuming that the underlying assumptions concerning total expenditure, relative prices, etc., are accurate) would probably have to start by recomputing our equations from the revised data for 1929–1961 then available. It will be interesting to see if these revised data give a better fit than the data we have used. If past experience is any guide, they probably will.

Table 5.6. 1962 and 1963 PCE Predictions (1954 dollars)

| Item | 1961 level | 1962 Level | | 1963 Level* | | | 1962 Change | | 1963 Change* | | |
|---|---|---|---|---|---|---|---|---|---|---|---|
| | | Actual | Predicted | Actual | Predicted (1) | Predicted (2) | Actual | Predicted | Actual | Predicted (1) | Predicted (2) |
| 1.0 | $53.23 | $54.14 | $53.25 | $54.77 | $53.72 | $54.06 | $ 0.91 | $0.02 | $0.63 | $0.47 | $−0.08 |
| 1.1 | 286.65 | 291.40 | 295.31 | 291.15 | 301.46 | 299.18 | 4.75 | 8.66 | −0.25 | 6.15 | 7.78 |
| 1.2 | 59.70 | 60.18 | 59.39 | 60.27 | 59.16 | 59.77 | 0.48 | −0.31 | 0.09 | −0.23 | −0.41 |
| 1.3 | 7.71 | 7.98 | 8.64 | 7.78 | 9.14 | 8.81 | 0.27 | 0.93 | −0.20 | 0.51 | 0.83 |
| 1.4 | 6.07 | 5.32 | 5.90 | 5.03 | 5.30 | 5.30 | −0.75 | −0.17 | −0.29 | −0.61 | −0.02 |
| 1.5 | 35.91 | 35.76 | 36.91 | 36.24 | 37.57 | 36.32 | −0.15 | 1.00 | 0.48 | 0.66 | 0.56 |
| 2.1 | 20.04 | 20.70 | 20.79 | 20.18 | 20.88 | 20.91 | 0.66 | 0.75 | −0.52 | 0.09 | 0.21 |
| 2.2 | 1.13 | 1.16 | 1.20 | 1.16 | 1.22 | 1.19 | 0.03 | 0.07 | 0.00 | 0.03 | 0.03 |
| 2.3 | 124.29 | 126.20 | 127.64 | 127.19 | 129.34 | 128.50 | 1.91 | 3.35 | 0.99 | 1.70 | 2.30 |
| 2.4 | 0.28 | 0.34 | 0.24 | 0.31 | 0.24 | 0.24 | 0.06 | −0.04 | −0.03 | 0.00 | −0.10 |
| 2.5 | 10.06 | 10.26 | 10.15 | 10.38 | 10.13 | 10.25 | 0.20 | 0.09 | 0.12 | −0.02 | −0.01 |
| 2.6 | 4.05 | 3.96 | 4.11 | 3.87 | 4.18 | 4.03 | −0.09 | 0.06 | −0.09 | 0.07 | 0.07 |
| 2.7 | 13.02 | 13.24 | 13.51 | 13.78 | 14.00 | 13.86 | 0.22 | 0.49 | 0.54 | 0.49 | 0.62 |
| 2.8 | 2.82 | 2.67 | 2.90 | 2.74 | 2.94 | 2.77 | −0.15 | 0.08 | 0.07 | 0.04 | 0.10 |
| 3.1 | 15.34 | 15.85 | 16.21 | 16.39 | 17.22 | 16.83 | 0.51 | 0.87 | 0.54 | 1.01 | 0.98 |
| 3.2 | 11.77 | 11.98 | 12.01 | 11.93 | 11.97 | 11.97 | 0.21 | 0.24 | −0.05 | −0.04 | −0.01 |
| 4.1 | 138.56 | 142.69 | 142.67 | 145.69 | 146.86 | 146.90 | 4.13 | 4.11 | 3.00 | 4.19 | 4.21 |
| 4.2 | 59.90 | 61.10 | 60.75 | 62.89 | 61.74 | 62.21 | 1.20 | 0.85 | 1.79 | 0.99 | 1.11 |
| 4.3 | 10.73 | 10.74 | 10.85 | 10.76 | 10.70 | 11.47 | 0.01 | 0.12 | 0.02 | −0.15 | 0.73 |
| 4.4 | 6.19 | 6.36 | 6.26 | 6.66 | 6.34 | 6.42 | 0.17 | 0.07 | 0.30 | 0.08 | 0.06 |
| 5.1 | 24.92 | 25.93 | 27.03 | 27.05 | 28.01 | 27.30 | 1.01 | 2.11 | 1.12 | 0.98 | 1.37 |
| 5.2 | 30.71 | 31.23 | 32.82 | 32.80 | 33.81 | 33.83 | 0.52 | 2.11 | 1.57 | 0.99 | 2.60 |
| 5.3 | 9.47 | 9.66 | 9.45 | 9.91 | 9.32 | 9.45 | 0.19 | −0.02 | 0.25 | −0.12 | −0.21 |
| 5.4 | 18.84 | 19.45 | 19.68 | 20.17 | 20.02 | 19.81 | 0.61 | 0.84 | 0.72 | 0.34 | 0.36 |
| 5.5 | 16.45 | 17.30 | 17.48 | 18.20 | 17.72 | 17.74 | 0.85 | 1.03 | 0.90 | 0.24 | 0.44 |
| 5.6 | 16.97 | 17.96 | 17.33 | 18.30 | 17.72 | 18.07 | 0.99 | 0.36 | 0.34 | 0.39 | 0.11 |
| 5.7 | 4.95 | 5.32 | 5.11 | 5.56 | 5.27 | 5.34 | 0.37 | 0.16 | 0.24 | 0.16 | 0.02 |
| 5.8a | 30.48 | 32.51 | 32.48 | 34.13 | 34.55 | 34.58 | 2.03 | 2.00 | 1.62 | 2.07 | 2.07 |
| 5.8b | 16.15 | 17.07 | 16.84 | 17.19 | 17.58 | 17.79 | 0.92 | 0.69 | 0.12 | 0.74 | 0.72 |
| 5.8c | 5.09 | 5.26 | 5.17 | 5.30 | 5.21 | 5.28 | 0.17 | 0.08 | 0.04 | 0.03 | 0.02 |
| 5.8d | 17.52 | 17.74 | 17.64 | 17.97 | 17.42 | 17.50 | 0.22 | 0.12 | 0.23 | −0.22 | −0.24 |
| 5.9 | 23.51 | 24.46 | 24.72 | 25.99 | 25.90 | 25.64 | 0.95 | 1.21 | 1.53 | 1.18 | 1.18 |
| 5.10 | 16.70 | 16.32 | 17.65 | 15.80 | 18.06 | 16.79 | −0.38 | 0.95 | −0.52 | 0.41 | 0.47 |
| 5.11 | 10.48 | 10.67 | 10.86 | 11.03 | 11.18 | 11.03 | 0.19 | 0.38 | 0.36 | 0.31 | 0.36 |
| 6.1 | 19.77 | 20.49 | 20.68 | 21.17 | 21.55 | 21.39 | 0.72 | 0.91 | 0.68 | 0.87 | 0.90 |
| 6.2 | 5.89 | 6.20 | 6.04 | 6.43 | 6.22 | 6.42 | 0.31 | 0.15 | 0.23 | 0.19 | 0.22 |
| 6.3 | 21.44 | 22.40 | 21.94 | 23.19 | 22.42 | 22.88 | 0.96 | 0.50 | 0.79 | 0.48 | 0.48 |
| 6.4 | 9.78 | 10.06 | 9.95 | 10.30 | 10.16 | 10.21 | 0.28 | 0.17 | 0.24 | 0.20 | 0.15 |
| 6.5 | 4.08 | 4.17 | 4.11 | 4.34 | 4.16 | 4.18 | 0.09 | 0.03 | 0.17 | 0.05 | 0.01 |
| 6.6 | 24.46 | 25.47 | 23.65 | 25.93 | 22.82 | 24.64 | 1.01 | −0.81 | 0.46 | [illegible] | [illegible] |

| | | | | | | | | | | | |
|---|---|---|---|---|---|---|---|---|---|---|---|
| 6.7 | 11.22 | 11.79 | 12.35 | 11.97 | 13.46 | 12.92 | 0.57 | 1.15 | 0.18 | 1.11 | 1.15 |
| 6.8 | 7.02 | 7.15 | 7.06 | 7.19 | 7.06 | 7.15 | 0.13 | 0.04 | 0.04 | 0.00 | 0.00 |
| 7.1 | 3.71 | 3.38 | 3.39 | 3.62 | 3.89 | 3.89 | −0.33 | −0.32 | 0.24 | 0.50 | 0.51 |
| 7.2 | 3.58 | 3.85 | 3.81 | 4.11 | 4.02 | 4.09 | 0.27 | 0.23 | 0.26 | 0.21 | 0.24 |
| 7.3 | 21.77 | 23.84 | 21.84 | 24.37 | 22.13 | 23.39 | 2.07 | 0.07 | 0.53 | 0.28 | −0.45 |
| 7.4 | 20.45 | 20.71 | 20.19 | 21.46 | 20.00 | 20.53 | 0.26 | −0.26 | 0.75 | −0.19 | −0.18 |
| 7.5 | 7.58 | 7.66 | 7.59 | 7.58 | 7.57 | 7.63 | 0.08 | 0.01 | −0.08 | −0.03 | −0.03 |
| 7.6 | 32.23 | 33.41 | 34.42 | 35.94 | 36.41 | 35.53 | 1.18 | 2.19 | 2.53 | 1.99 | 2.12 |
| 7.7 | 5.00 | 5.11 | 4.66 | 5.15 | 4.78 | 4.78 | 0.11 | −0.34 | 0.04 | 0.12 | −0.33 |
| 8.1a | 67.12 | 80.35 | 76.44 | 88.32 | 79.35 | 81.48 | 13.23 | 9.32 | 7.97 | 2.91 | 1.13 |
| 8.1b | 16.20 | 18.00 | 16.73 | 18.75 | 16.97 | 17.36 | 1.80 | 0.53 | 0.75 | 0.24 | −0.64 |
| 8.1c | 22.75 | 23.47 | 23.72 | 24.16 | 24.49 | 24.31 | 0.72 | 0.97 | 0.69 | 0.77 | 0.84 |
| 8.1d | 58.26 | 59.37 | 60.17 | 60.97 | 61.81 | 61.12 | 1.11 | 1.91 | 1.60 | 1.64 | 1.75 |
| 8.1e | 1.62 | 1.67 | 1.73 | 1.74 | 1.85 | 1.79 | 0.05 | 0.11 | 0.07 | 0.12 | 0.12 |
| 8.1f | 8.98 | 9.67 | 9.51 | 9.55 | 9.93 | 10.06 | 0.69 | 0.53 | −0.12 | 0.42 | 0.39 |
| 8.2a | 5.10 | 4.89 | 5.02 | 4.66 | 4.61 | 4.62 | −0.21 | −0.08 | −0.23 | −0.41 | −0.27 |
| 8.2b | 2.73 | 2.70 | 2.68 | 2.63 | 2.62 | 2.64 | −0.03 | −0.05 | −0.07 | −0.06 | −0.06 |
| 8.2c | 0.45 | 0.43 | 0.46 | 0.43 | 0.47 | 0.44 | −0.02 | 0.01 | 0.00 | 0.01 | 0.01 |
| 8.3a | 1.53 | 1.45 | 1.57 | 1.18 | 1.50 | 1.40 | −0.08 | 0.04 | −0.27 | −0.07 | −0.05 |
| 8.3b | 1.39 | 1.46 | 1.42 | 1.45 | 1.47 | 1.52 | 0.07 | 0.03 | −0.01 | 0.05 | 0.06 |
| 8.3c | 4.23 | 4.60 | 4.71 | 5.21 | 5.30 | 5.16 | 0.37 | 0.48 | 0.61 | 0.58 | 0.56 |
| 8.3d | 0.12 | 0.12 | 0.14 | 0.12 | 0.13 | 0.13 | 0.00 | 0.02 | 0.00 | −0.01 | 0.01 |
| 9.1 | 7.35 | 7.06 | 7.31 | 6.83 | 7.25 | 7.10 | −0.29 | −0.04 | −0.23 | −0.05 | 0.04 |
| 9.2 | 11.11 | 11.10 | 11.13 | 10.87 | 11.13 | 11.11 | −0.01 | 0.02 | −0.23 | 0.01 | 0.01 |
| 9.3 | 13.39 | 13.83 | 13.82 | 14.20 | 14.14 | 14.15 | 0.44 | 0.43 | 0.37 | 0.32 | 0.32 |
| 9.4 | 11.59 | 11.93 | 11.81 | 12.52 | 11.86 | 12.06 | 0.34 | 0.22 | 0.59 | 0.05 | 0.13 |
| 9.5 | 20.32 | 22.06 | 21.28 | 23.88 | 21.85 | 22.38 | 1.74 | 0.96 | 1.82 | 0.57 | 0.32 |
| 9.6 | 3.92 | 4.05 | 3.88 | 4.21 | 4.11 | 4.11 | 0.13 | −0.04 | 0.16 | 0.23 | 0.06 |
| 9.7 | 5.92 | 5.81 | 5.81 | 5.94 | 5.99 | 6.00 | −0.11 | −0.11 | 0.13 | 0.19 | 0.19 |
| 9.8a | 5.17 | 4.72 | 5.36 | 4.59 | 5.45 | 4.88 | −0.45 | 0.19 | −0.13 | 0.09 | 0.16 |
| 9.8b | 1.67 | 1.67 | 1.72 | 1.62 | 1.76 | 1.73 | 0.00 | 0.05 | −0.05 | 0.04 | 0.06 |
| 9.8c | 1.39 | 1.41 | 1.39 | 1.40 | 1.45 | 1.45 | 0.02 | 0.00 | −0.01 | 0.06 | 0.04 |
| 9.9 | 3.61 | 3.57 | 3.67 | 3.55 | 3.68 | 3.62 | −0.04 | 0.06 | −0.02 | 0.01 | 0.05 |
| 9.10 | 4.52 | 4.69 | 4.51 | 4.80 | 4.71 | 4.72 | 0.17 | −0.01 | 0.11 | 0.20 | 0.03 |
| 9.11 | 2.42 | 2.45 | 2.58 | 2.58 | 2.70 | 2.62 | 0.03 | 0.16 | 0.13 | 0.12 | 0.17 |
| 9.12 | 6.13 | 6.23 | 6.37 | 6.46 | 6.57 | 6.47 | 0.10 | 0.24 | 0.23 | 0.20 | 0.24 |
| 10.1 | 8.70 | 9.40 | 9.24 | 9.67 | 9.85 | 10.01 | 0.70 | 0.54 | 0.27 | 0.61 | 0.61 |
| 10.2 | 6.40 | 6.63 | 6.71 | 6.76 | 7.03 | 6.97 | 0.23 | 0.31 | 0.13 | 0.32 | 0.34 |
| 10.3 | 3.95 | 3.80 | 4.14 | 3.89 | 4.32 | 4.05 | −0.15 | 0.19 | 0.09 | 0.18 | 0.25 |
| 11.0 | 22.78 | 23.52 | 23.44 | 24.13 | 24.36 | 24.42 | 0.74 | 0.66 | 0.61 | 0.92 | 0.90 |
| 12.1 | 12.13 | 13.00 | 12.65 | 13.88 | 13.16 | 13.61 | 0.87 | 0.52 | 0.88 | 0.51 | 0.61 |
| 12.2 | 7.42 | 7.88 | 7.76 | 7.92 | 8.25 | 8.39 | 0.46 | 0.34 | 0.04 | 0.49 | 0.51 |
| 12.3 | 1.42 | 1.54 | 1.06 | 1.69 | 1.16 | 1.16 | 0.12 | −0.36 | 0.15 | 0.09 | −0.38 |
| 12.4 | −4.94 | −4.95 | −5.99 | −5.06 | −6.47 | −6.47 | −0.01 | −1.05 | −0.11 | −0.47 | −1.52 |

* Predicted (1) uses predicted 1962; predicted (2) uses actual 1962.

the individual PCE items. The other way is to predict 1963 using the actual values for 1962.

In analyzing these predictions, it would be misleading to compare directly the predicted level with the actual level. A more meaningful and stringent test is to compare the predicted changes between 1961 and 1962 and 1962 and 1963 with the actual changes. These calculations are also tabulated in Table 5.6.

Inspection of the table shows that with respect to *direction of change*, the equations correctly predict 55 of the 65 increases between 1961 and 1962 and correctly predict 7 of the 17 decreases.[4] This means that compared to naive forecasting, that is, forecasting no change, our equations are better in 62 of the 84 cases. With respect to levels, 41 of the predictions are too high, 42 are too low, while one is correct. Hence there is no systematic over-prediction.[5]

The performance for 1963 is much poorer. The equations correctly predict 52 of the 60 increases and 8 of the 21 decreases when the predicted values for 1962 are used,[6] and only 48 of the increases and 8 of the decreases when the actual values for 1962 are used. In each instance, the projections are substantially better than using naive forecasts.

The largest overpredictions in dollars are for 1.1 (food consumed in the home). The prediction is close to $4 too high in 1962 and is over $8 too high in 1963 (using 1962 actual), when there was a small decline. Preliminary data suggest, however, that 1.1 in 1964 may be back on the regression line.

The largest underpredictions in dollars are for 8.1a (new cars and net purchases of used cars). The projection for 1962 is about $4 too low, and is about $6.80 too low for 1963. This is in keeping with our earlier reservation that the projections in 1970 for automobiles may be too low.

On the brighter side, it is encouraging to observe that, in spite of earlier reservations, the equations for 5.8a (electricity) and 4.1 (space rental value of owner-occupied housing) do very well, especially for 1962.

As summary statistics for measuring the accuracy of the predictions, we have calculated $R^2$'s and Theil $U$'s between the actual and predicted changes. The categories have been weighted by their respective budget shares in order to compensate for the largest category being many times larger than the smallest. These statistics are presented in Table 5.7.

Table 5.7. Summary Statistics for Projections

| Year | $R^2$ | Theil $U$ |
|---|---|---|
| 1962 | .8642 | .2619 |
| 1963 (1) | .0349 | .6893 |
| 1963 (2) | .0063 | .7489 |

[4] A "no change" for either the actual or the predicted is excluded.

[5] The predictions have been made to add up.

[6] The predicted changes have been computed from the predicted levels for 1962, not the actual levels.

The weighted $R^2$ is quite high for 1962, but is extremely low for both sets of projections for 1963. The low values for 1963 are due to the poor predictions for 1.1 and 8.1a, particularly for 1.1 which is the largest category of the 84. The high values of the Theil $U$ for 1963 also reflect this fact. One interesting result is that the changes between 1962 and 1963 are predicted better by using 1962 predicted than using 1963 actual. This suggests that the data revisions for 1960 and 1961 may have affected the intercepts, but data errors could also be a factor. Further discussion of this point is in the next chapter.

The next step is to aggregate the categories to the 12 larger categories of consumption and to the level of durables, nondurables and services parallel to the way we did for the projections. These aggregates and their respective budget shares are tabulated in Table 5.8.

The largest dollar discrepancies in the predictions are for food and tobacco (Group I) and transportation (Group VIII). These two results, as we have noted, are due to the poor predictions for the large food item and automobiles. The prediction for household operation (Group V) is off over $3 in 1962, but improves considerably in 1963. The predictions for the other groups are quite good, especially for rent (Group IV), although the percentage error for foreign travel and remittances (Group XII) is substantial.

In terms of budget shares, the predictions do very well in general. Except for Groups I, V, and VIII, the predicted budget shares are equal to or within .1 percent of the actual values. For the durable-nondurable-service breakdown, the predicted budget shares are about one-half point too high for nondurables and too low, particularly in 1963, for durables. Nondurables reflect the overprediction for food, while durables reflect the underprediction for automobiles.

As a whole, the results from the accuracy analysis of the predictions for 1962 and 1963, particularly 1962, are favorable to the set of equations. Despite a few large errors, they add to our confidence in the projections for 1970. Presumably the results would have been still more favorable, especially for 1963, had the equations been re-estimated with the revised data for 1960 and 1961. The data for 1962 and 1963 used here will no doubt be revised in the future. However, to forestall any tendency toward smugness, we must remember that no model can be adequately tested by data for only two years.[7]

[7] A fundamental assumption of our time-series analysis is, of course, that the relationships between expenditure and the factors excluded from the regression equation are constant over time. We had hoped to make use of the data from the 1960 Bureau of Labor Statistics budget survey together with the data from 1950 Survey, in order to see whether expenditure patterns had altered between 1950 and 1960. However, time and resource constraints precluded our doing full justice to this intent. Instead, we have concentrated on food and clothing, two of the largest categories of expenditure, and have used functions estimated with 1950 data to predict 1960 expenditure using 1960 total expenditure and prices. The food equation used is the one estimated by Jean Crockett (1960), while the clothing equation used is the one estimated by Morris Hamburg (1960). Yoel Haitovsky of the Harvard Economic Research Project performed the analysis.

Haitovsky's principal findings, which involve ten large cities in the North, were that

[note continued on p. 167]

Table 5.8. PCE Predictions for 1962 and 1963, Twelve Group Aggregates and Durables, Nondurables, and Services

| | Level | | | | | | Budget share | | | | | |
|---|---|---|---|---|---|---|---|---|---|---|---|---|
| | | 1962 | | 1963* | | | | 1962 | | 1963* | | |
| Group | 1961 | Actual | Predicted | Actual | Predicted (1) | Predicted (2) | 1961 | Actual | Predicted | Actual | Predicted (1) | Predicted (2) |
| I | $449.27 | $454.78 | $459.40 | $455.24 | $466.35 | $463.44 | .271 | .266 | .269 | .261 | .267 | .265 |
| II | 175.69 | 178.53 | 180.54 | 179.61 | 182.93 | 181.75 | .106 | .105 | .106 | .103 | .105 | .104 |
| III | 27.11 | 27.83 | 28.22 | 28.32 | 29.19 | 28.80 | .016 | .016 | .017 | .016 | .017 | .016 |
| IV | 215.38 | 220.89 | 220.53 | 226.00 | 225.64 | 227.00 | .130 | .129 | .129 | .129 | .129 | .130 |
| V | 242.24 | 250.88 | 254.26 | 259.40 | 261.77 | 260.15 | .146 | .147 | .149 | .148 | .150 | .149 |
| VI | 103.66 | 107.73 | 105.78 | 110.52 | 107.85 | 109.79 | .063 | .063 | .062 | .063 | .062 | .063 |
| VII | 94.32 | 97.96 | 95.90 | 102.23 | 98.80 | 99.84 | .057 | .057 | .056 | .059 | .057 | .057 |
| VIII | 190.48 | 208.18 | 204.30 | 219.17 | 210.50 | 212.03 | .115 | .122 | .120 | .125 | .120 | .121 |
| IX | 98.51 | 100.58 | 100.64 | 103.45 | 102.65 | 102.40 | .060 | .059 | .059 | .059 | .059 | .059 |
| X | 19.05 | 19.83 | 20.09 | 20.32 | 21.20 | 21.03 | .012 | .012 | .012 | .012 | .012 | .012 |
| XI | 22.78 | 23.52 | 23.44 | 24.13 | 24.36 | 24.42 | .014 | .014 | .014 | .014 | .014 | .014 |
| XII | 16.03 | 17.47 | 15.48 | 18.43 | 16.10 | 16.69 | .010 | .010 | .009 | .011 | .009 | .010 |
| Total | 1654.52 | 1708.18 | 1708.58 | 1746.82 | 1747.34 | 1747.34 | — | — | — | — | — | — |
| Durables | 225.43 | 245.11 | 242.10 | 260.44 | 248.66 | 251.05 | .136 | .143 | .142 | .149 | .142 | .144 |
| Nondurables | 780.98 | 794.67 | 801.21 | 800.41 | 815.03 | 810.73 | .472 | .465 | .469 | .458 | .466 | .464 |
| Services | 648.11 | 668.40 | 665.27 | 685.97 | 683.65 | 685.56 | .392 | .391 | .389 | .393 | .391 | .392 |

* Predicted (1) uses predicted 1962; predicted (2) uses actual 1962.

## *IV. Comparison with European Projections*

Our results can be put in an interesting perspective by comparing them with similar studies for European countries. A recent book, edited by Sandee (1964) under the auspices of the European Scientific Association for Medium and Long Term Forecasting (ASEPELT), brings together a number of country studies whose purpose was much the same as ours, namely, to project consumption in 1970 on the basis of past experience (mostly time series). A uniform classification into sixteen categories of expenditure was provided to the authors, most of whom appear to have observed it fairly closely. In his introduction the editor has used the results for six countries (Belgium, France, Italy, the Netherlands, Norway, and Sweden) in an international comparison, from which he concludes that "consumption functions are nearly the same all over Europe." Perhaps this statement is somewhat too sweeping, though it agrees with the conclusion reached by Houthakker (1963) on the basis of a somewhat different approach. In any case, it is interesting to see how United States consumption fits into the European pattern.

Because of differences in definition, especially in the food items, it was not possible to adapt our results entirely to the ASEPELT classification. By condensing the latter into eleven categories, however, the American figures can be made comparable; at the least, they can be made as comparable to the European figures as these are among themselves, for complete uniformity is not to be expected. The condensed classification includes the following PCE items for the United States as numbered and defined in Chapter 4:

| | |
|---|---|
| Food and beverages | 1.0 through 1.4, excluding 1.2 |
| Tobacco | 1.5 |
| Clothing and footwear | 2.1 through 2.5 |
| Household durables | 2.7, 2.8; 5.1 through 5.4; 9.4 through 9.6 |
| Heat and light | 5.8a, 5.8b, 5.8d |
| Rent | 4.1 through 4.3; 5.8c |
| Health and hygiene | 6.1 through 6.7 |
| Public transport and communications | 5.9; 8.2a, 8.2b, 8.2c, 8.3a through 8.3d |
| Private transport (equipment) | 8.1a |
| Private transport (operation) | 8.1b through 8.1f |
| Miscellaneous | 1.2; 2.6; 4.4; 5.10, 5.11; 7.1 through 7.7; 9.1, 9.2, 9.3, and 9.7 through 9.12; 10.1, 10.2, 10.3; 11; 12.1, 12.2, 12.3 |

[footnote continued from p. 165]
for both food and clothing expenditures cities which were above the regression line in 1950 were also above the regression line in 1960. A similar relationship held for those cities which were below the regression line in 1950. Hence we can conclude that, for food and clothing anyway, there were no marked shifts in expenditure patterns between 1950 and 1960.

However, we cannot go on to conclude that our regression equations for food and clothing are therefore "right." Haitovsky's findings only say that the underlying structure was reasonably stable between 1950 and 1960 and that a plausible case can be made for the structure remaining stable until 1970. But even at worst, if our equations are only empirical relationships, stability of structure implies that we can nonetheless place confidence in the projections from these equations.

Next the figures have to be expressed in common units. In Sandee's analysis the dollar is used for this purpose, all conversions being made at official rates of exchange. He acknowledges, however, that these rates do not fully reflect differences in price levels among countries but refrains from using more realistic exchange rates on the ground that sufficiently recent data were not then available. Actually, the United Nations Statistical Office, in the *1963 Yearbook of National Accounts Statistics,* has presented newly calculated purchasing-power parities which are more suitable for use in international comparisons than official exchange rates. There are, as is well known, many controversies about purchasing-power parities, but we feel that their weaknesses are outweighed by their advantages and shall therefore use them here. The use of such parities is especially indicated in any comparison involving the United States because the dollar is generally agreed to be overvalued at official exchange rates. The parities used (in foreign currency units per dollar) are given in the bottom line of Table 5.9, together with the official rates. The parities refer to 1960 (except for France, where the initial data are for 1959). They have also been applied to the 1970 figures, which is appropriate because all the data are at constant domestic prices.

The overall purchasing-power parities, of course, do not tell the whole story about intercountry price differences. There are also differences in the relative prices of consumption categories; thus the price ratio of personal services to other commodities is higher in the United States than in Europe, while household durables are relatively cheaper in the United States. The United Nations figures used here, however, are not broken down by category, and we have therefore not attempted any adjustment for differences in relative prices.

The data for the seven countries are tabulated in Table 5.9, but they can be more easily compared by means of the ten diagrams in Figure 5.1, which are similar to those presented by Sandee (1964). The two points for each country are linked by an arrow whose tip corresponds to 1970. The scale is logarithmic on both axes, so that the slope indicates the elasticity with respect to total PCE. Generally speaking, the arrows for the United States are within the range suggested by the European arrows, and all arrows are also reasonably parallel. A more exact test could have been made by analysis of covariance, as is done in Houthakker (1965) on other data, but this would carry us too far. Visual inspection suggests that the United States demand functions are not markedly different from those for the six European countries.

The reader will be able to draw his own conclusions from the divergencies apparent in these diagrams, some of which are also discussed by Sandee. The greatest dispersion occurs in tobacco and can presumably be explained in part by differences in the relative price of tobacco resulting from excise taxes. The European countries foresee large increases in the expenditure on household durables and on private transport, no doubt because their stocks

Table 5.9. Personal Consumption Expenditures in Seven Countries in Dollars per capita at 1960 Prices and Purchasing-power Parity Rates

| Item | Belgium | | France* | | Italy | | Netherlands | | Norway | | Sweden | | United States† | |
|---|---|---|---|---|---|---|---|---|---|---|---|---|---|---|
| | 1960 | 1970 | 1959 | 1970 | 1960 | 1970 | 1960 | 1970 | 1960 | 1970 | 1960 | 1970 | 1961 | 1970 |
| Food and beverages | 328.58 | 413.34 | 317.72 | 410.82 | 270.40 | 347.75 | 233.87 | 294.32 | 324.37 | 399.60 | 363.38 | 429.55 | 353.10 | 421.60 |
| Tobacco | 19.07 | 23.21 | 18.10 | 21.41 | 24.33 | 36.16 | 29.76 | 38.10 | 27.40 | 30.64 | 36.10 | 44.67 | 35.89 | 46.29 |
| Clothing and footwear | 85.37 | 119.58 | 110.25 | 169.15 | 55.74 | 81.16 | 99.74 | 146.17 | 145.24 | 185.85 | 131.00 | 196.84 | 154.92 | 184.74 |
| Household durables | 80.33 | 114.54 | 61.27 | 133.90 | 13.05 | 25.01 | 85.85 | 162.84 | 129.27 | 196.31 | 101.04 | 163.08 | 135.40 | 181.56 |
| Heat and light | 43.39 | 59.34 | 43.06 | 67.66 | 15.36 | 27.19 | 37.96 | 50.93 | 31.14 | 43.35 | 52.80 | 69.40 | 64.00 | 91.16 |
| Rent | 98.39 | 105.45 | 44.12 | 70.97 | 20.39 | 29.09 | 48.55 | 61.64 | 63.15 | 90.31 | 106.72 | 170.44 | 212.50 | 268.46 |
| Health and hygiene | 44.10 | 67.41 | 81.15 | 163.95 | 23.38 | 36.03 | 31.22 | 54.90 | 36.75 | 48.83 | 33.86 | 55.48 | 96.84 | 134.11 |
| Public transport and communications | 27.35 | 35.72 | 24.49 | 33.95 | 19.58 | 35.48 | 18.25 | 22.09 | 42.47 | 51.82 | 38.77 | 47.23 | 39.50 | 55.87 |
| Private transport (equipment) | 52.27 | 93.55 | 17.74 | 40.57 | 8.56 | 18.22 | 16.01 | 34.66 | 19.81 | 75.24 | 47.79 | 91.23 | 67.03 | 94.77 |
| Private transport (operation) | | | 24.13 | 54.65 | 17.27 | 41.06 | 5.42 | 11.51 | 10.34 | 33.76 | 51.47 | 95.13 | 110.07 | 141.95 |
| Miscellaneous | 150.06 | 244.72 | 121.36 | 199.08 | 72.19 | 124.12 | 117.33 | 190.35 | 112.86 | 149.35 | 125.32 | 169.65 | 387.75 | 524.49 |
| Total PCE‡ | 928.91 | 1276.86 | 863.39 | 1366.12 | 540.26 | 801.27 | 723.97 | 1067.51 | 942.95 | 1267.32 | 1088.25 | 1533.39 | 1657.00 | 2145.00 |
| Official exchange rate | 49.70 | Belg. francs | 4.909 | Fr. francs | 620.60 | lire | 3.77 | guilders | 7.15 | kroner | 5.18 | kronor | 1.00 | dollar |
| PPP rate§ | 49.25 | Belg. francs | 4.150 | Fr. francs | 456.50 | lire | 2.85 | guilders | 5.74 | kroner | 4.65 | kronor | 1.00 | dollar |

* 1959 prices.
† 1954 prices.
‡ Items do not always add up to totals obtained separately.
§ Purchasing-power parity rate interpolated from *UN Yearbook of National Accounts Statistics 1963*, table 3B, pp. 327–331.

of these items are now much smaller than in America. It may be noted that Sandee questions the low Italian figures for household durables.

As Sandee puts it, international comparison provides "mutual encouragement [because] nearly all of these estimates follow closely related patterns [and] therefore reinforce each other." The inclusion of the United States certainly lends support to this view.

Figure 5.1

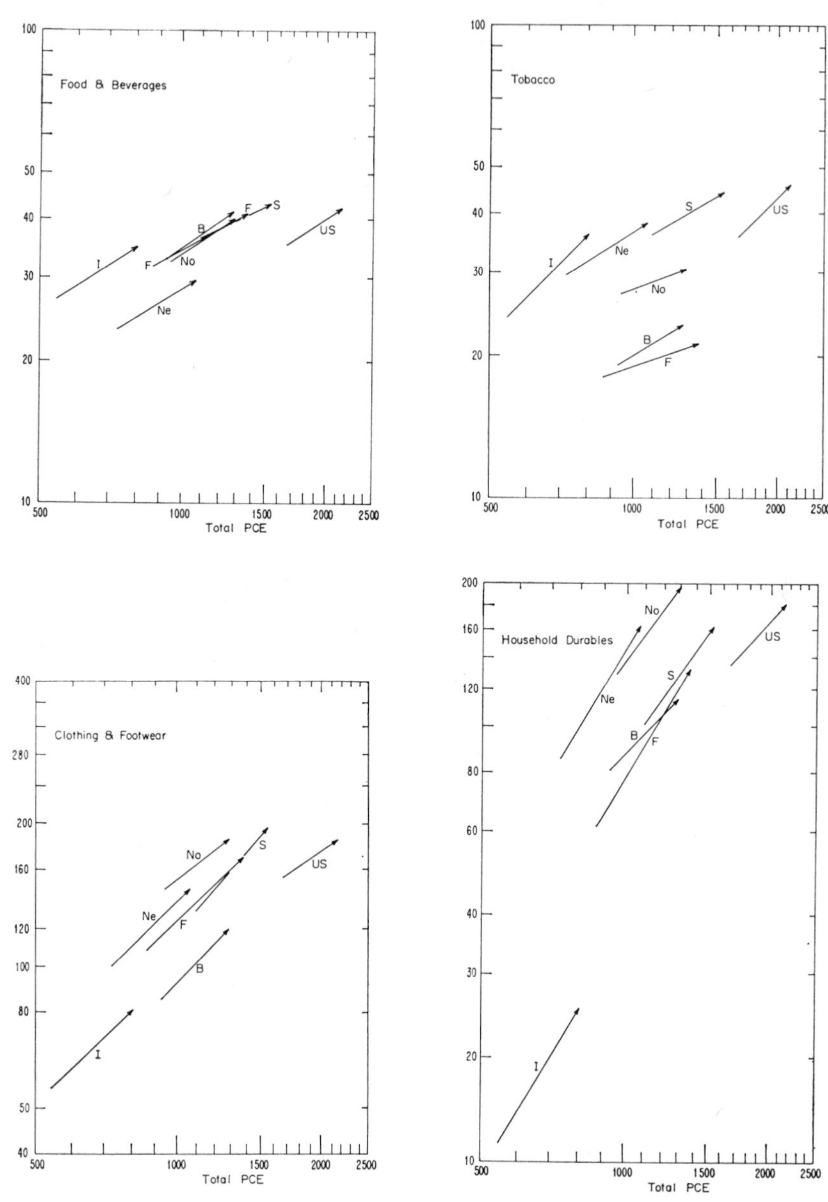

Figure 5.1—*continued*

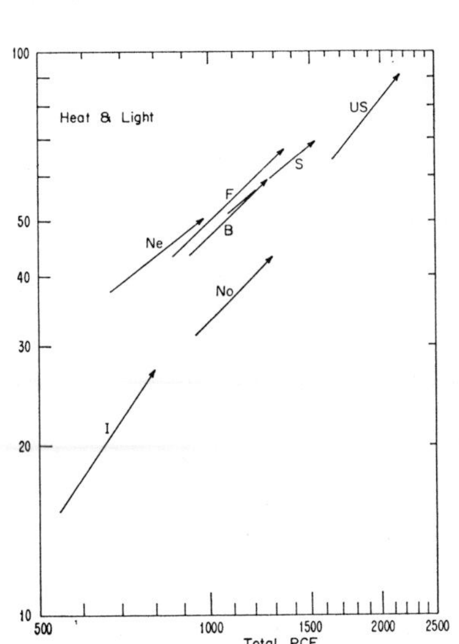


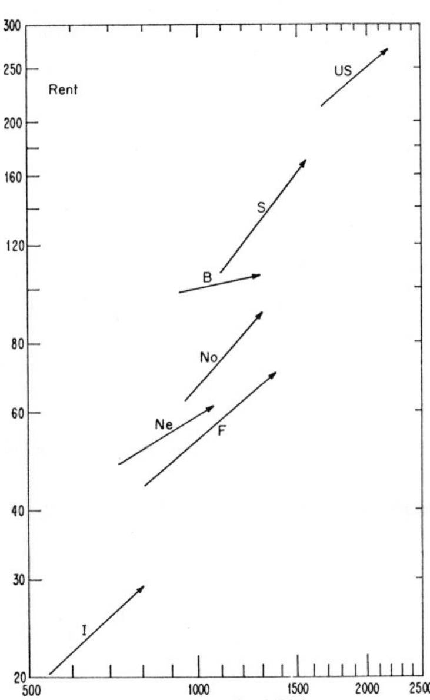


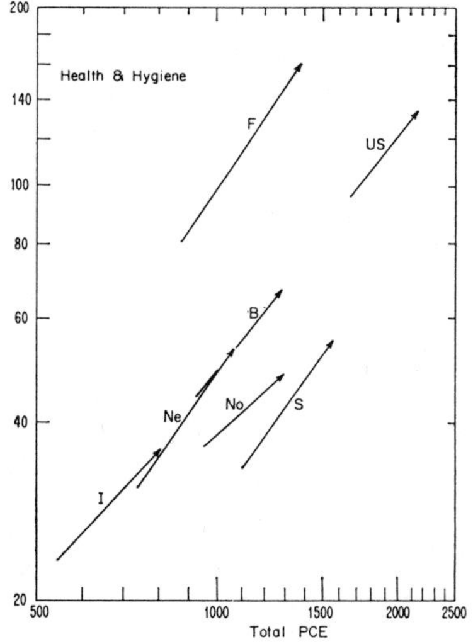


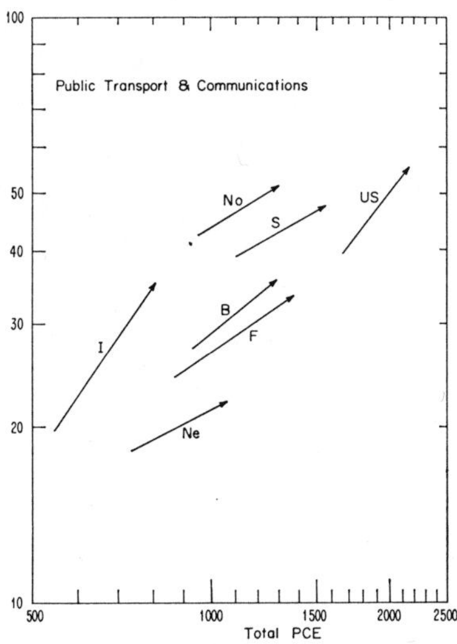

Figure 5.1—*continued*

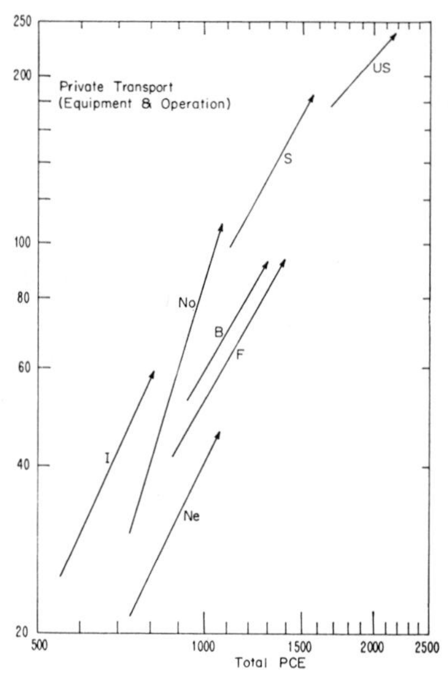


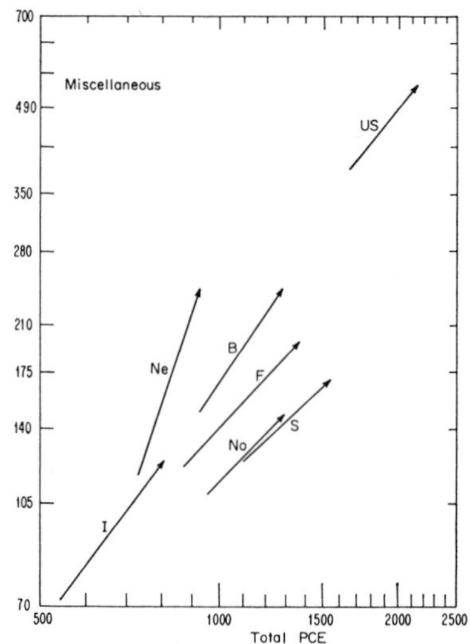

# 6

# *The Dynamics of Total Consumption and Saving*

In this chapter we apply dynamic models of demand to total consumption and its complement, savings. To do so we merely have to interpret $x_t$ as (measured) income and $q_t$ as total consumption, and omit the price terms.[1] Various modifications of this simple approach will also be considered. The empirical results obtained in this chapter refer not only to annual observations for the United States, as in previous chapters, but also to quarterly figures that are available only for the postwar period. In addition, Canadian data (both annual and quarterly) are analyzed.

We shall first discuss the basic model (section I), which turns out to do well at first sight but has some unsatisfactory features on closer examination. The incorporation of a permanent-income hypothesis into the dynamic model (section II) does not improve matters and indeed leads to unacceptable results. Returning then to the basic model, we specialize it by requiring the depreciation rate on consumers' financial assets to be zero (section III), which provides a very simple savings function with reasonable empirical properties, though there is also evidence of a change in the function during the postwar period. As a further variation, the population effect mentioned in Chapter 2, section II, is taken into account; it appears to be of minor importance. The last section is devoted to the projection of total consumption and savings in 1970.

## *I. The Basic Dynamic Model Applied to Total Consumption*

The model described in section II of Chapter 1, which underlies most of the results in this book, can be applied immediately to total consumer expenditure, provided we interpret $x_t$ as disposable income and not as PCE, which now becomes $q_t$. It is then compatible with much contemporary thinking on the consumption function. In particular, linearity with respect to income has been found a good approximation by most students of the subject. Perhaps more important, the basic model gives prominence to habit formation, which has often been stressed in this context, for instance by Duesenberry and Modigliani (1947), Brown (1952) and Duesenberry, Eckstein, and Fromm

[1] Prices are irrelevant except for the Pigou effect, a possible money illusion, and similar phenomena. Strictly speaking, capital gains should also be taken into account. These problems are not investigated here.

(1960). As we shall see in section III below, the model also has a bearing on the effect of asset holdings on saving, which has been stressed by Tobin (1953), Zellner (1957), and others; in fact it will there be shown that habit formation in consumption and asset effects on saving are really two sides of the same coin.

Concerning habit formation, we need only recall the usual argument. When income rises, consumers will not immediately attain the higher level of consumption made possible; when income falls, they will wish to maintain the previously reached consumption level as much as possible. The result is inertia or sluggishness in the adjustment of consumption to income, and this is precisely what our basic model is designed to represent.

While there is nothing new in this emphasis on dynamic adjustment, our model has an advantage over earlier formulations because it is derived from an underlying theory expressed in continuous time. It thereby avoids the arbitrariness common to models initially expressed as difference equations. The length of the period of observation (usually a quarter or a year) does not have any particular significance for the dynamic adjustment process, and should therefore not be used in the theoretical specification of the process. From this point of view, the use of "previous peak income" in the Duesenberry-Modigliani theory of the consumption function is also a crude approximation at best.

The derivation from a continuous-time theory is especially useful when both quarterly and annual data are available. It has often been observed that the marginal propensity to consume (MPC) is lower when estimated from quarterly data than when estimated from annual data. Explanations for this discrepancy vary.[2] They usually run in terms of a permanent-income theory, which will be considered in the next section. Without appealing to the latter theory, our basic model can also shed light on this difficulty. The apparent MPC appears in our estimating equation (36) of Chapter 1 as the coefficient $A_2$ of $\Delta x_t$, and we shall see that $A_2$ is indeed greater in annual than in quarterly equations. However, what matters from the present point of view is not $A_2$ but $\gamma$, the short-run MPC, or $\gamma'$, its long-run counterpart, and these should be independent of the period of observation. This independence therefore constitutes an important test of the underlying dynamic theory.

While on this subject, it is also interesting to consider the other structural parameters in their relation to the period of observation. To do so we have to go back to equation (34) of Chapter 1; rewritten in the same form as (36) it becomes

$$(1)\quad q_t = \frac{\alpha\delta\tau^2}{1 - \frac{\tau}{2}(\beta - \delta)} + \frac{1 + \frac{\tau}{2}(\beta - \delta)}{1 - \frac{\tau}{2}(\beta - \delta)} q_{t-\tau} + \frac{\gamma\left(1 + \frac{\tau\delta}{2}\right)}{1 - \frac{\tau}{2}(\beta - \delta)} \Delta x_t$$

$$+ \frac{\gamma\delta\tau}{\frac{\tau}{1} - 2(\beta - \delta)} x_{t-\tau},$$

[2] See, for instance, Ackley (1961, ch. II), Griliches (1962), and Suits (1963).

where $\Delta x_t$ now stands for $x_t - x_{t-\tau}$. We see then that the parameters $\alpha$, $\beta$, and $\delta$ always appear in the combination $\alpha\tau$, $\beta\tau$, and $\delta\tau$, so that $\gamma$ is the only one that is not multiplied by $\tau$, the period of observation. Hence if we put $\tau = 1/4$, which amounts to using quarterly data if $\tau = 1$ corresponds to a year, then we obtain $\alpha/4$, $\beta/4$, $\gamma$, and $\delta/4$. The $\alpha$, $\beta$, and $\delta$ estimated from quarterly data therefore must be one-fourth of the $\alpha$, $\beta$, and $\delta$ estimated from annual data; this is a further test on the basic model.[3]

The empirical results for the United States are as follows:

U.S. annual (1929–1941, 1947–1961)

$$q_t = \underset{(44.16)}{108.31} + \underset{(.219)}{.372}\, q_{t-1} + \underset{(.054)}{.641}\, \Delta x_t + \underset{(.181)}{.497}\, x_{t-1} + \underset{(19.92)}{39.78}d_t \tag{2}$$

$$\hat{\alpha} = 124.84 \qquad \hat{\beta} = .350 \qquad \hat{\gamma} = .512 \qquad \hat{\gamma}' = .791 \qquad \hat{\delta} = 1.266$$

$$R^2 = .997 \qquad D.W. = 1.97$$

$$R^2 = .868 \quad (\Delta q_t \text{ as dependent variable})$$

U.S. annual (1947–1962)

$$q_t = \underset{(74.52)}{105.70} + \underset{(.283)}{.240}\, q_{t-1} + \underset{(.128)}{.650}\, \Delta x_t + \underset{(.243)}{.646}\, x_{t-1} \tag{3}$$

$$\hat{\alpha} = 86.34 \qquad \hat{\beta} = .748 \qquad \hat{\gamma} = .528 \qquad \hat{\gamma}' = .850 \qquad \hat{\delta} = 1.973$$

$$R^2 = .977 \qquad D.W. = 1.70$$

U.S. quarterly (1947–1962, seasonally adjusted annual rates)

$$q_t = \underset{(31.66)}{38.35} + \underset{(.106)}{.682}\, q_{t-1} + \underset{(.119)}{.263}\, \Delta x_t + \underset{(.091)}{.275}\, x_{t-1} \tag{4}$$

$$\hat{\alpha} = 20.77 \qquad \hat{\beta} = 1.817 \qquad \hat{\gamma} = .149 \qquad \hat{\gamma}' = .866 \qquad \hat{\delta} = 2.195$$

$$R^2 = .965 \qquad D.W. = 2.24$$

$$R^2 = .17 \quad (\Delta q_t \text{ as dependent variable})$$

Of these three equations, (2) and (4) are the most important; the annual postwar equation is given only because it covers the same period as the quarterly equation. The two principal equations are both quite satisfactory when taken by themselves: the estimated coefficients are all highly significant —except for the intercept in equation (4)—and the derived structural parameters all have the expected sign; moreover, the fit is good in both cases,[4] and there is no *prima facie* evidence of serial correlation. Equation (3),

[3] The matter is slightly complicated by the fact that quarterly national accounts data are customarily expressed as annual rates. This does not change what has just been said about $\beta$ and $\delta$, but it implies that the quarterly and annual $\alpha$'s should be the same.

[4] The $R^2$ with $\Delta q_t$ as dependent variable is given for (2) and (4), and also for (5) and (6) because it is needed for comparison with the permanent-income equations of the next section; it may be ignored for the moment.

based on only sixteen observations, is rather less satisfactory. The coefficient of $q_{t-1}$ is not significant, and the coefficients of $\Delta x_t$ and $x_{t-1}$ are very close to each other, which suggests that a purely static consumption function would have done just as well.

When we consider (2) and (4) more closely, however, our initial satisfaction has to give way to considerable doubt. In the first place, they are by no means consistent with each other in view of the preceding discussion of the effect of different periods of observations. Even substituting (3) for (2) does not help much in this respect. The calculated values of $\beta$ and $\delta$, which in theory should be a fourth in (4) of what they are in (2) or (3), are actually much larger. The calculated values of $\alpha$ and $\gamma$, which should be the same, are obviously different, even though we cannot calculate the significance of the difference. The only encouraging result of the comparison is that $\gamma'$, the long-run MPC, is quite similar in (2) and (4), and in fact virtually identical in (3) and (4). Even here it may be objected that a long-run MPC of about .85 is rather low.

Further doubts, especially about the quarterly equation, arise from inspection of Figures 6.1 and 6.2, showing actual and computed values of per capita consumption. The fit of the annual equation (2) in the postwar period clearly leaves much to be desired, though it does well in the prewar period. More serious, however, are the defects of the quarterly equation. In the years 1950–1951 predicted consumption appears to lag one quarter behind actual consumption. Of course we can hardly expect our equation to predict the two buying waves resulting from the Korean War (one in the third quarter of 1950 and the other in the first quarter of 1951), but it is a little disturbing that it is also unable to handle the aftermath of these buying waves. The reason is presumably that the equation treats consumption as habit-forming, whereas the hoarding that then took place had just the opposite effect on subsequent consumption.

Even if this defect is charitably overlooked, another and more fundamental inadequacy is revealed by Figure 6.2, particularly in the years after the Korean War. There is a distinct tendency for predicted consumption to be lower than actual consumption in the upswing of the various business cycles, and to exceed it in the downswings. This is especially clear in 1953–1955, in the winter of 1957–1958, and in 1961–1962. Here again predicted consumption appears to be one quarter behind actual consumption.

It is instructive to consider the effect of these two inadequacies on the Durbin–Watson coefficient, which in the case of equation (4) failed to reveal anything peculiar in the residuals. The Korean War problem, as is clear from Figure 6.2, leads to sharp swings in the residuals from negative to positive, hence to strong negative serial correlation. The cyclical problem, on the other hand, manifests itself in long strings of residuals of like sign, corresponding to positive serial correlation. As it happens, these two forms of serial correlation virtually cancel each other over the period as a whole, so that the *D.W.* coefficient cannot give a warning.

Figure 6.1

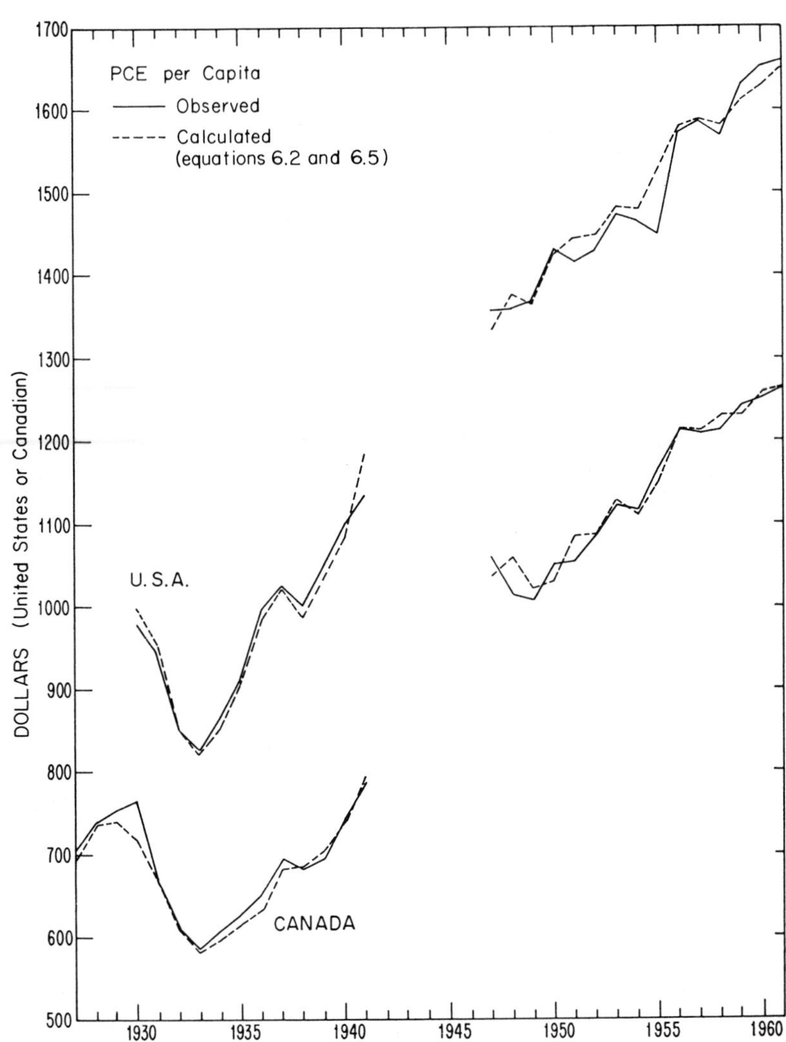


The empirical results for Canada are as follows:

Canada annual (1927–1941, 1947–1961)

(5)
$$q_t = \underset{(.102)}{.619}\, q_{t-1} + \underset{(.069)}{.605}\, \Delta x_t + \underset{(.096)}{.364}\, x_{t-1}$$

$$\hat{\alpha} = 0 \qquad \hat{\beta} = .391 \qquad \hat{\gamma} = .522 \qquad \hat{\gamma}' = .955 \qquad \hat{\delta} = .862$$

$$R^2 = .997 \qquad D.W. = 2.27$$

$$R^2 = .79 \quad (\Delta q_t \text{ as dependent variable})$$

Figure 6.2

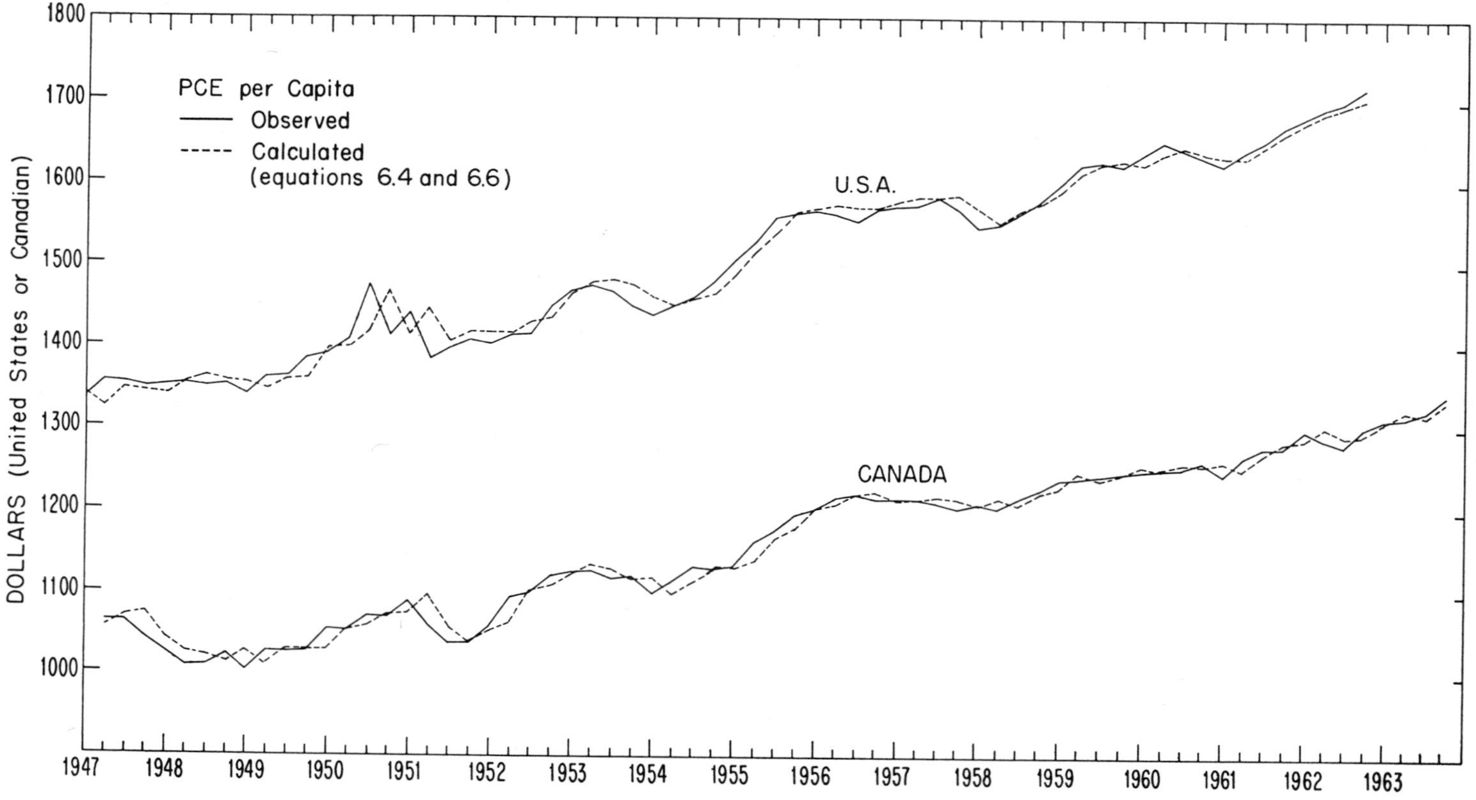

PCE per Capita
Observed
Calculated
(equations 6.4 and 6.6)
U.S.A.
CANADA
DOLLARS (United States or Canadian)
1800
1700
1600
1500
1400
1300
1200
1100
1000
1947
1948
1949
1950
1951
1952
1953
1954
1955
1956
1957
1958
1959
1960
1961
1962
1963

Canada quarterly (1946–1962)

$$q_t = .917\, q_{t-1} + .170\, \Delta x_t + .080\, x_{t-1} \tag{6}$$
$$(.073) \qquad (.064) \qquad (.068)$$

$$\hat{\alpha} = 0 \qquad \hat{\beta} = .527 \qquad \hat{\gamma} = .135 \qquad \hat{\gamma}' = .415 \qquad \hat{\delta} = .613$$

$$R^2 = .983 \qquad D.W. = 1.88$$

$$R^2 = .18 \quad (\Delta q_t \text{ as dependent variable})$$

Many of the comments made on the United States equations apply equally to the Canadian equations. Again the estimates are superficially plausible, but unsatisfactory on closer examination. In the Canadian case the failure of the long-run MPC calculated from (5) to agree with the one calculated from (6) is particularly disturbing. The fault is no doubt with the quarterly equation, where $\gamma' = .415$, and it is probably due to the high intercorrelation between $q_{t-1}$ and $x_{t-1}$ in the quarterly observations. It will be noted that the estimated coefficient of $x_{t-1}$, which is one of the two determinants of $\gamma'$—see equation (45) in Chapter 1—has a large standard error.

Despite all these difficulties, the results of this section are basically encouraging: they are good enough to suggest that we are on the right track and that a refinement of the basic dynamic models will overcome some or all of the anomalies observed. Various refinements are considered in the next three sections.

## *II. A Permanent-Income Variant of the Basic Dynamic Model*

Ever since the publication of *A Theory of the Consumption Function* (Friedman, 1957), the permanent-income hypothesis has dominated research in this area. It is still too early for a definitive evaluation of the empirical relevance of the hypothesis, but it is undeniable that it has contributed greatly to our understanding of statistical estimates of the consumption function. As is well known, the hypothesis is essentially concerned with errors of measurement in the income variable and with the bias they cause in the apparent MPC if it is not estimated with due attention to the Friedman effect. In the strict form proposed by Friedman himself, consumption depends only on the "permanent component" of income and not at all on the "transitory component." For our purposes, however, we need not fully commit ourselves to this hypothesis;[5] rather we shall allow permanent and transitory income to have different MPC's. On the other hand, we are compelled to introduce a special assumption relating measured income to permanent income, since the latter concept is not directly observable.

[5] Friedman does not include the purchase of durables in consumption. For total consumption as analyzed in this chapter, which includes durables, the strict hypothesis is not appropriate. Previous studies—for instance, Houthakker and Haldi (1960) for cars—indicated that transitory income does affect expenditure on durables.

Fortunately this assumption appears to be in line with Friedman's own ideas concerning the use of the permanent-income hypothesis in time-series analysis.

The continuous-time model used in this section looks as follows:

$$q(t) = \alpha + \beta s(t) + \gamma_p x_p(t) + \gamma_t x_t(t), \tag{7}$$

$$\dot{s}(t) = q(t) - \delta s(t), \tag{8}$$

$$x(t) = x_p(t) + x_t(t), \tag{9}$$

$$\dot{x}_p(t) = \kappa \dot{x}(t), \tag{10}$$

where $x_p$ is permanent income and $x_t$ transitory income. Equations (7) and (8) are essentially the same as in the basic model, and (9) is a definition. The special assumption just mentioned is embodied in (10), according to which the change over time of permanent income is proportional to the change in measured income. The constant $\kappa$ should normally be less than one. This assumption corresponds to one used by Friedman for measuring permanent income when measured income is growing exponentially.[6] At least during the postwar period, growth has been roughly of this type. We must admit, however, that this way of introducing the Friedman effect is crude and that it may not do justice to the permanent-income hypothesis. The difficulty is that the hypothesis is hard to translate into an operational procedure without special assumptions, such as (10), whose consistency with the hypothesis is open to question.[7]

However this may be, the model described by equations (7) through (10) can be transformed into an estimating equation by similar devices as were applied to the basic dynamic model in sections II and III of Chapter 1. First differentiate (7) with respect to time and substitute from (8) to obtain

$$\dot{q}(t) = \beta\{q(t) - \delta s(t)\} + \gamma_p \dot{x}_p(t) + \gamma_t \dot{x}_t(t). \tag{11}$$

According to (9) we have

$$\dot{x}(t) = \dot{x}_p(t) + \dot{x}_t(t), \tag{12}$$

and hence, using (10),

$$\dot{x}_t = (1 - \kappa)\dot{x} \tag{13}$$

so that (12) becomes

$$\dot{q}(t) = \beta\{q(t) - \delta s(t)\} + \{\gamma_p \kappa + \gamma_t(1 - \kappa)\}\dot{x}(t), \tag{14}$$

[6] Differentiating equation (5.17) on p. 144 of Friedman (1957), we get (in Friedman's notation)

$$\dot{y}_p^* (t) = \beta y^*(t).$$

Hence if

$$\dot{y}^*(t) = \frac{\beta}{\kappa} y^*(t) \qquad \text{[our } \kappa\text{]},$$

which implies exponential growth, our equation (10) is equivalent to Friedman's.

[7] On this subject, see also Friedman (1963).

where for convenience we shall write

$$\gamma_p k + \gamma_t(1 - \kappa) = \gamma^*. \tag{15}$$

Hence $\gamma^*$ is the marginal propensity to consume out of measured income. Next we eliminate $s(t)$ by solving (7):

$$\beta s(t) = q(t) - \alpha - \gamma_p x_p - \gamma_t x_t, \tag{16}$$

which transforms (14), using (15), into

$$\dot{q}(t) = \alpha\delta + (\beta - \delta)q(t) + \gamma_p \delta x_p(t) + \gamma_t \delta x_t(t) + \gamma^* \dot{x}(t). \tag{17}$$

The only thing that remains is to eliminate $x_p(t)$ and $x_t(t)$, which are not observable. This is done by differentiating again and using (9), (13), and (15), leading to

$$\ddot{q}(t) = (\beta - \delta)\dot{q}(t) + \gamma^* \delta \dot{x}(t) + \gamma^* \ddot{x}(t). \tag{18}$$

Except for the appearance of second derivatives, this equation is similar to (8) of Chapter 1, and can be approximated by a finite model in the same manner. We can therefore write immediately

$$\Delta q_t = A_1^* \Delta q_{t-1} + A_2^* \Delta^2 x_t + A_3^* \Delta x_{t-1}, \tag{19}$$

where

$$A_1^* = \frac{1 + \frac{1}{2}(\beta - \delta)}{1 - \frac{1}{2}(\beta - \delta)}, \tag{20}$$

$$A_2^* = \frac{\gamma^*(1 - \delta/2)}{1 - \frac{1}{2}(\beta - \delta)}, \tag{21}$$

$$A_3^* = \frac{\gamma^* \delta}{1 - \frac{1}{2}(\beta - \delta)}. \tag{22}$$

From (20) through (22) unique estimates of $\beta$, $\gamma^*$, and $\delta$ can be derived, but it is not possible to estimate $\gamma_p$, $\gamma_t$, and $\kappa$ separately. Since these structural parameters are unidentifiable, it may seem that there is little to be gained from the permanent-income version of the dynamic model. However, if the permanent-income version were to provide more plausible estimates of $\beta$ and $\delta$, and also do a better job of explaining the historical record, then this would be evidence favoring use of the model.

Let us now turn to the empirical results:

U.S. annual (1929–1942, 1947–1961)

$$\underset{}{\Delta^2 q_t} = \underset{(.196)}{-.278\,\Delta q_{t-1}} + \underset{(.058)}{.624\,\Delta^2 x_t} + \underset{(.151)}{.832\,\Delta x_{t-1}} + \underset{(4.900)}{5.972\,d_t} \tag{23}$$

$$\hat{\beta} = .449 \qquad \hat{\gamma}^* = .578 \qquad \hat{\gamma}^{*\prime} = .651 \qquad \hat{\delta} = 3.988$$

$R^2 = .850$ ($\Delta q_t$ as dependent variable) $\qquad D.W. = 1.62$

$R^2 = .989$ ($q_t$ as dependent variable)

U.S. quarterly (1947–1962)

(24)
$$\Delta q_t = \underset{(.138)}{.283}\,\Delta q_{t-1} + \underset{(.122)}{.278}\,\Delta^2 x_t + \underset{(.161)}{.527}\,\Delta x_{t-1}$$

$$\hat{\beta} = 32.114 \qquad \hat{\gamma}^* = .041 \qquad \hat{\gamma}^{*\prime} = .410 \qquad \hat{\delta} = 35.695$$

$$R^2 = .133 \quad (\Delta q_t \text{ as dependent variable}) \qquad D.W. = 2.03$$

$$R^2 = .975 \quad (q_t \text{ as dependent variable})$$

Canada annual (1927–1941, 1947–1961)

(25)
$$\Delta q_t = \underset{(.143)}{-.296}\,\Delta q_{t-1} + \underset{(.074)}{.602}\,\Delta^2 x_t + \underset{(.124)}{.914}\,\Delta x_{t-1} + \underset{(4.17)}{7.85}d_t$$

$$\hat{\beta} = 2.716 \qquad \hat{\gamma}^* = .412 \qquad \hat{\gamma}^{*\prime} = .992 \qquad \hat{\delta} = 6.299$$

$$R^2 = .81 \quad (\Delta q_t \text{ as dependent variable}) \qquad D.W. = 2.06$$

$$R^2 = .997 \quad (q_t \text{ as dependent variable})$$

Canada quarterly (1947–1963)

(26)
$$\Delta q_t = \underset{(.134)}{.056}\,\Delta q_{t-1} + \underset{(.069)}{.169}\,\Delta^2 x_t + \underset{(.168)}{.198}\,\Delta x_{t-1}$$

$$\hat{\beta} = 1.051 \qquad \hat{\gamma}^* = .124 \qquad \hat{\gamma}^{*\prime} = .197 \qquad \hat{\delta} = .197$$

$$R^2 = .49 \quad (\Delta q_t \text{ as dependent variable}) \qquad D.W. = 1.99$$

$$R^2 \geqslant .999 \quad (q_t \text{ as dependent variable})$$

When these estimates are compared with those of the preceding section, it cannot be said that they represent an improvement. The two quarterly equations are especially unsatisfactory, but the $\beta$'s and $\delta$'s in both annual equations, and the long-run MPC for the United States, are also implausible. This may be due to the fitting procedure[8] or to the underlying model. In any case equations (23) through (26) suggest that the permanent-income approach is not the answer to the difficulties encountered in the preceding section.

## *III. Savings as the Acquisition of Nondepreciating Assets*

The more elaborate version of the dynamic model that has just been described proved to be useless. In the present section we shall see what a simplified version can do.

The simplification is based on a peculiarity of savings as an object of choice, namely, that the assets acquired through saving are durable and in fact may be assumed to have a depreciation rate of zero. Under the national accounting

[8] The equations were actually fitted with $\Delta^2 q_t$ as the dependent variable. Curiously enough, the $R^2$ with $\Delta^2 q_t$ as dependent variable is considerably better than those with $\Delta q_t$, though not as high as with $q_t$. In any case, goodness of fit is not much of a problem with any of the consumption functions tested here; nor for that matter is autocorrelation of the residuals.

definition observed in our basic data, saving is essentially the net accumulation of *financial* assets and liabilities, such as money, bonds, shares, equities in unincorporated business,[9] and various forms of nonbusiness debt. Financial assets frequently earn interest or dividends so that it might seem that they have a negative depreciation rate, but this is not the case. Current revenues from investments are included in income and are not counted as an addition to capital, and interest on consumer debt is regarded as an item of expenditure.[10] Capital gains and losses do not appear in the national accounts at all; in principle they may influence consumption and savings, but in practice their influence is hard to detect, and we shall leave them out of the present analysis. The crucial assumption of this section (and of the next) is that, for savings, $\delta = 0$.

The basic model then becomes

$$y(t) = \alpha + \beta s(t) + \gamma x(t), \tag{27}$$

$$\dot{s}(t) = y(t), \tag{28}$$

where $y(t)$ is savings and $s(t)$ the stock of financial assets. Eliminating $s(t)$ by differentiation we get

$$\dot{y}(t) = \beta y(t) + \gamma \dot{x}(t), \tag{29}$$

and in terms of discrete time periods, with the usual approximation,

$$y_t = \frac{1 + \frac{1}{2}\beta}{1 - \frac{1}{2}\beta} y_{t-1} + \frac{\gamma}{1 - \frac{1}{2}\beta} \Delta x_t, \tag{30}$$

or more simply

$$y_t = B_1 y_{t-1} + B_2 \Delta x_t. \tag{31}$$

The result of assuming $\delta = 0$ is therefore to lose two parameters in the estimating equation. It is to be noted, however, that we have not assumed $\alpha = 0$; but $\alpha$ cannot be determined from the estimating equation (31).

The assumption $\delta = 0$ leads to an apparent difficulty with the long-run concepts. In Chapter 1 we defined the static long run by the condition $\dot{s} = 0$, and we see then from (28) that $\hat{y} = 0$. This is as it should be, for in static long-run equilibrium there would be no point in continuing to accumulate a nondepreciating asset. But what about the case of steady long-run growth? We saw in section II of Chapter 1 that the long-run MPC is the same for long-run equilibrium as for steady (linear) growth in income. In the present instance the long-run MPS is evidently zero in the static case, in

[9] In the national accounts, all real estate, including owner-occupied dwellings, is assumed to be owned by the business sector. Increases in the stock of durable consumer goods are not included in saving.

[10] There is perhaps an inconsistency here, since such interest might more logically be treated as a deduction from income. The point at issue is not affected by this.

accordance with (1.11), and (1.14) implies that the growth rate of savings is also zero. It then follows from (1.15) and (28) that

$$g_s = \hat{y} = -\frac{\gamma}{\beta}g_x. \tag{32}$$

Hence, *in steady linear growth savings are proportional to the (absolute) growth in income.*[11] If, in accordance with most of the literature, we put the matter in terms of the savings rate and the (relative) growth rate, we find that

$$\frac{\hat{y}}{x} = -\frac{\gamma}{\beta}\frac{g_x}{x}, \tag{33}$$

so that in steady linear growth the savings ratio is proportional to the growth rate. Since $\gamma > 0$ and $\beta < 0$ (financial assets being durable), the constant of proportionality is positive. In view of (1.15) it may be interpreted as a long-run marginal wealth–income ratio.

Similar results can be derived for the case of exponential growth in per capita income, provided the structural equation (27) is made homogeneous by putting $\alpha = 0$. If we assume

$$\dot{x}(t) = \rho x(t), \tag{34}$$

where $\rho$ is the growth rate of per capita income, then it is easy to show that $y$ and $s$ will ultimately grow at the same rate $\rho$. It also follows that

$$\hat{y}(t) = \frac{\gamma\rho x(t)}{\rho - \beta} = \frac{\gamma\dot{x}(t)}{\rho - \beta}, \tag{35}$$

where $\hat{y}(t)$ represents savings in "equilibrium growth," also known as the "golden age." The stock of assets, $s(t)$, does not play any independent part in determining $\hat{y}(t)$, but follows a similarly defined growth path $\hat{s}(t)$.

Translating (35) into a savings ratio we find

$$\frac{\hat{y}(t)}{x(t)} = \frac{\gamma\rho}{\rho - \beta}, \tag{36}$$

which may be compared to (33) by putting $g_x = \rho x$. Although the steady-growth savings ratio is proportional to the growth rate of income in both cases, the proportionality factor is not the same. In (33) this factor is independent of the growth rate, but in (36) it is not. For the growth rates typical in the United States, the difference between (33) and (36) is not negligible; in order to facilitate this comparison, we shall give for each empirical equation not only $-(\gamma/\beta)$ as required by (33) but also $\gamma\rho^*/(\rho^* - \beta)$ according to (36), where $\rho^*$ has been put at .025 for the annual equations and at .006 for the

[11] The theory of savings developed in this section is therefore closely related to that of Modigliani and Brumberg (developed in 1953), at least in its long-run aspects. In the next section we shall bring our theory even closer to the Modigliani–Brumberg view by expressing it in aggregate rather than in per capita terms. It should be noted that so far in this chapter, as everywhere in this book, consumption, savings, and income are expressed per capita.

quarterly equations to reflect a typical growth rate of per capita disposable personal income. As was pointed out earlier, exponential growth is in general more plausible than linear growth, but linear growth between 1961 and 1970 was one of the assumptions of our projection exercise.

There is more to be said about the theoretical aspects of the present model of savings, but we must leave this to another occasion and confine ourselves to a few brief remarks here. The consumption equation corresponding to (31) can be obtained from the identity $x_t = q_t + y_t$, where $q_t$ stands for consumption as before. It is then easily seen that since (31) has no intercept, the consumption equation cannot have one either. Moreover, the absence of a term with $x_{t-1}$ in (31) implies that, in the consumption equation, $A_2 = A_3$. We know from section 1.V that $A_2 = A_3$ corresponds to $\delta = 2$, which sheds further light on the significance of this rather obscure special case.[12] We also note that the condition $A_2 = A_3$ is approximately satisfied in (3) and (4), though less obviously in (2) and (6).

We now come to the empirical results obtained with the model of this section.

U.S. annual (1929–1941, 1947–1961), Pass 1

(37)
$$y_t = \underset{(.045)}{.936}\, y_{t-1} + \underset{(.056)}{.376}\, \Delta x_t$$

$$R^2 = .845 \qquad D.W. = 2.43$$

$$\hat{\beta} = 2\frac{A_1 - 1}{A_1 + 1} = -.0663 \qquad \hat{\gamma} = \frac{2A_2}{A_1 + 1} = .389 \qquad -\frac{\hat{\gamma}}{\hat{\beta}} = 5.86$$

$$\frac{\hat{\gamma}\rho^*}{\rho^* - \hat{\beta}} = .106$$

Same, Pass 3

(38)
$$y_t = \underset{(.045)}{.911}\, y_{t-1} + \underset{(.063)}{.350}\, \Delta x_t - \underset{(.202)}{.317}\, z_t$$

$$R^2 = .867 \qquad D.W. = 1.97$$

$$\hat{\beta} = -.0926 \qquad \hat{\gamma} = .367 \qquad -\frac{\hat{\gamma}}{\hat{\beta}} = 3.96 \qquad \frac{\gamma\rho^*}{\rho^* - \hat{\beta}} = .078$$

In (37) the *D.W.* coefficient is high enough to warrant application of the three-pass method for the first time in this chapter, leading to a distinct improvement. The third-pass equation is more plausible because the steady-growth coefficients are closer to actual experience, especially in recent years. The linear-growth coefficients of 5.86 would imply a savings ratio of nearly 15 percent for $\rho^* = .025$, and even for exponential growth the savings ratio

[12] In this case, the consumption function can be written in the form $q_t = A_1 q_{t-1} + A_2^* x_t$. But for technical reasons all computations have been made with (31).

is too high at 10.6 percent. The corresponding coefficients in (38), especially for exponential growth, make much better sense. The different effect of linear and exponential growth on savings can be clearly observed.

U.S. quarterly (1947–1962), Pass 1

(39)
$$y_t = \underset{(.021)}{.944}\, y_{t-1} + \underset{(.110)}{.872}\, \Delta x_t$$

$$R^2 = .675 \qquad D.W. = 2.48$$

$$\hat{\beta} = -.0580 \qquad \hat{\gamma} = .897 \qquad -\frac{\hat{\gamma}}{\hat{\beta}} = 15.45 \qquad \frac{\hat{\gamma}\rho^*}{\rho^* - \hat{\beta}} = .073$$

In view of the high $D.W.$ coefficient for the quarterly data, a Pass 3 equation was also computed, but it was unacceptable because $B_1 = 1.000$, which is inconsistent with the underlying theory since it makes $\beta = 0$ and the steady-growth savings ratios indeterminate. Moreover in this equation the three-pass variable $z_t$ was so highly correlated with $y_{t-1}$ as to make all the estimates suspect. We shall therefore take (39) as the best quarterly equation.

The steady-growth savings ratios from (39) are again plausible and agree very well with those derived from (38); we recall that $\rho^* = .025$ for the annual equations and $\rho^* = .006$ for the quarterly equations. This is an important point in favor of the structural model. On the other hand, the $\beta$'s and $\gamma$'s for (38) and (39) are again not in the expected pattern mentioned at the outset, though the discrepancies are not as striking as they were in section I. This may result in part from the different periods covered by the annual and quarterly equations; we have not computed postwar annual equations for this section, but do so for the United States in the next.

Equation (39), like its counterparts in the two preceding sections, appears to be much affected by the violent fluctuations associated with the Korean War. We therefore present a quarterly equation covering only the post-Korean period:

U.S. quarterly (1953–1962), Pass 1

(40)
$$y_t = \underset{(.013)}{.980}\, y_{t-1} + \underset{(.100)}{.356}\, \Delta x_t$$

$$R^2 = .538 \qquad D.W. = 2.03$$

$$\hat{\beta} = -.0202 \qquad \hat{\gamma} = .360 \qquad -\frac{\hat{\gamma}}{\hat{\beta}} = 18.9 \qquad \frac{\hat{\gamma}\rho^*}{\rho^* - \hat{\beta}} = .078$$

It is interesting to observe the very close agreement of this equation with (38). The steady-growth savings ratios and $\gamma$'s are virtually identical, and the quarterly $\beta$ is close to a fourth of the annual $\beta$. In view of this, we should perhaps prefer (40) to (39).

The goodness of fit of the equations of this section cannot be directly compared with those of section I, at least not by means of $R^2$, because the dependent variables are different. However the "standard error of estimate," which is the estimated standard deviation of the dependent variable when the explanatory variables are held constant, is conceptually comparable between the consumption and the savings equations, for when income $x_t$ is held constant the standard deviation of $q_t$ is the same as that of $x_t - q_t$. Empirically the standard errors of estimate are very close to each other, but in the consumption equations they are slightly smaller.

Canada annual (1927–1941, 1947–1961), Pass 1

(41)
$$y_t = \underset{(.047)}{.849}\, y_{t-1} + \underset{(.075)}{.423}\, \Delta x_t$$

$$R^2 = .820 \qquad D.W. = 2.53$$

$$\hat{\beta} = -.163 \qquad \hat{\gamma} = .458 \qquad -\frac{\hat{\gamma}}{\hat{\beta}} = 2.83 \qquad \frac{\hat{\gamma}\rho^*}{\rho^* - \hat{\beta}} = .0605$$

Canada quarterly (1947–1963), Pass 1

(42)
$$y_t = \underset{(.018)}{.957}\, y_{t-1} + \underset{(.053)}{.845}\, \Delta x_t$$

$$R^2 = .795 \qquad D.W. = 1.92$$

$$\hat{\beta} = -.0437 \qquad \hat{\gamma} = .862 \qquad -\frac{\hat{\gamma}}{\hat{\beta}} = 19.6 \qquad \frac{\hat{\gamma}\rho^*}{\rho^* - \hat{\beta}} = .104$$

These two equations are both good, but the first appears to be the more satisfactory despite the high *D.W.* coefficient (the three-pass method failed to correct this). The exponential steady-growth ratio of 6 percent is in line with Canadian historical experience, whereas the 10.4 percent resulting from the quarterly equation is too high. The latter figure may be due in part to the inclusion of the years 1962 and 1963, during which the savings ratio rose sharply. The annual $\beta$ is about four times the quarterly $\beta$, as it should be, but the annual $\gamma$ differs substantially from the quarterly $\gamma$. Further research on the Canadian savings function is clearly required.[13]

To conclude this section, it seems fair to say that the interpretation of savings as the acquisition of nondepreciating assets is a useful step forward. Though some problems remain, it has led both to simpler formulas and to more plausible empirical results. A variation on the same theme will be discussed next.

[13] Our colleague Thomas Wilson has pointed out to us that the Canadian savings and income data are seriously influenced by fluctuations in farm inventories. There appears to be no simple way of eliminating this disturbance.

## *IV. Savings and the Population Effect*

We have already referred to the similarity between the zero-depreciation theory of savings just presented and the Modigliani–Brumberg theory. The similarity is most marked in the long-run behavior predicted by the two theories; whether it extends also to the short-run savings function is less clear, since Modigliani's views have not so far been spelled out in detail.[14] There is another aspect that has been emphasized by Modigliani, namely the population effect already discussed in Chapter 2, section II. As was noted there, the growth rate of population is normally too small to cause a perceptible bias in the estimates of the depreciation rate. However, in the interpretation of savings now under consideration, $\delta$ is assumed to be zero, so it is conceivable that $\psi$ (the growth rate of population) may affect the estimates more seriously.

The population effect can be taken into account by writing

$$S = \pi s, \qquad Y = \pi y, \qquad X = \pi x, \tag{43}$$

where $\pi$ is population. The structural equations (27)–(28) then become

$$Y(t) = \alpha\pi(t) + \beta S(t) + \gamma X(t), \tag{44}$$

$$\dot{S}(t) = Y(t), \tag{45}$$

in accordance with (2.2) for zero depreciation. Consequently

$$\dot{Y}(t) = \beta Y(t) + \gamma \dot{X}(t), \tag{46}$$

which is of the same form as (29) and can therefore also be written in the estimating form

$$Y_t = C_1 Y_{t-1} + C_2 \Delta X_t. \tag{47}$$

All we have to do, therefore, is to work with aggregate rather than per capita savings and income. The only other change we have to make is in the growth rate of aggregate income $\rho^{**}$ which is now put at .041 for annual equations and .01 for quarterly equations.

U.S. annual (1929–1941, 1947–1961)

$$Y_t = \underset{(.045)}{.845}\, Y_{t-1} + \underset{(.058)}{.408}\, \Delta X_t \tag{48}$$

$$R^2 = .968 \qquad D.W. = 2.58$$

$$\hat{\beta} = -.168 \qquad \hat{\gamma} = .442 \qquad -\frac{\hat{\gamma}}{\hat{\beta}} = 2.63 \qquad \frac{\hat{\gamma}\rho^{**}}{\rho^{**} - \hat{\beta}} = .087$$

[14] His most important writings on the subject, notably the 1953 paper with Brumberg and his presidential address to the Econometric Society in 1962, remain unpublished. We have been privileged to read the former and hear the latter.

U.S. quarterly (1947–1962)

(49)
$$Y_t = \underset{(.022)}{.900}\, Y_{t-1} + \underset{(.109)}{.828}\, \Delta X_t$$

$$R^2 = .978 \qquad D.W. = 2.27$$

$$\hat{\beta} = -.106 \qquad \hat{\gamma} = .872 \qquad -\frac{\hat{\gamma}}{\hat{\beta}} = 8.25 \qquad \frac{\hat{\gamma}\rho^{**}}{\rho^{**} - \hat{\beta}} = .075$$

These are both Pass 1 equations; the three-pass method has not been applied to the United States equations in this section. The savings ratios for exponential growth are reasonably close to each other and to the observed ratios, but the pattern of the $\beta$'s and $\gamma$'s is not what it should be. We have therefore also tried different time periods.

U.S. annual (1947–1962)

(50)
$$Y_t = \underset{(.064)}{.809}\, Y_{t-1} + \underset{(.112)}{.450}\, \Delta X_t$$

$$R^2 = .964 \qquad D.W. = 2.47$$

$$\hat{\beta} = -.211 \qquad \hat{\gamma} = .498 \qquad -\frac{\hat{\gamma}}{\hat{\beta}} = 2.35 \qquad \frac{\hat{\gamma}\beta^{**}}{\rho^{**} - \hat{\beta}} = .081$$

This equation agrees somewhat better with (49), but it is still not very close to it.

U.S. quarterly (1953–1962)

(51)
$$Y_t = \underset{(.016)}{.960}\, Y_{t-1} + \underset{(.100)}{.380}\, \Delta X_t$$

$$R^2 = .995 \qquad D.W. = 1.92$$

$$\hat{\beta} = -.0406 \qquad \hat{\gamma} = .388 \qquad -\frac{\hat{\gamma}}{\hat{\beta}} = 9.56 \qquad \frac{\hat{\gamma}\rho^{**}}{\rho^{**} - \hat{\beta}} = .077$$

This is a very satisfactory equation, which agrees closely with (48) and (50). The good fit is worth noting: the equation comes within 10 percent of actual savings in nearly every quarter, and we shall see in the next section that it also predicts the 1963 and 1964 figures very well. Translated into the same dependent variable, however, the fit of (51) is not markedly better than that of (40).

We have not computed any Canadian equations for aggregate savings. However, the following equation for aggregate consumption $Q_t$ is of some interest, if only because it shows that the condition $\delta = 0$ for savings, which implies $\delta = 2$ for consumption (see the preceding section), is not too restrictive. By this we mean that an only slightly better fit can be obtained by ignoring the condition, as was indeed done in section I.

Canadian quarterly (1947–1963)

$$Q_t = \underset{(.074)}{.906}\, Q_{t-1} + \underset{(.067)}{.201}\, \Delta X_t + \underset{(.069)}{.095}\, X_{t-1} \tag{52}$$

$$R^2 = .997 \qquad D.W. = 2.02$$

Here $A_2 \neq A_3$, so that (52) does not fully agree with the zero-depreciation theory of saving; the depreciation rate for financial assets implied by (52) is about .1. But the difference $A_2 - A_3$, which has a standard error of about .07, is not very significant; consequently the fit, which is excellent, would not be much reduced by putting $A_2 = A_3$. It is interesting to note that $A_2 \sim 2A_3$, suggesting that for Canadian consumption the Bergstrom model might be appropriate.

The United States equations in this section do not indicate much empirical advantage in working with aggregate rather than per capita figures; the advantage is primarily theoretical. These equations, however, provide some further support for the theory of savings outlined in section II. We shall now subject this theory to a more stringent test.

## *V. Forecasting Performance of the United States Equations*

The criteria by which the underlying models have been judged so far are plausibility of the estimated parameters, consistency between annual and quarterly equations, and goodness of fit. The application of these criteria has led to encouraging results, particularly for the savings equations where $\delta = 0$. Nevertheless it is useful to test these equations more searchingly by looking at their forecasting performance after the period of observation. Since the annual equations use data through 1961 or 1962 and the quarterly equations data through 1962, there is now enough new evidence to make such a test worthwhile.[15] The principal limitation of this test is that 1962, 1963, and 1964 were years of fairly steady growth. A downturn would have added interest to the test.

With dynamic equations containing lagged values of the dependent variable, there are two ways of making conditional forecasts, as we saw in section III of Chapter 5. For instance, if data through period $t$ have been used in estimating the equation, and we need a forecast for period $t + 2$, we can use either

$$\hat{y}_{t+2} = B_1 y_{t+1} + B_2 \Delta x_{t+2} \tag{53}$$

or

$$\hat{y}_{t+2} = B_1 \hat{y}_{t+1} + B_2 \Delta x_{t+2}, \tag{54}$$

[15] The following calculations are all based on the figures appearing in the February 1965 *Survey of Current Business*. These figures will no doubt be revised in subsequent issues.

where

$$\hat{y}_{t+1} = B_1 y_t + B_2 \Delta x_{t+1}. \quad (55)$$

In (53) the actual value of $y_{t+1}$ is used, while in (54) the value of $y_{t-1}$ used is itself a forecast. This distinction is of considerable importance in evaluating an equation, especially when it is to be used for long-term projection. Projections based on (53) are to some extent self-correcting, because they use intervening information, whereas (54) is in the nature of a straightforward extrapolation. The latter test is therefore more stringent and also more relevant. We can rely on (53) only if we are primarily interested in short-term projection; in fact, for $t + 1$, (53) coincides with (54).

In order to achieve comparability between the per capita equations of section III and the aggregate equations of section IV, all the forecasts and actual values are shown in terms of the savings ratio in the accompanying tables. Except for Table 6.3, they are based on (54).

It appears from Table 6.1 that all the annual equations tend to overestimate savings in 1963 and 1964, but the postwar equations are better than the 1929–1961 equations. This is not due to the inclusion of 1962 in the data for the postwar equations, since the whole-period equations forecast the 1962 savings ratio accurately. The aggregate equations perform distinctly better than the per capita equations.

Table 6.1. U.S. Annual Equations: Actual and Projected Values of the Savings Ratio (in %)

| Equation | 1962 | 1963 | 1964 |
|---|---|---|---|
| Actual | 7.9 | 6.8 | 7.5 |
| (37) Per capita 1929–1961 | 7.9 | 8.0 | 8.7 |
| (56) Per capita 1947–1962* | – | 7.3 | 8.3 |
| (48) Aggregate 1929–1961 | 7.8 | 7.7 | 8.4 |
| (50) Aggregate 1947–1962 | – | 7.1 | 8.0 |

* The equation is

$$y_t = \underset{(.048)}{.888}\, y_{t-1} + \underset{(.116)}{.512}\, \Delta x_t. \quad (56)$$

Among the quarterly equations in Table 6.2, those estimated from post-Korean observations are markedly superior to those based on 1947–1962; the latter overpredict recent savings substantially. Of the 1947–1962 equations, the aggregate equations are somewhat better than the per capita equations, but in the 1953–1962 equations there is virtually no difference on this score. The 1953–1962 equations, on the other hand, underestimate the effect of the tax cut that first showed up in the second quarter of 1964, and they do not explain the odd behavior of the savings ratio in the last two quarters of 1964. But this is not too serious, for these very recent figures are preliminary.

Table 6.2. U.S. Quarterly Equations: Actual and Projected Values of the Savings Ratio (in %)

| Equation | 1963 I | 1963 II | 1963 III | 1963 IV | 1964 I | 1964 II | 1964 III | 1964 IV |
|---|---|---|---|---|---|---|---|---|
| Actual | 6.5 | 6.8 | 6.7 | 7.3 | 7.0 | 7.9 | 7.1 | 8.0 |
| (39) Per capita 1947–1962 | 6.8 | 6.8 | 6.9 | 7.2 | 7.8 | 8.9 | 8.9 | 9.0 |
| (40) Per capita 1953–1962 | 6.8 | 6.8 | 6.8 | 6.9 | 7.1 | 7.5 | 7.6 | 7.6 |
| (49) Aggregate 1947–1962 | 6.7 | 6.6 | 6.8 | 7.0 | 7.6 | 8.5 | 8.4 | 8.4 |
| (51) Aggregate 1953–1962 | 6.7 | 6.7 | 6.8 | 6.9 | 7.1 | 7.5 | 7.6 | 7.6 |

It is also interesting to note that the 1953–1962 equations forecast the annual savings ratios for 1963 and 1964 very accurately: the projected figures for both (40) and (51), obtained by adding up the quarterly projections, are 6.8 for 1963 and 7.5 for 1964. The 1947–1962 quarterly equations, however, do not project the 1963 and 1964 annual ratios as well as the 1947–1962 annual equations.

The above test of the quarterly equations suggests that there may have been a change in savings behavior sometime in the early 1950s. The reasons for this change are still obscure. Two phenomena suggest themselves as possibly relevant. One was the steep rise in stock-market prices, which caused huge capital gains (mostly unrealized). In some years during the middle and late 1950s, these capital gains exceeded aggregate personal savings by a considerable margin. Another possible factor was the emergence of considerable unemployment during and after the 1953–54 recession, which has not yet disappeared even now. Further research into these aspects is necessary.

To illustrate the difference between the forecasting equations (53) and (54), Table 6.3 shows the quarterly projections from (51), which appears to be our

Table 6.3. U.S. Quarterly Equation (51): Projected Savings Ratios, Using (53) and (54)

| Base of projection | 1963 I | 1963 II | 1963 III | 1963 IV | 1964 I | 1964 II | 1964 III | 1964 IV |
|---|---|---|---|---|---|---|---|---|
| Actual | 6.5 | 6.8 | 6.7 | 7.3 | 7.0 | 7.9 | 7.1 | 8.0 |
| Savings in 1962–IV | 6.7 | 6.7 | 6.8 | 6.9 | 7.1 | 7.5 | 7.6 | 7.6 |
| Actual savings in preceding quarter | 6.7 | 6.5 | 6.8 | 6.8 | 7.5 | 7.4 | 7.9 | 7.2 |

best savings equation, using either the fourth quarter from 1962 or the quarter preceding the projection as the base. The second line is identical with the corresponding one in Table 6.2. It is clear that (54), which uses more information, does not project as well as (53). This result, it will be recalled, was also found in Chapter 5 with the PCE categories. The reason presumably is that this information, though no doubt relevant conceptually, is too much affected by error. The savings ratio computed from quarterly National Accounts data is rather erratic, and the minor fluctuations in the "actual" figures may be merely errors of measurement. Consequently a forecast based on (53), which pays no attention to these minor fluctuations, is more reliable than one that does.

This also suggests that, in the presence of errors of measurement, we should not rely too much on the comparison of actual and calculated values of the observations in judging a regression equation containing a lagged dependent variable. In such a comparison it is natural to use (54), that is, to use actual values for the lagged dependent variable. Perhaps it is more illuminating to use the equivalent of (53). But then the problem arises of what value of the dependent value should be used as a point of departure. This question needs further study.

## *VI. Conclusions and Projections for 1970*

The application of the dynamic model to total consumption or savings appears to be a definite advance. If the dynamic model is specialized by putting the depreciation rate of net financial assets at zero, very satisfactory savings equations result. However, there is evidence of a change in savings behavior, so that the equations for 1953–1962 (computed only from quarterly data) perform better than those computed from longer periods of observation. There is some gain in applying the equations to aggregate, as opposed to per capita, data. The best equations obtained are satisfactory in at least five respects.

1. The structural parameters derived from them are in accordance with expectations.
2. These parameters are consistent between the best quarterly equations, (40) and (51), and at least some of the annual equations, namely (38) and (48) respectively.
3. The equations fit well during the period of observation.
4. They provide fairly reliable projections after the period of observation.
5. They fit in with the best previous work on savings, especially with the work of Modigliani and his associates.

Even so, a number of problems remain, which have been noted as they became apparent in the preceding sections. In particular it is not clear why our best equations do not perform well before 1953.

Finally, we give some projections for 1970 in line with the original purpose of this book. Since all our projections are based on assumed average annual growth rates of 4 per cent or 5 per cent in aggregate GNP, it is natural to use the aggregate savings equations of section IV for this purpose.

The best of these appears to be (51). In the absence of a more specific assumption, we have taken the growth rate of aggregate disposable personal income to be the same as the growth rate of aggregate GNP. Moreover, it is sufficiently accurate to assume that by 1970 the quarterly equation will have reached the equilibrium corresponding to steady linear growth. We find then that $\rho = .04$, with linear growth, leads to a 1970 savings ratio of 9.5 per cent and $\rho = .05$ to a ratio of 11.5 per cent. If growth in 1970 were exponential at these same rates, the savings ratios would be respectively 7.7 per cent and 9.0 per cent.

# 7

# *Evaluation*

At this point we shall draw together what we consider the major results and conclusions of our investigation. Though we have never lost sight of the fact that the final objective was to provide several sets of projections of personal consumption expenditures in 1970, much of our research energy has fallen into two other clearly defined areas. These are the derivation and empirical estimation of the dynamic model of consumer behavior and the treatment of several formal econometric problems encountered in estimating the equations and making the projections. Hence the investigation as a whole can be described as a thoroughgoing study in econometrics.

## *I. Empirical Results*

We feel that the empirical results have justified our initial enthusiasm for the dynamic model, if only because in many instances the long-run elasticities differ markedly from the short-run elasticities. Of the 83 regression equations estimated in Chapter 4, 72 are dynamic, and in most cases the stock coefficient, depreciation rate, total PCE, and price elasticities are plausible. The results of Chapter 6 show the dynamic model to even better advantage. In addition, use of the dynamic model has largely sidestepped the problems associated with autocorrelation of the error term, though the Monte Carlo results of Chapter 3 suggests that autocorrelation in a projection context may not be as serious a problem as many (including ourselves) had previously believed.

Moreover, use of the dynamic model has enabled us to obtain the highly interesting result that consumption in the United States is characterized more by habit formation than by inventory adjustment. This conclusion is based on the fact that, of the 68 categories with stock coefficients, 50 have positive stock coefficients. These 50 categories account for 58.4 percent of total expenditure in 1961. In addition, the positive stock coefficients for the aggregate consumption functions estimated in Chapter 6 corroborate the predominance of habit formation.

The widespread occurrence of habit formation is in keeping with another major result, namely, that prices play a more modest role than total expenditure in explaining United States consumption. Prices appear in only 45 of the 83 equations, while total expenditure appears in 80. These two results may be due to the relatively high level of income in the United States: If income is high enough, it is possible for nearly all commodities to become subject to habit formation, and, of course, prices become less of a factor. Additional empirical support for this contention is offered by the Swedish consumption study of Taylor (1964). There it was found that, at income levels roughly half those in the United States, inventory adjustment is more widespread than habit formation, while prices play a more important role than in the United States. It should be interesting in future research to study consumption in other countries, such as Canada, the United Kingdom, and the Netherlands, to see whether they also fit into this pattern.

Though the dynamic model is a step forward, it is still a fairly simple model in that there are only a few parameters to estimate. The largest number of parameters that we ever estimate is six, while in most instances we estimate only four or five. However, in view of the fact that our data have been aggregate time-series data, these still may be too many parameters. Econometricians for years have been plagued by the multicollinearity seemingly inherent in time-series data, and our dynamic model cannot solve this problem.

In order to get some feel for the multicollinearity in the data, we have performed a principal components analysis on the independent variables used in Chapter 4.[1] In principle, the variables analyzed should include the first differences of the 83 relative prices, their lagged values, and the lagged values of the dependent variables, in addition to total PCE and the other predictors found in the various static equations. But this would make a total of 260 variables, an unmanageable total for our present computer program. In order to reduce the number of variables to more manageable proportions, we have restricted the set to the current values of the variables that actually appear in one or more of the final equations. Thus, the set includes 45 prices and 9 other variables in addition to total PCE.

Let us denote the set of independent variables (adjusted for their means) by the matrix $X$ and the principal components of $X$ by the matrix $Z$. Then $Z = XK$, where $K$ is an orthogonal transformation matrix.

For the situation at hand, both $X$ and $Z$ are 29 by 55 in dimension, and $K$ is 55 by 55. The total variation in $X$ is equal to the trace of $X'X$, which is also equal to the trace of $Z'Z$. The trace of $Z'Z$ in turn is simply the sum of the latent roots of $Z'Z$. The principal components of $X$ are computed in such a manner that the one associated with the largest latent root, thus accounting for the largest proportion of the total variation in $X$, is extracted first, and so on.

Since by definition the principal components are uncorrelated with one another, a convenient way of analyzing the dimensions of variation in $X$ is to look at the percentage of total variation in $X$ accounted for by each of the principal components. These percentages are tabulated for the first ten principal components of $X$ in Table 7.1. We see that the first component

[1] For a general discussion of principal components, see Kendall (1957) or Anderson (1958).

Table 7.1. Percentage of the Total Variation in 55 Independent Variables Used in the U.S. Consumption Study Accounted for by the First Ten Principal Components

| Principal components | % | Cumulative % |
|---|---|---|
| 1 | 92.21 | 92.21 |
| 2 | 3.73 | 95.94 |
| 3 | 1.98 | 97.92 |
| 4 | 0.99 | 98.91 |
| 5 | 0.31 | 99.22 |
| 6 | 0.18 | 99.39 |
| 7 | 0.15 | 99.54 |
| 8 | 0.14 | 99.68 |
| 9 | 0.09 | 99.77 |
| 10 | 0.05 | 99.81 |

accounts for over 92 percent of the total variation in the 55 variables included in $X$, a very large percentage indeed.[2] The next two components account for 3.73 percent and 1.98 percent, respectively, while the fourth accounts for only 1 percent of the total. These four together account for close to 99 percent of the total variation, thereby implying that four linear combinations of the 55 original variables can effectively describe their variation. Hence there is not enough independent variation in these 55 variables to estimate more than four parameters with precision.

This somewhat harsh conclusion is tempered by the fact that the lagged values of the expenditure series and the first differences of prices have been excluded from our principal-component analysis. Presumably these would add at least one more dimension to the variation, and possibly two or more. Hence we are probably not squeezing our data too hard on those occasions when we estimate five or more parameters.

Though somewhat ancillary to our main purpose, it is an interesting extension of the analysis to correlate the principal components back with the 55 original variables. By this procedure, we may be able to interpret the principal components in terms of underlying economic influences. To our knowledge, this has never been done with United States time-series consumption data, though Stone (1947) in a pioneering paper performed a principal-component analysis on some seventeen constituent series of United States national income for the period 1922–1938.[3] Stone found that 97.45 percent of the total variation in these series could be accounted for by three "factors" that were very closely associated with income, the rate of change of income, and a trend.

[2] This result is not surprising, however. In an extensive principal-component analysis of the predetermined variables of the Klein–Goldberger 1929–1952 model (Klein and Goldberger, 1955), Taylor (1965) found that the first principal component also accounted for over 90 percent of the total variation.

[3] This method was first developed by psychologists; for references see Kendall (1957).

In keeping with what we already know, we should expect to find the first principal component closely associated with total expenditure. Beyond this, we might expect one of the components to be associated with the distribution of income, another with the stock of autos, and perhaps still another associated with TV stocks. Of the prices, ideally we would expect durables to be associated with one principal component, nondurables with another, and so on.[4] However, it is unlikely that this will be the case; whether a good is classified as durable or nondurable is often arbitrary. The simple correlations between the 55 original variables and their first four principal components are tabulated in Table 7.2.

Table 7.2. Correlation Between the First Five Principal Components and the 55 Variables Included in $X$

| | Principal components | | | |
|---|---|---|---|---|
| Variable | 1 | 2 | 3 | 4 |
| Total PCE | .9966 | −.0746 | −.0032 | .0278 |
| Population over 18 | .5677 | .6423 | −.0406 | .3645 |
| Farm population | −.9797 | .0939 | .1332 | .0887 |
| Income distribution | −.9753 | −.1769 | −.0182 | .1051 |
| Car stocks | .9365 | −.1949 | −.2325 | .0073 |
| TV stocks | .8383 | −.3042 | −.3853 | −.0712 |
| Population in labor unions | .9426 | .2509 | .1342 | .0259 |
| Nonimmigrant aliens | .8667 | −.3200 | −.2632 | −.0036 |
| Population foreign-born | −.9748 | −.1535 | .1434 | −.0184 |
| Shares sold on NYSE | −.1296 | −.9152 | .0615 | −.0339 |
| Price of | | | | |
| 1.2 | .1353 | .4277 | .7571 | −.2936 |
| 1.4 | −.7223 | −.0142 | −.6229 | .0821 |
| 2.1 | .7110 | −.4105 | −.2414 | −.2854 |
| 2.2 | .6688 | .4545 | .4607 | −.1021 |
| 2.5 | −.8928 | .0020 | −.4402 | .0005 |
| 2.6 | −.3735 | −.1791 | −.8811 | −.1675 |
| 2.7 | −.8065 | .3977 | .1701 | −.1582 |
| 3.1 | −.9519 | −.0044 | −.2288 | −.0593 |
| 5.2 | −.9068 | .0964 | .3431 | −.1193 |
| 5.3 | .4117 | −.0581 | −.7481 | .2236 |
| 5.7 | .2611 | −.5751 | −.4555 | .0922 |
| 5.8a | −.9857 | −.1229 | −.0958 | −.0237 |
| 5.11 | .5471 | .1144 | −.7605 | .0287 |
| 6.3 | .0111 | −.0679 | −.7763 | .5539 |
| 6.7 | −.7481 | .4297 | .1746 | .4419 |
| 6.8 | .8784 | −.0517 | −.3802 | .1221 |
| 7.1 | .7664 | −.5376 | −.3107 | .0767 |

[4] Stone also noted that principal components offer a way of introducing a complex of prices into a demand equation. We had anticipated possible use of this procedure had we run into a severe adding-up problem, for if the entire set of prices can be represented by a few principal components, then all prices can in principle be included in the equation. Fortunately, we have not had to do this.

Table 7.2—*continued*

| Variable | Principal components 1 | 2 | 3 | 4 |
|---|---|---|---|---|
| 7.2 | .2792 | .5284 | −.5986 | .4312 |
| 7.4 | .4390 | −.4839 | −.7131 | .1177 |
| 7.5 | .7367 | −.3508 | −.5665 | −.0315 |
| 7.6 | .9576 | −.0356 | .0673 | .0550 |
| 7.7 | −.1887 | −.0867 | −.9116 | −.2524 |
| 8.1a | .8618 | .1055 | −.1389 | −.2974 |
| 8.1b | −.9667 | .0596 | .0309 | .1184 |
| 8.1c | −.7740 | −.4449 | −.3669 | .1139 |
| 8.1d | −.8819 | .0288 | −.3294 | .2069 |
| 8.1f | −.3303 | .2398 | −.1883 | .5259 |
| 8.2a | .1387 | −.2678 | −.9080 | .0575 |
| 8.2b | −.6563 | −.1004 | .0194 | .6604 |
| 8.2c | .0518 | −.3835 | −.8636 | .0181 |
| 8.3a | −.8534 | −.4192 | .0931 | −.2012 |
| 8.3c | −.8937 | −.3887 | .1600 | .0586 |
| 8.3d | −.8999 | .1184 | −.1229 | .1516 |
| 9.2 | −.1460 | −.0279 | −.8850 | .1772 |
| 9.3 | −.5696 | .6548 | −.1643 | .1149 |
| 9.4 | −.9732 | −.0409 | −.0437 | −.0228 |
| 9.5 | −.6567 | −.5287 | .5275 | .0280 |
| 9.6 | −.3174 | −.8905 | .2591 | .1093 |
| 9.7 | .2819 | .3995 | .6171 | .0266 |
| 9.9 | .7487 | −.1316 | −.5724 | −.0819 |
| 9.10 | .8621 | −.1315 | −.4652 | −.0304 |
| 9.12 | −.3435 | .1004 | −.8754 | .2703 |
| 10.3 | .7005 | −.2723 | −.5875 | −.1838 |
| 12.1 | −.7870 | .0766 | .2010 | .4944 |
| 12.3 | .3172 | .3965 | .5274 | .4857 |

Our expectation that the first principal component would be very highly associated with total expenditure is certainly borne out, for the simple correlation between the two is .9966. However, the first principal component is also very highly correlated with a large number of the other variables, including many prices. This is a necessary consequence of the fact that the first component accounts for over 92 percent of the total variation in the 55 variables whereas total PCE by itself accounts for only 65 percent of the total.[5] Hence the correlations in the first column of Table 7.2 give a striking picture of the multicollinearity in the variables.

The picture with regard to the other principal components is less clear. The distribution of income and the stock of autos per capita are very collinear with the first component, and therefore do not stand apart as independent influences. The second principal component is most closely associated with

[5] The figure of 65 percent is obtained by dividing the sum of squared deviations of total PCE by the trace of $X'X$.

the number of shares sold per capita on the New York Stock Exchange and the percentage of the population older than eighteen, the relationship being negative with the former and positive with the latter. Though highly tentative, the positive association with the percentage of the population older than eighteen suggests that the second principal component may reflect the age distribution of the population.

If we disregard prices for the moment, the third and fourth principal components are most closely associated with the stock of TV sets and the percentage of the population older than eighteen respectively, though in neither case are the correlations high enough to warrant an identification of these components.

When we look at the correlations between principal components and prices, nothing very illuminating is apparent. As already noted, many of the prices are highly correlated with the first component, and therefore with total PCE. Presumably the 38 remaining prices excluded from the analysis are also highly collinear with total PCE. If this were the case, it can provide a statistical rationalization for the modest over-all importance of prices in the study. The correlations between prices and the remaining principal components are typically lower than with the first principal component. Moreover, no clear-cut pattern is apparent. In particular, there is no discernible clustering of the prices for durable, nondurables, and services around any particular principal component.[6]

## *II. The Projections for 1970*

The two major results concerning the projections in 1970 are:

1. With few exceptions, the projections are insensitive to the relative prices in 1970.
2. In terms of budget shares, the projections are also not very sensitive to the growth rate of total expenditure.

[6] We have also performed a principal-component analysis on the 45 prices by themselves. The first component accounts for over 78 percent of the total variation in these prices, a high percentage in view of the fact that they are relative prices. The first four principal components account for 97.28 percent of the total variation.

In order to provide an additional test for possible clustering of the prices for durables, nondurables, and services into three groups, we correlated the first four principal components of the 45 prices with the relative prices for durables, nondurables, and services (as defined by the Commerce Department). These correlations are as follows:

| | Principal component | | | |
|---|---|---|---|---|
| | 1 | 2 | 3 | 4 |
| Durables | −.1256 | .3856 | −.6368 | −.3690 |
| Nondurables | .7667 | .2211 | −.4944 | −.0769 |
| Services | −.7147 | −.2193 | .5655 | .1725 |

This correlation matrix suggests that the first is associated with nondurables, while the second and third are associated with durables and services, respectively. However, the correlations are too low, particularly for the second and third, to be very specific.

Beyond these two results, it is difficult to conclude much from the four sets of projections, for if we know what the projections should be in 1970 the whole exercise would be unnecessary.

The accuracy of the predictions for 1962 and 1963, discussed in section III of Chapter 5, serves to increase the confidence that we can place in the projections. As an overall measure of the accuracy of the predicted *changes* in constant-dollar expenditures for each of the categories between 1961 and 1962, the $R^2$ (where each category is weighted by its budget share in 1961) between the actual and predicted changes is .86. The results for 1963 may be improved by subsequent data revisions. There is a slight tendency to overpredict the aggregate (obtained by summing the predictions before they are made to add up), but the distribution of over- and underpredictions is unsystematic.[7]

## III. Formal Econometric Results

Perhaps the most interesting formal econometric results are those obtained in the Monte Carlo experiments of Chapter 3. Though much still remains to be done on both formal and empirical levels, the Monte Carlo results provide several interesting insights into the small sample estimating and projecting properties of dynamic equations. In particular, it was interesting to find that projecting from the structural equation is inefficient, and results in considerable bias. It was also interesting to find that the projections from the three-pass equations are unbiased, though they are less efficient than the biased OLS projections.

The Monte Carlo results also bring home the fact that choosing the projection equation cannot be done in a vacuum. Clearly, there is a difference between a structural equation and a good projection equation. In order to assess properly a projection equation, we need to know how and in what context a projection is to be used. In particular, we need to know the utility function (or at least the cost function) of the policy-maker using the projections, for with this knowledge we could weight such "costs" as bias and variance in choosing the projection equation.

In estimating the dynamic equation, we were led to develop a simple quadratic programing procedure for taking into account an overidentifying restriction on the depreciation rate. Though the procedure itself is short of novel, it does offer some insights into the multicollinearity (which we found earlier in this chapter to be quite substantial) of the predictors. The results here are certainly suggestive for additional research.

Our study also served as an empirical testing ground for the new three-pass least-squares method for estimating models with the lagged dependent variable as a predictor. In general, we must conclude that the technique has

[7] The fact that there is a slight tendency to overpredict the aggregate is an interesting result in itself, for usually aggregate time-series models have a tendency to underpredict actual changes. For detailed discussions of this point, see Theil (1961).

"worked" in the sense that we were able to estimate many equations in the face of substantial autocorrelation in the OLS residuals.

It is time to bring this econometric investigation to a close. If we confess to some satisfaction with the results, this may be merely because experience has taught us not to expect too much. It is not often that a relatively untried theoretical approach (such as our dynamic model) survives an extensive confrontation with a broad range of stubborn facts (such as the detailed personal-consumption-expenditure data for the United States). On the whole it survived better than we had dared to hope. In view of somewhat similar results achieved by Stone and his associates, we may conclude that *an explicitly dynamic formulation should now become part and parcel of demand analysis.* Although improvements can and should be made both in the dynamic theory and in its application, the days of the traditional, essentially static, approach would seem to be numbered.

For obvious reasons, we have to be less confident about the projections for 1970. The dynamic model is useful in explaining the past; whether it is equally good in predicting the future remains to be seen, though the test for 1962 and 1963 provides some encouragement. Here, too, there is more work to be done, especially on extrapolation from the dynamic equation and on measures of reliability of the projection.

In turning this book over to the reader we wish to emphasize, perhaps unnecessarily, that the core of our work is Chapter 4. A detailed discussion of over eighty commodities may not make exciting reading, but it is mostly by the results of that chapter that our work should be judged. Those with less time or patience will find Chapter 6 equally indicative of the possibilities opened by the dynamic model of demand. It is likely that the empirical results of these two chapters can be improved, but the essentially dynamic nature of consumption phenomena now seems to be firmly established.

*Data Sources*

*References*

*Index*

# *Data Sources*

## *I. Annual United States Data*

(1) Total personal consumption expenditure (in 1954 dollars). Source: Bureau of Labor Statistics worksheets. Data in current dollars are in *National Income* (1954), *U.S. Income and Output* (1958), and the successive July issues of the *Survey of Current Business* (all of these are publications of the Office of Business Economics, U.S. Department of Commerce). The regressions in Chapter 4 incorporate revisions made through July 1962.

(2) Percentage of the population older than eighteen years. Sources: For 1930, 1940, and 1950, figures were taken from the *Census of the Population.* The in-between years were obtained by interpolating by the formula $x_{10} = x_0 (1 + r)^{10}$ where $x_{10}$ represents the census year ten years ahead of $x_0$. For 1951–1958, the figures were taken from the *Statistical Abstract* for each year. Finally, 1959–1961 were obtained in the U.S. Department of Commerce, Bureau of the Census, *Current Population Estimates, Series P*-25.

(3) Percentage of the population living on farms. Source: *Economic Report of the President,* 1963, table C-76.

(4) Stock of automobiles per capita. Sources: American Petroleum Institute, *Petroleum Facts and Figures,* 1959 (p. 238) and 1961 (p. 153), and *Wards Automotive Yearbook,* 1962 (p. 146). The data refer to car registrations.

(5) Income distribution. Source: Unpublished data were provided by the Bureau of Labor Statistics. The variable is defined in Chapter 2.

(6) Number of shares sold on the New York Stock Exchange per capita. Sources: *Historical Statistics of the United States from Colonial Times to* 1957, Series x-373 (p. 659), and *Statistical Abstract,* 1962 (p. 467).

(7) Percentage of the population that are members of a labor union. Sources: *Historical Statistics of the United States from Colonial Times to* 1957, Series D-735 and 741 (pp. 97–98), and *Statistical Abstract,* 1962 (p. 241).

(8) Stock of television sets per capita. Sources: *Electrical Merchandising* (for years 1946 and 1947), and *The Economic Almanac,* 1962 (p. 404).

(9) Percentage of the population foreign-born. Source: *Statistical Abstract,* 1960 (p. 32) and 1962 (p. 29). The 1960 *Abstract* provides estimates of the proportion of the United States population (of all races) foreign-born by decades 1920, 1930, 1940, and 1950. The 1962 *Abstract* provides only an estimate of the white United States population foreign-born, which is 5.2 per cent of the total population. During the earlier decades, an average of .2 per cent of the United States population was both nonwhite and foreign-born. Hence the estimate is taken to be 5.4 per cent for 1960. The estimates for the other years are obtained by linear interpolation between successive decades.

(10) Nonimmigrant aliens admitted per capita. Sources: *Historical Statistics of the United States from Colonial Times to* 1957 (p. 63), and annual issues of the *Statistical Abstract.*

(11) Total consumption expenditure per capita (in 1954 dollars). Source: U.S. Department of Commerce as found in the *Economic Report of the President,* 1963. These data differ slightly from those given for (1) above. (11) and (12) are the data used in Chapter 6. Figures for 1963 and 1964 are from the *Survey of Current Business,* February 1965.

(12) Disposable income per capita (in 1954 dollars). Source: U.S. Department of Commerce as found in the *Economic Report of the President,* 1963.

(13) Total population of the United States in thousands (including armed forces overseas). Sources: *Statistical Abstract of the United States,* 1962 (for 1929–1960), and *The Economic Almanac,* 1962 (for 1961).

(14) Disposable farm income per capita (in 1954 dollars). Sources: Data for average disposable income per farm-operator family were obtained from various issues of the *Survey of Current Business.* The number of farm-operator families was obtained from *Historical Statistics* and the *Statistical Abstract,* 1962. Finally, the farm population was obtained from the *Economic Report of the President,* 1963.

## *II. Quarterly United States Data*

(15) Total personal consumption expenditure per capita (in 1954 dollars; seasonally adjusted annual rates). Sources: *U.S. Income and Output* and various issues of the *Survey of Current Business.* Quarterly population figures were obtained by linear interpolation between successive annual figures, and from the *Economic Report of the President,* 1965.

(16) Disposable income per capita in 1954 dollars (seasonally adjusted annual rates). Sources: Same as for (15).

## *III. Annual Canadian Data*

(17) Total consumption expenditure per capita (in 1957 dollars). Sources: Dominion Bureau of Statistics, *National Accounts Income and Expenditure,* 1926–1956, and various quarterly issues of *National Accounts.* Population figures are from various volumes of the *Canada Year Book.*

(18) Disposable income per capita (in 1957 dollars). Sources: Same as for (17).

## *IV. Quarterly Canadian Data*

(19) Total personal consumption expenditure (in 1957 dollars; seasonally adjusted annual rates). Sources: Dominion Bureau of Statistics, various quarterly issues of *National Accounts.* Quarterly population estimates were obtained by linear interpolation between successive annual figures.

(20) Disposable income per capita (in 1957 dollars; seasonally adjusted annual rates). Sources: Same as for (19).

# *References*


Ackley, G. N. (1961), *Macroeconomic Theory*, Macmillan and Company.

Allen, R. G. D., and Bowley, A. (1935), *Family Expenditure*, P. S. King and Son.

Anderson, T. W. (1958), *An Introduction to Multivariate Statistical Analysis*, John Wiley and Sons.

Barten, A. P. (1964), "Consumer Demand Functions under Conditions of Almost Additive Preferences," *Econometrica*, vol. 32, no. 1–2.

Brown, T. M. (1952), "Habit Persistence and Lags in Consumer Behavior," *Econometrica*, vol. 20, no. 1.

Christ, C. F. (1956), "Aggregate Econometric Models," *American Economic Review*, vol. 46, no. 3.

Crockett, J. (1960), "Demand Relationships for Food," in *Consumption and Savings*, Friend and Jones, eds., University of Pennsylvania.

Duesenberry, J. S. (1947), "Some New Income-Consumption Relationships and Their Implications" (abstract), *Econometrica*, vol. 15, no. 2.

Duesenberry, J. S. (1949), *Income, Saving, and the Theory of Consumer Behavior*, Harvard University Press.

Duesenberry, J. S., Eckstein, O., and Fromm, G. (1960). "A Simulation of the United States Economy in Recession," *Econometrica*, vol. 28, no. 4.

Durbin, J. R., and Watson, G. S. (1951), "Testing for Serial Correlation in Least Squares Regression, II," *Biometrica*, vol. 38.

Farrell, M. J. (1959), "The New Theories of the Consumption Function," *Economic Journal*, vol. 69.

Ferber, R., and Verdoorn, P. J. (1962), *Research Methods in Economics and Business*, Macmillan and Company.

Fisher, F. M., and Kaysen, C. (1962), *A Study in Econometrics: The Demand for Electricity in the United States*, North-Holland Publishing Company.

Friedman, M. (1957), *A Theory of the Consumption Function*, Princeton University Press.

Friedman, M. (1963), "Windfalls, the Horizon, and Related Concepts in the Permanent Income Hypothesis," in *Measurement in Economics*, ed. C. F. Christ et al., Stanford University Press.

Griliches, Z. (1961), "A Note on Serial Correlation Bias in Estimates of Distributed Lags," *Econometrica*, vol. 29, no. 1.

Griliches, Z., Maddala, G. S., Lucas, R., and Wallace, N. (1962), "Notes on Estimated Aggregate Quarterly Consumption Functions," *Econometrica*, vol. 30, no. 3.

Hamburg, M. (1960), "Demand for Clothing," in *Consumption and Savings*, Friend and Jones, eds., University of Pennsylvania.

Houthakker, H. S. (1951), "Some Calculations on Electricity Consumption in Great Britain," *Journal of the Royal Statistical Society*, vol. 114, part III.

Houthakker, H. S. (1961), "An International Comparison of Personal Savings," *Bulletin de l'Institut International de Statistique*, vol. 38, no. 2.

Houthakker, H. S. (1962), "On a Class of Dynamic Demand Functions" (abstract), *Econometrica*, vol. 30, no. 3.

Houthakker, H. S. (1963), "Some Problems in the International Comparison of Consumption Patterns," in *Le Rôle et l'évaluation des besoins de bien de consommation*, ed. R. Mossé, CNRS, Paris.

Houthakker, H. S. (1965), "New Evidence on Demand Elasticities," *Econometrica*, vol. 33, no. 2.

Houthakker, H. S., and Haldi, J. (1960), "Household Investment in Automobiles," in *Consumption and Savings*, Friend and Jones, ed., University of Pennsylvania.

Houthakker, H. S., and Tobin, J. (1952), "Estimates of the Free Demand for Rationed Foodstuffs," *Economic Journal*, vol. 62, no. 245.

Kendall, M. G. (1957), *A Course in Multivariate Analysis*, Griffin.

Klein, L. R. (1958), "The Estimation of Distributed Lags," *Econometrica*, vol. 26, no. 4.

Klein, L. R., and Goldberger, A. S. (1955), *An Econometric Model of the United States*, 1929–1952, North-Holland Publishing Company.

Koyck, L. M. (1954), *Distributed Lags and Investment Analysis*, North-Holland Publishing Company.

Leser, C. E. V. (1963), "Forms of Engel Functions," *Econometrica*, vol. 31, no. 4.

Malinvaud, E. (1961), "Estimation et prévision dans les modèles autorégressifs," *Revue de L'Institut International de Statistique*, vol. 29, no. 2.

Meyer, J. R., and Glauber, R. R. (1964), *Investment Decisions, Economic Forecasting, and Public Policy*, Harvard Business School.

Meyer, J. R., and Kuh, E. (1957), *The Investment Decision*, Harvard University Press.

Modigliani, F. (1947), "Fluctuations in the Savings Ratio: A Problem in Economic Forecasting" (abstract), *Econometrica*, vol. 15, no. 2.

Modigliani, F., and Brumberg, R. (1954), "Utility Analysis and the Consumption Function: An Interpretation of Cross Section Data," in *Post-Keynesian Economics*, ed. K. K. Kurihara, Rutgers University Press.

Nerlove, M. (1958), *Distributed Lags and Demand Analysis*, Agricultural Handbook Number 141, United States Department of Agriculture.

Nerlove, M. (1960), "The Market Demand for Durable Goods: A Comment," *Econometrica*, vol. 28, no. 1.

Nicholson, J. L. (1949), "Variations in Working Class Family Expenditure," *Journal of the Royal Statistical Society*, vol. 112.

Prais, S. J. (1952), "Non-Linear Estimates of the Engel Curve," *Review of Economic Studies*, vol. 20.

Prais, S. J., and Houthakker, H. S. (1955), *The Analysis of Family Budgets*, Cambridge University Press.

Prest, A. R. (1948), "National Income of the United Kingdom," *Economic Journal*, vol. 58, no. 229.

Sandee, J. (1964), ed., *Europe's Future Consumption*, North-Holland Publishing Company.

Stone, J. R. N. (1947), "On the Interdependence of Blocks of Transactions," Supplement to the *Journal of the Royal Statistical Society*, vol. 9, nos. 1–2.

Stone, J. R. N. (1954), "Linear Expenditure Systems and Demand Analysis: An Application to the Pattern of British Demand," *Economic Journal*, vol. 64.

Stone, J. R. N., and Prais, S. J. (1953), "Forecasting from Econometric Models: A Further Note on Derationing," *Economic Journal*, vol. 63.

Stone, J. R. N., and others (1954), *The Measurement of Consumers' Expenditure and Behaviour in the United Kingdom*, 1920–1938, vol. 1, Cambridge University Press.

Stone, J. R. N., and Croft-Murray, G. (1959), *Social Accounting and Economic Models*, Bowes and Bowes.

Stone, J. R. N., and Rowe, D. A. (1960), "The Durability of Consumers' Durable Goods," *Econometrica*, vol. 28, no. 2.

Suits, D. B. (1958), "The Demand for New Automobiles in the United States, 1929–1956," *Review of Economics and Statistics*, vol. 40.

Suits, D. B. (1963), "The Determinants of Consumer Expenditure: A Review of Present Knowledge," in *Impacts of Monetary Policy*, one of the research studies prepared for the Commission on Money and Credit, Prentice-Hall, Inc.

Taylor, L. D. (1964), "Personal Consumption Expenditure in Sweden, 1931–1958," paper presented at the Zürich meetings of the Econometric Society.

Taylor, L. D. (1965), "Multicollinearity in Equation Systems," abstract to appear in *Econometrica*, vol. 33.

Taylor, L. D., and Wilson, T. A. (1964), "Three-Pass Least Squares: A Method for Estimating Models with a Lagged Dependent Variable," *Review of Economics and Statistics*, vol. 46.

Theil, H. (1961), *Economic Forecasts and Policy*, North-Holland Publishing Company.

Tobin, J. (1951), "Relative Income, Absolute Income and Savings" in *Money, Trade, and Economic Growth, Essays in Honor of John Henry Williams*, Macmillan and Company.

Tsujimura, K., and Sato, T. (1964), "Irreversibility of Consumer Behavior in Terms of Numerical Preference Fields," *Review of Economics and Statistics*, vol. 46.

Wold, H., and Juréen, L. (1953), *Demand Analysis, A Study in Econometrics*, John Wiley and Sons.

Yule, G. U. (1926), "Why Do We Sometimes Get Nonsense Correlation Between Time Series?" *Journal of the Royal Statistical Society*, vol. 89, no. 1.

Zellner, A. (1957), "The Short-Run Consumption Function," *Econometrica*, vol. 25, no. 4.

# *Index*